TODD McFARLANE AND IMAGE COMICS PRESENT

SPAWN BOOK ELEVEN
CROSSROADS

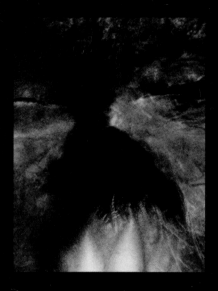

STORY
TODD McFARLANE

ART
TODD McFARLANE
GREG CAPULLO
TONY DANIEL
KEVIN CONRAD
DANNY MIKI

COPY EDITOR AND LETTERING
TOM ORZECHOWSKI

PRESIDENT OF
ENTERTAINMENT
TERRY FITZGERALD

COLOR
BRIAN HABERLIN
DAN KEMP
TODD BROEKER
ROY YOUNG

EXECUTIVE DIRECTOR
OF PUBLISHING
BEAU SMITH

COVER PENCILS
TODD McFARLANE
GREG CAPULLO
TONY DANIEL

MANAGING EDITOR
MELANIE SIMMONS

ART DIRECTOR
BRENT ASHE

COVER INKS
TODD McFARLANE
KEVIN CONRAD
DANNY MIKI

DESIGNER
BOYD WILLIAMS

PUBLISHER FOR
IMAGE COMICS
JIM VALENTINO

PUBLICATION COVER
ASHLEY WOOD

PUBLICATION DESIGN
BRENT ASHE

The alley's deepest reaches. The place even hard-case sociopaths fear.

A place where dark souls attempt to vanish. None entirely successful.

–THE SYSTEM

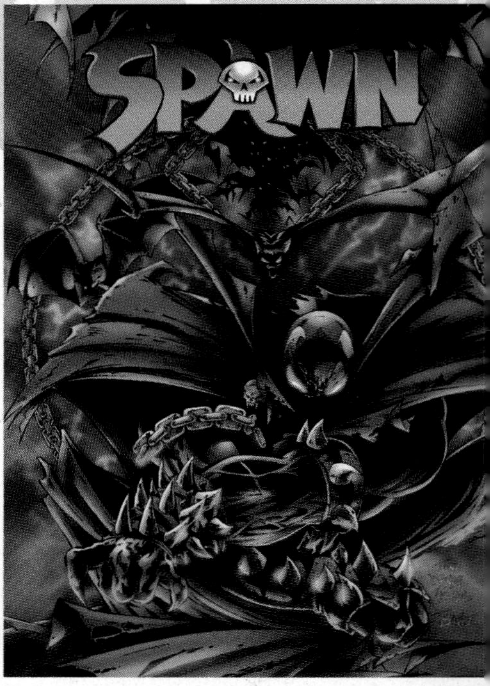
SPAWN

FORTY-EIGHT

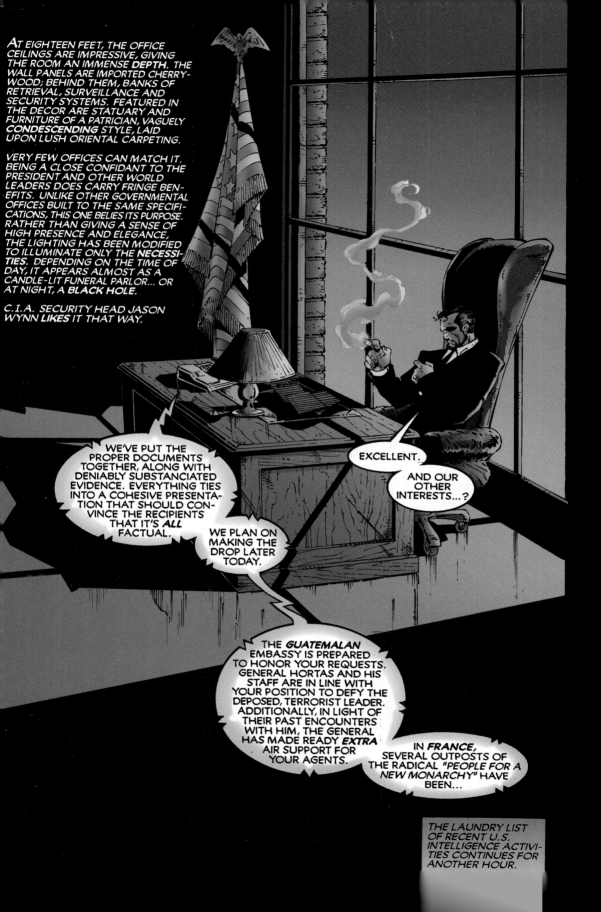

AT EIGHTEEN FEET, THE OFFICE CEILINGS ARE IMPRESSIVE, GIVING THE ROOM AN IMMENSE *DEPTH*. THE WALL PANELS ARE IMPORTED CHERRY-WOOD; BEHIND THEM, BANKS OF RETRIEVAL, SURVEILLANCE AND SECURITY SYSTEMS. FEATURED IN THE DECOR ARE STATUARY AND FURNITURE OF A PATRICIAN, VAGUELY *CONDESCENDING* STYLE, LAID UPON LUSH ORIENTAL CARPETING.

VERY FEW OFFICES CAN MATCH IT. BEING A CLOSE CONFIDANT TO THE PRESIDENT AND OTHER WORLD LEADERS DOES CARRY FRINGE BEN-EFITS. UNLIKE OTHER GOVERNMENTAL OFFICES BUILT TO THE SAME SPECIFI-CATIONS, THIS ONE BELIES ITS PURPOSE. RATHER THAN GIVING A SENSE OF HIGH PRESENCE AND ELEGANCE, THE LIGHTING HAS BEEN MODIFIED TO ILLUMINATE ONLY THE *NECESSI-TIES*. DEPENDING ON THE TIME OF DAY, IT APPEARS ALMOST AS A CANDLE-LIT FUNERAL PARLOR... OR AT NIGHT, A *BLACK HOLE*.

C.I.A. SECURITY HEAD JASON WYNN *LIKES* IT THAT WAY.

WE'VE PUT THE PROPER DOCUMENTS TOGETHER, ALONG WITH DENIABLY SUBSTANCIATED EVIDENCE. EVERYTHING TIES INTO A COHESIVE PRESENTA-TION THAT SHOULD CON-VINCE THE RECIPIENTS THAT IT'S *ALL* FACTUAL.

WE PLAN ON MAKING THE DROP LATER TODAY.

EXCELLENT.

AND OUR OTHER INTERESTS...?

THE *GUATEMALAN* EMBASSY IS PREPARED TO HONOR YOUR REQUESTS. GENERAL HORTAS AND HIS STAFF ARE IN LINE WITH YOUR POSITION TO DEFY THE DEPOSED, TERRORIST LEADER. ADDITIONALLY, IN LIGHT OF THEIR PAST ENCOUNTERS WITH HIM, THE GENERAL HAS MADE READY *EXTRA* AIR SUPPORT FOR YOUR AGENTS.

IN *FRANCE*, SEVERAL OUTPOSTS OF THE RADICAL "PEOPLE FOR A NEW MONARCHY" HAVE BEEN...

THE LAUNDRY LIST OF RECENT U.S. INTELLIGENCE ACTIVI-TIES CONTINUES FOR ANOTHER HOUR.

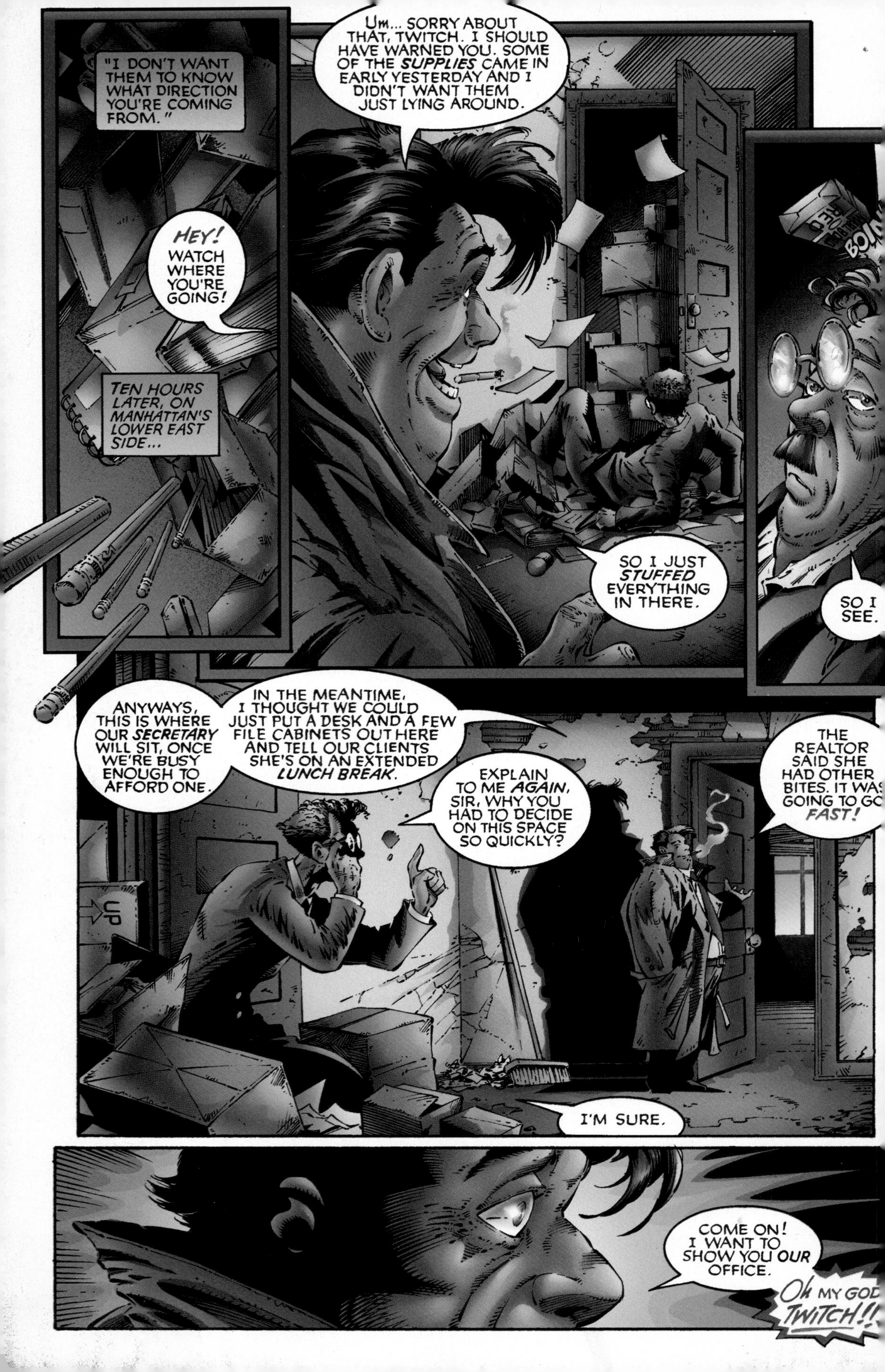
"I DON'T WANT THEM TO KNOW WHAT DIRECTION YOU'RE COMING FROM."
HEY! WATCH WHERE YOU'RE GOING!
TEN HOURS LATER, ON MANHATTAN'S LOWER EAST SIDE...
Um... SORRY ABOUT THAT, TWITCH. I SHOULD HAVE WARNED YOU. SOME OF THE SUPPLIES CAME IN EARLY YESTERDAY AND I DIDN'T WANT THEM JUST LYING AROUND.
SO I JUST STUFFED EVERYTHING IN THERE.
BOINK
SO I SEE.
ANYWAYS, THIS IS WHERE OUR SECRETARY WILL SIT, ONCE WE'RE BUSY ENOUGH TO AFFORD ONE.
IN THE MEANTIME, I THOUGHT WE COULD JUST PUT A DESK AND A FEW FILE CABINETS OUT HERE AND TELL OUR CLIENTS SHE'S ON AN EXTENDED LUNCH BREAK.
EXPLAIN TO ME AGAIN, SIR, WHY YOU HAD TO DECIDE ON THIS SPACE SO QUICKLY?
THE REALTOR SAID SHE HAD OTHER BITES. IT WAS GOING TO GO FAST!
UP
I'M SURE.
COME ON! I WANT TO SHOW YOU OUR OFFICE.
Oh MY GOD TWITCH!!

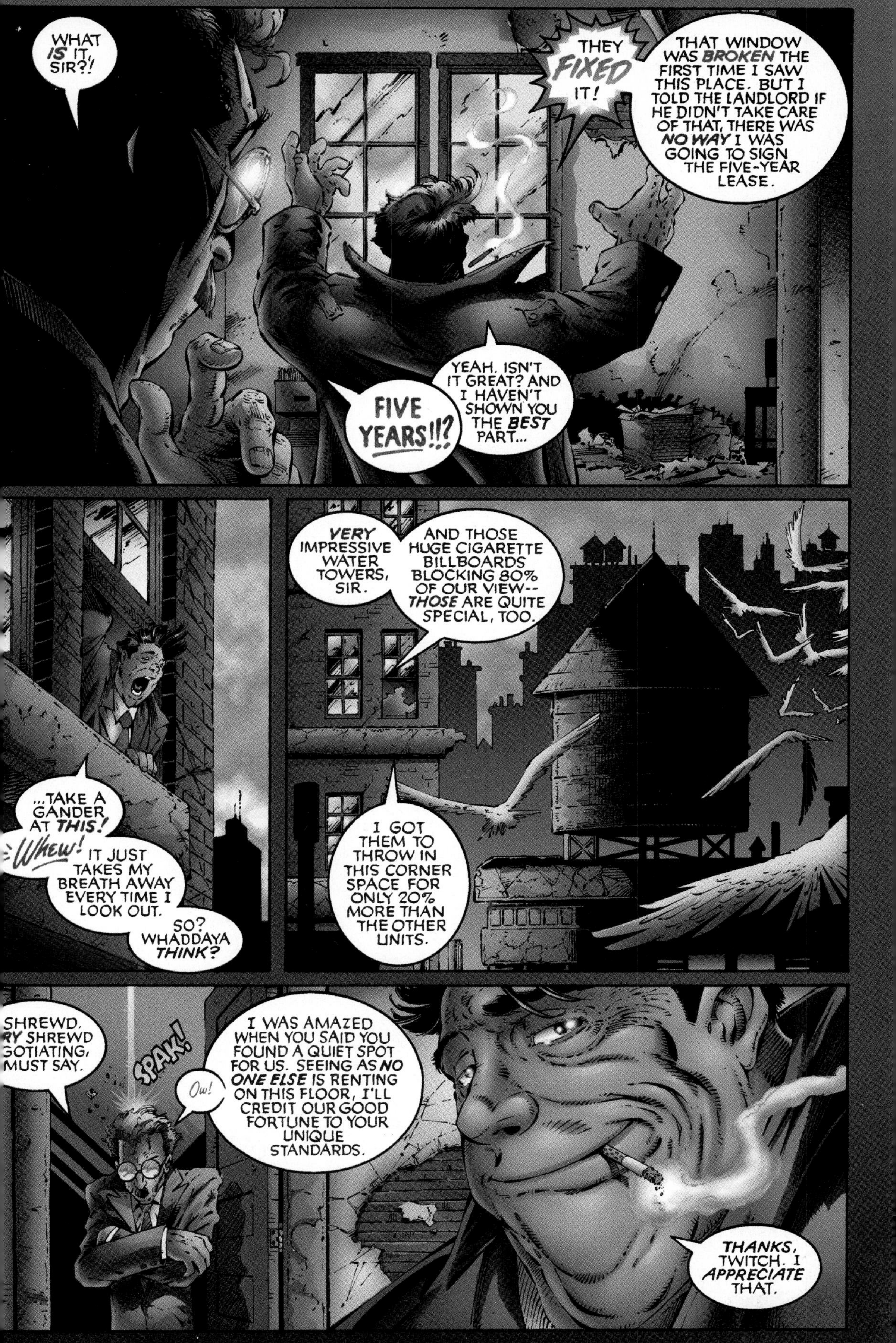
WHAT IS IT, SIR?!
THEY FIXED IT!
THAT WINDOW WAS BROKEN THE FIRST TIME I SAW THIS PLACE. BUT I TOLD THE LANDLORD IF HE DIDN'T TAKE CARE OF THAT, THERE WAS NO WAY I WAS GOING TO SIGN THE FIVE-YEAR LEASE.
FIVE YEARS!!?
YEAH. ISN'T IT GREAT? AND I HAVEN'T SHOWN YOU THE BEST PART...
...TAKE A GANDER AT THIS!
Whew!
IT JUST TAKES MY BREATH AWAY EVERY TIME I LOOK OUT.
SO? WHADDAYA THINK?
VERY IMPRESSIVE WATER TOWERS, SIR.
AND THOSE HUGE CIGARETTE BILLBOARDS BLOCKING 80% OF OUR VIEW-- THOSE ARE QUITE SPECIAL, TOO.
I GOT THEM TO THROW IN THIS CORNER SPACE FOR ONLY 20% MORE THAN THE OTHER UNITS.
SHREWD. RY SHREWD GOTIATING, MUST SAY.
SPAK!
Ow!
I WAS AMAZED WHEN YOU SAID YOU FOUND A QUIET SPOT FOR US. SEEING AS NO ONE ELSE IS RENTING ON THIS FLOOR, I'LL CREDIT OUR GOOD FORTUNE TO YOUR UNIQUE STANDARDS.
THANKS, TWITCH. I APPRECIATE THAT.

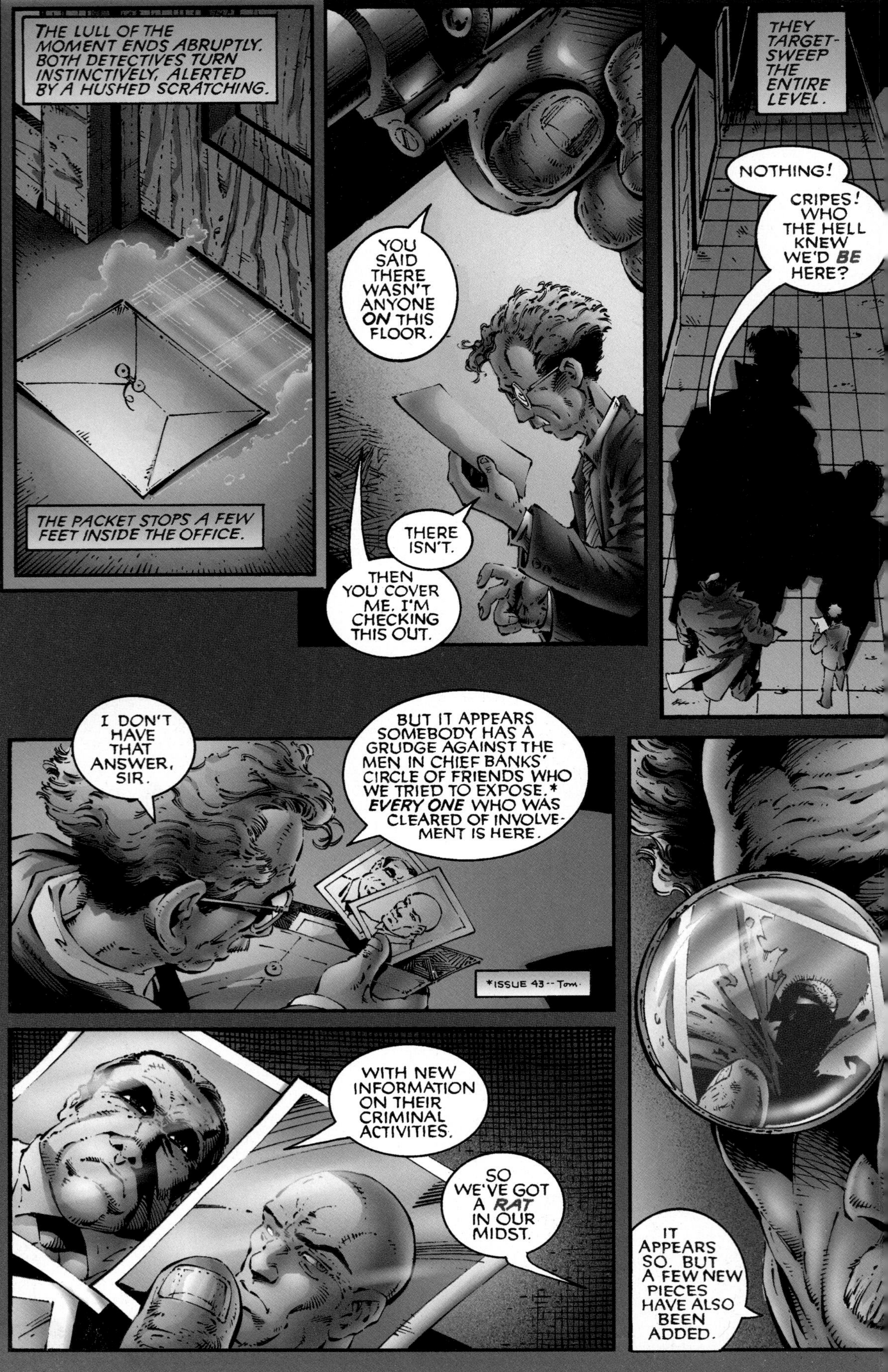

THE LULL OF THE MOMENT ENDS ABRUPTLY. BOTH DETECTIVES TURN INSTINCTIVELY, ALERTED BY A HUSHED SCRATCHING.
THE PACKET STOPS A FEW FEET INSIDE THE OFFICE.
YOU SAID THERE WASN'T ANYONE ON THIS FLOOR.
THERE ISN'T.
THEN YOU COVER ME. I'M CHECKING THIS OUT.
THEY TARGET-SWEEP THE ENTIRE LEVEL.
NOTHING!
CRIPES! WHO THE HELL KNEW WE'D BE HERE?
I DON'T HAVE THAT ANSWER, SIR.
BUT IT APPEARS SOMEBODY HAS A GRUDGE AGAINST THE MEN IN CHIEF BANKS' CIRCLE OF FRIENDS WHO WE TRIED TO EXPOSE.* EVERY ONE WHO WAS CLEARED OF INVOLVEMENT IS HERE.
*ISSUE 43 -- Tom.
WITH NEW INFORMATION ON THEIR CRIMINAL ACTIVITIES.
SO WE'VE GOT A RAT IN OUR MIDST.
IT APPEARS SO. BUT A FEW NEW PIECES HAVE ALSO BEEN ADDED.

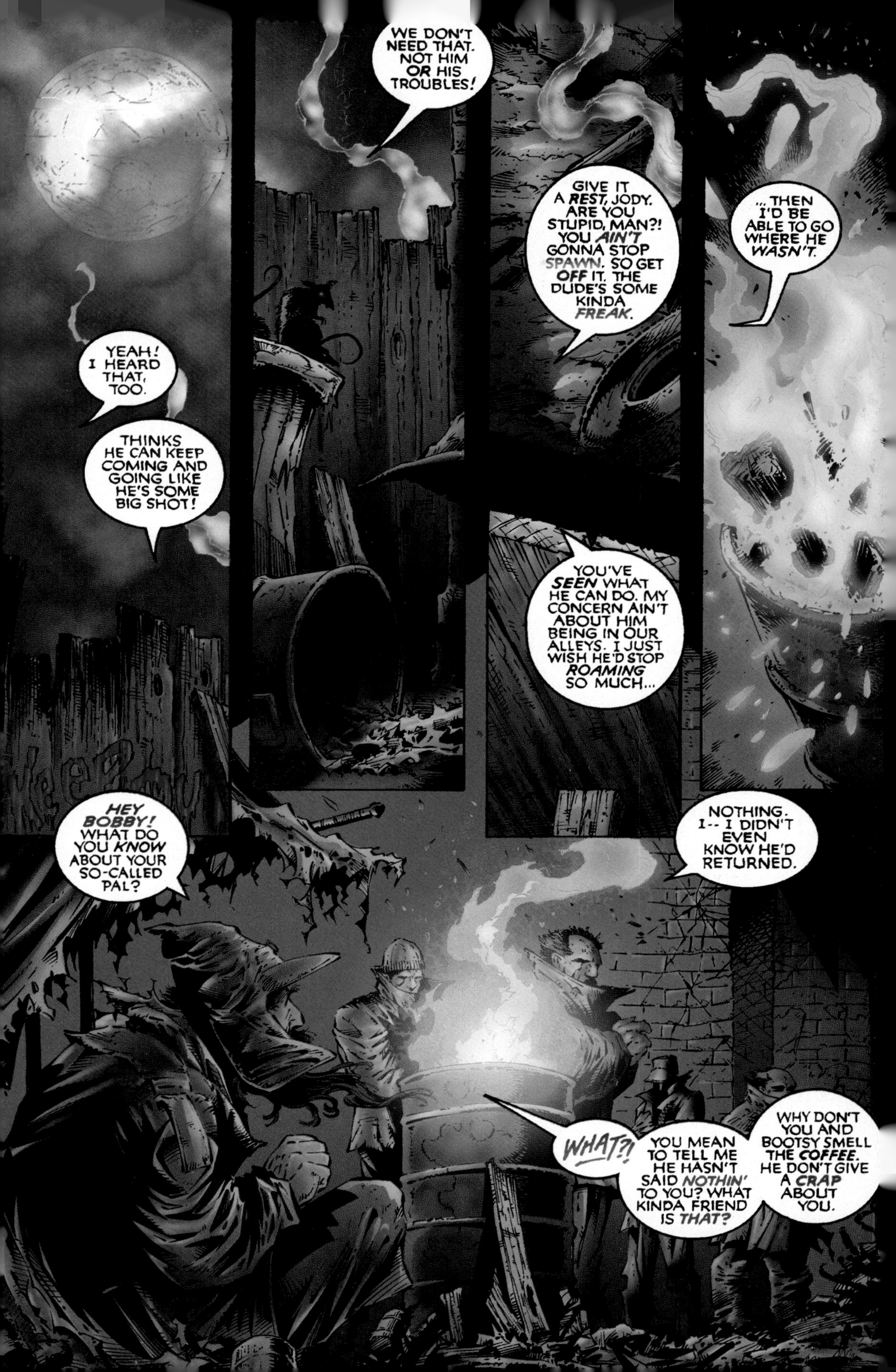
YEAH! I HEARD THAT, TOO.
THINKS HE CAN KEEP COMING AND GOING LIKE HE'S SOME BIG SHOT!
WE DON'T NEED THAT. NOT HIM OR HIS TROUBLES!
GIVE IT A REST, JODY. ARE YOU STUPID, MAN?! YOU AIN'T GONNA STOP SPAWN. SO GET OFF IT. THE DUDE'S SOME KINDA FREAK.
YOU'VE SEEN WHAT HE CAN DO. MY CONCERN AIN'T ABOUT HIM BEING IN OUR ALLEYS. I JUST WISH HE'D STOP ROAMING SO MUCH...
...THEN I'D BE ABLE TO GO WHERE HE WASN'T.
HEY BOBBY! WHAT DO YOU KNOW ABOUT YOUR SO-CALLED PAL?
NOTHING. I-- I DIDN'T EVEN KNOW HE'D RETURNED.
WHAT?!
YOU MEAN TO TELL ME HE HASN'T SAID NOTHIN' TO YOU? WHAT KINDA FRIEND IS THAT?
WHY DON'T YOU AND BOOTSY SMELL THE COFFEE. HE DON'T GIVE A CRAP ABOUT YOU.

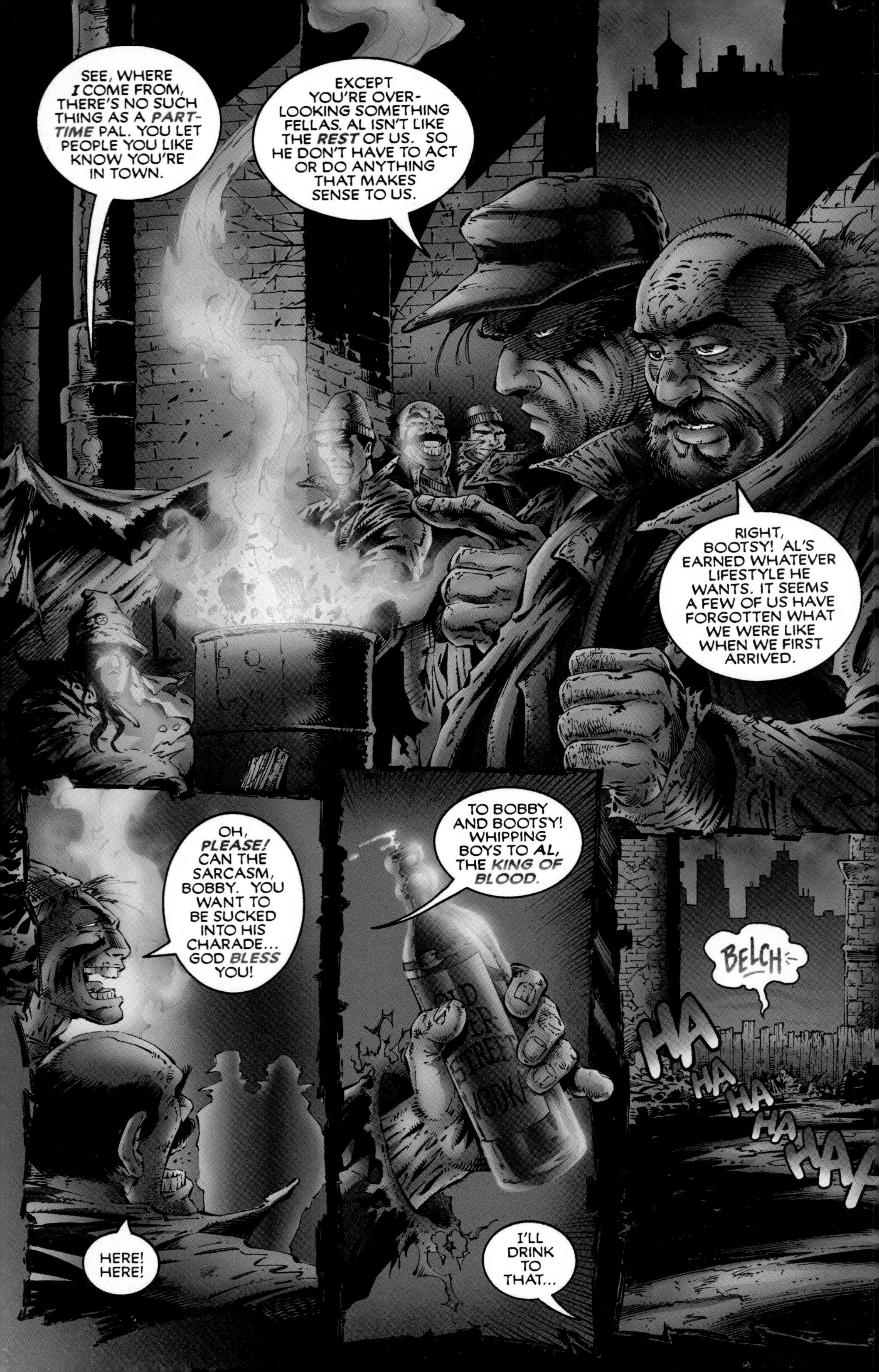
SEE, WHERE I COME FROM, THERE'S NO SUCH THING AS A PART-TIME PAL. YOU LET PEOPLE YOU LIKE KNOW YOU'RE IN TOWN.
EXCEPT YOU'RE OVER-LOOKING SOMETHING FELLAS. AL ISN'T LIKE THE REST OF US. SO HE DON'T HAVE TO ACT OR DO ANYTHING THAT MAKES SENSE TO US.
RIGHT, BOOTSY! AL'S EARNED WHATEVER LIFESTYLE HE WANTS. IT SEEMS A FEW OF US HAVE FORGOTTEN WHAT WE WERE LIKE WHEN WE FIRST ARRIVED.
OH, PLEASE! CAN THE SARCASM, BOBBY. YOU WANT TO BE SUCKED INTO HIS CHARADE... GOD BLESS YOU!
HERE! HERE!
TO BOBBY AND BOOTSY! WHIPPING BOYS TO AL, THE KING OF BLOOD.
I'LL DRINK TO THAT...
BELCH
HA HA HA HA HA HAA

IT GOES ESSENTIALLY UNNOTICED, THE POUNDING.

LOST AMONGST THE COUNTLESS OTHER SOUNDS.

THOSE WHO DO ACKNOWLEDGE IT ARE AWARE OF WHERE IT COMES FROM:

RAT CITY.

THE ALLEY'S DEEPEST REACHES.

BAM BAM   KRAK BAM

KRISH BAM BAM BAM

BAM BAM SCRAAPE BAM

BAM BAM CRUNK SKREEK BAM

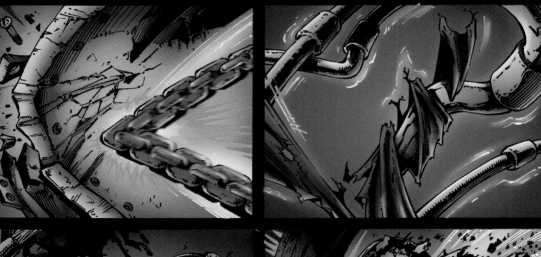

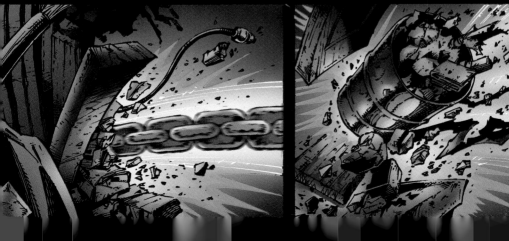

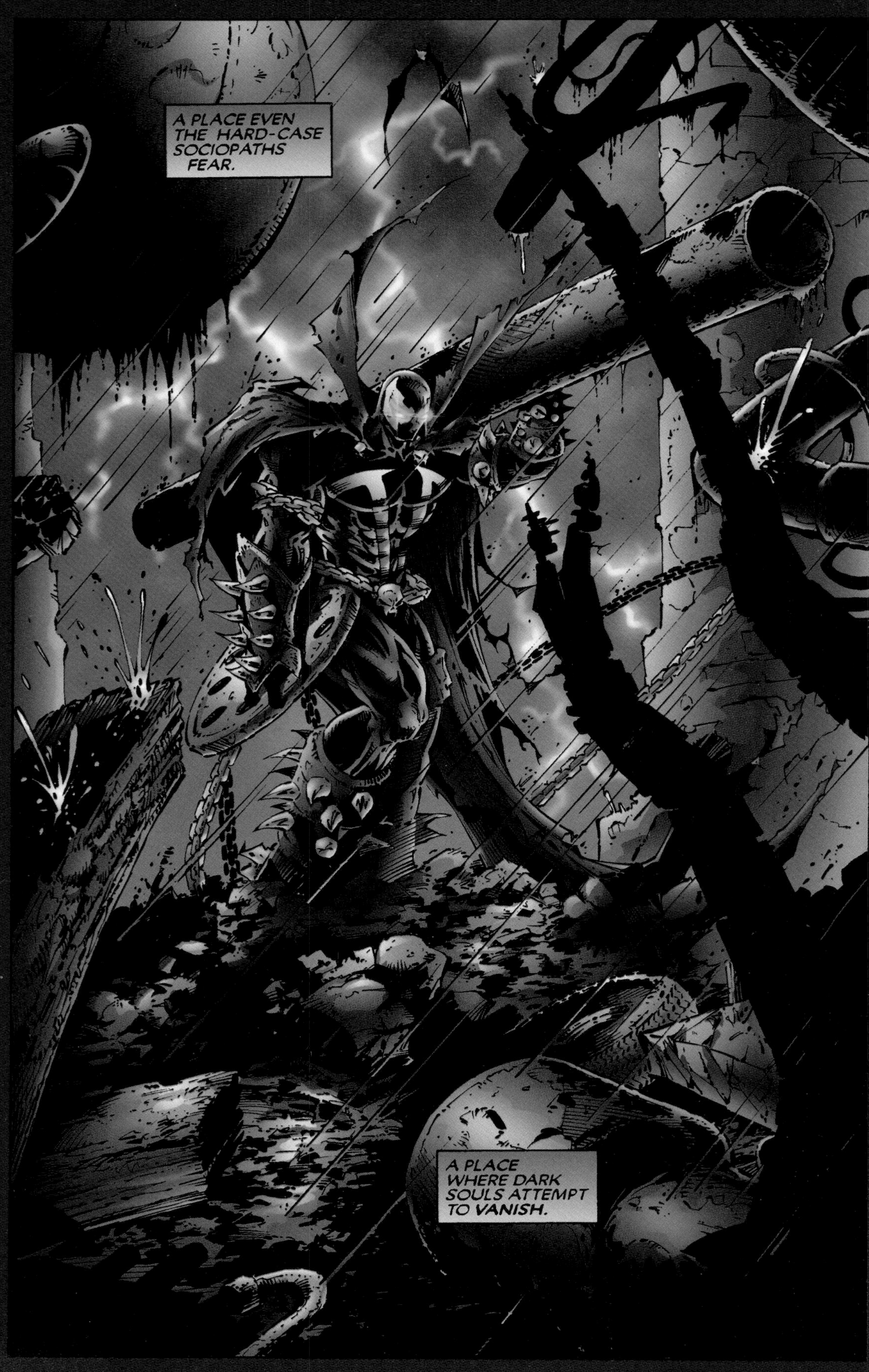
A PLACE EVEN THE HARD-CASE SOCIOPATHS FEAR.
A PLACE WHERE DARK SOULS ATTEMPT TO VANISH.

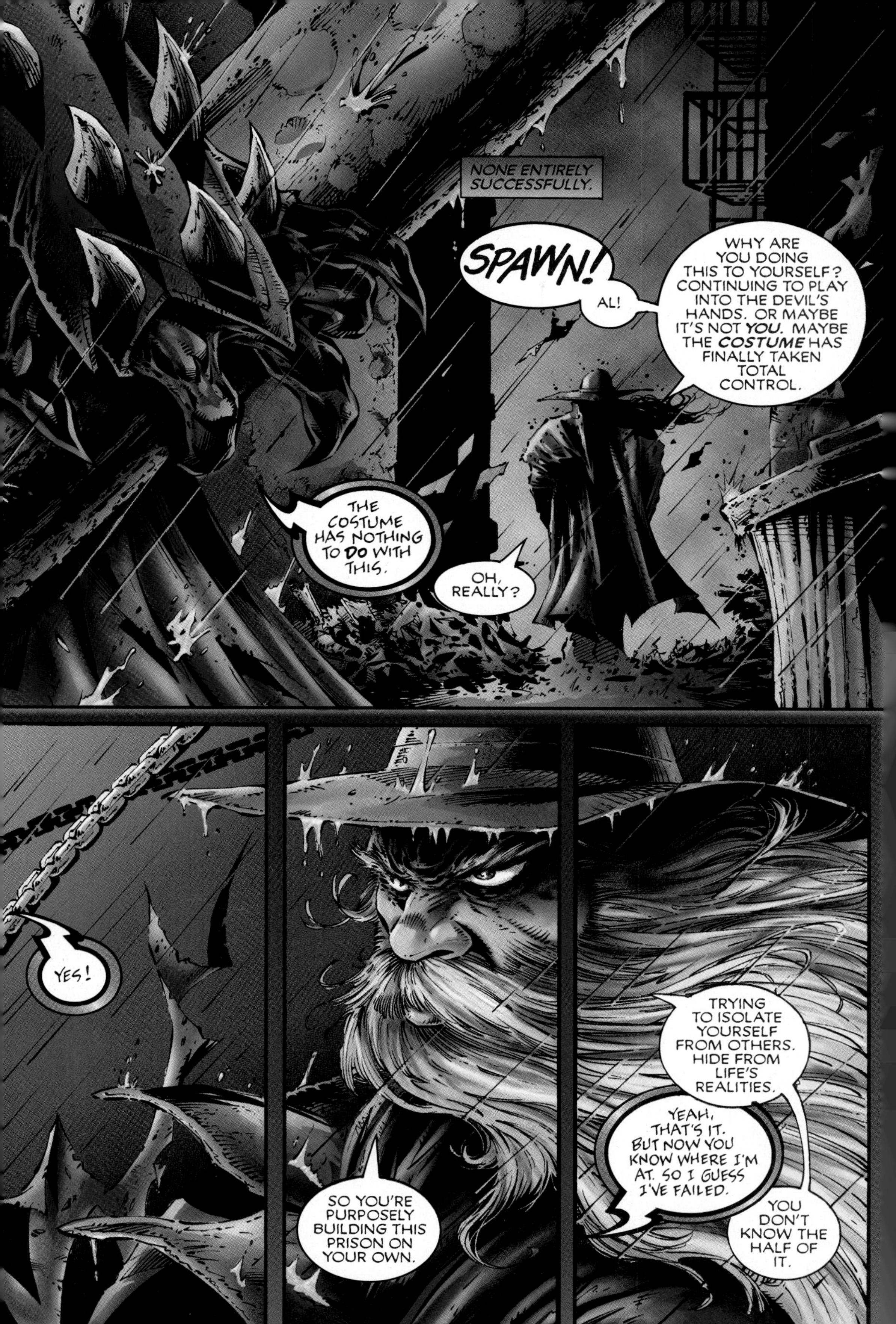
NONE ENTIRELY SUCCESSFULLY.
SPAWN!
AL!
WHY ARE YOU DOING THIS TO YOURSELF? CONTINUING TO PLAY INTO THE DEVIL'S HANDS. OR MAYBE IT'S NOT YOU. MAYBE THE COSTUME HAS FINALLY TAKEN TOTAL CONTROL.
THE COSTUME HAS NOTHING TO DO WITH THIS.
OH, REALLY?
YES!
SO YOU'RE PURPOSELY BUILDING THIS PRISON ON YOUR OWN.
TRYING TO ISOLATE YOURSELF FROM OTHERS. HIDE FROM LIFE'S REALITIES.
YEAH, THAT'S IT. BUT NOW YOU KNOW WHERE I'M AT. SO I GUESS I'VE FAILED.
YOU DON'T KNOW THE HALF OF IT.

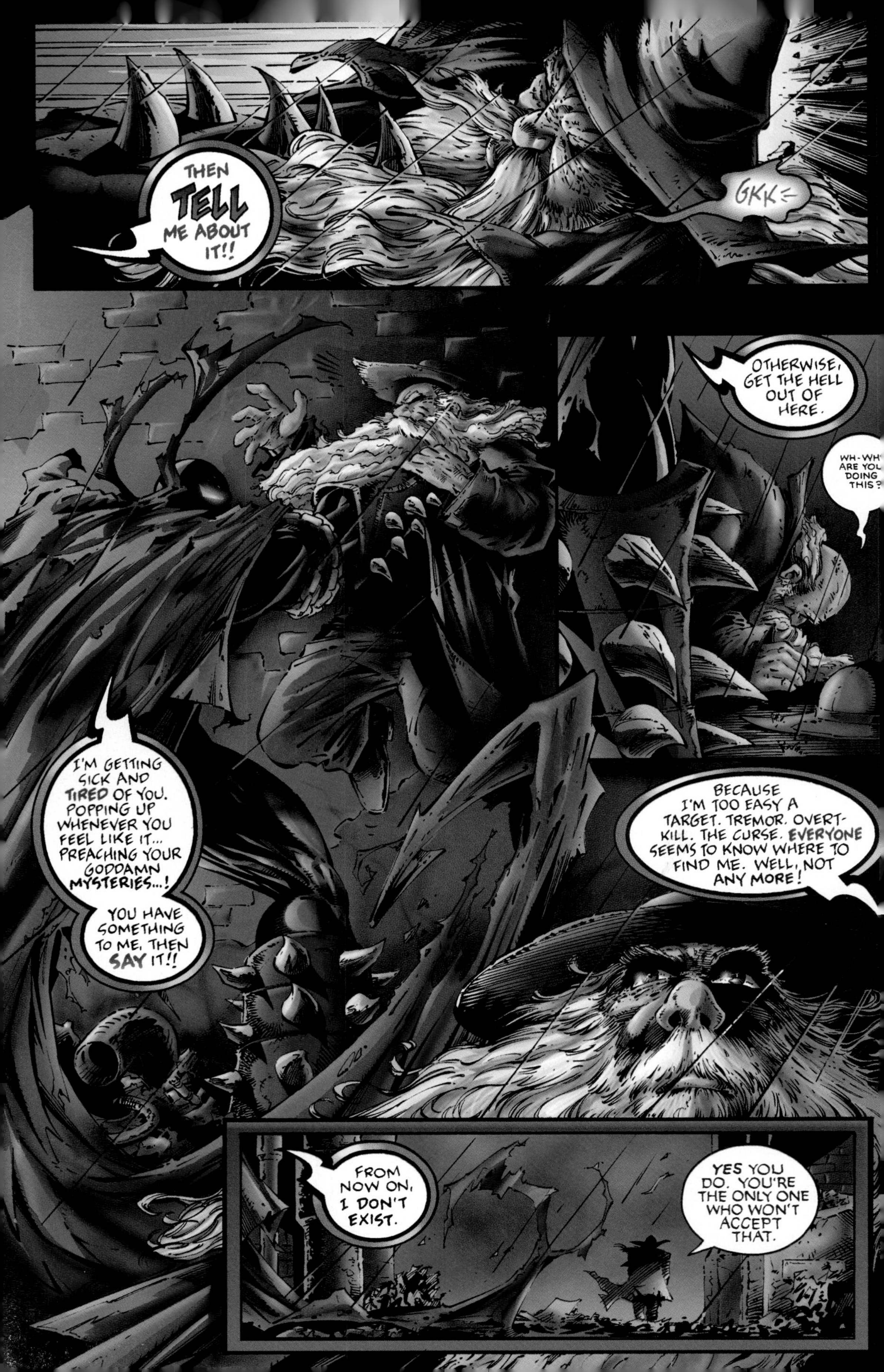

THEN TELL ME ABOUT IT!!
GKK
OTHERWISE, GET THE HELL OUT OF HERE.
WH-WH ARE YOU DOING THIS?
I'M GETTING SICK AND TIRED OF YOU. POPPING UP WHENEVER YOU FEEL LIKE IT... PREACHING YOUR GODDAMN MYSTERIES...!
YOU HAVE SOMETHING TO ME, THEN SAY IT!!
BECAUSE I'M TOO EASY A TARGET. TREMOR. OVERT-KILL. THE CURSE. EVERYONE SEEMS TO KNOW WHERE TO FIND ME. WELL, NOT ANY MORE!
FROM NOW ON, I DON'T EXIST.
YES YOU DO. YOU'RE THE ONLY ONE WHO WON'T ACCEPT THAT.

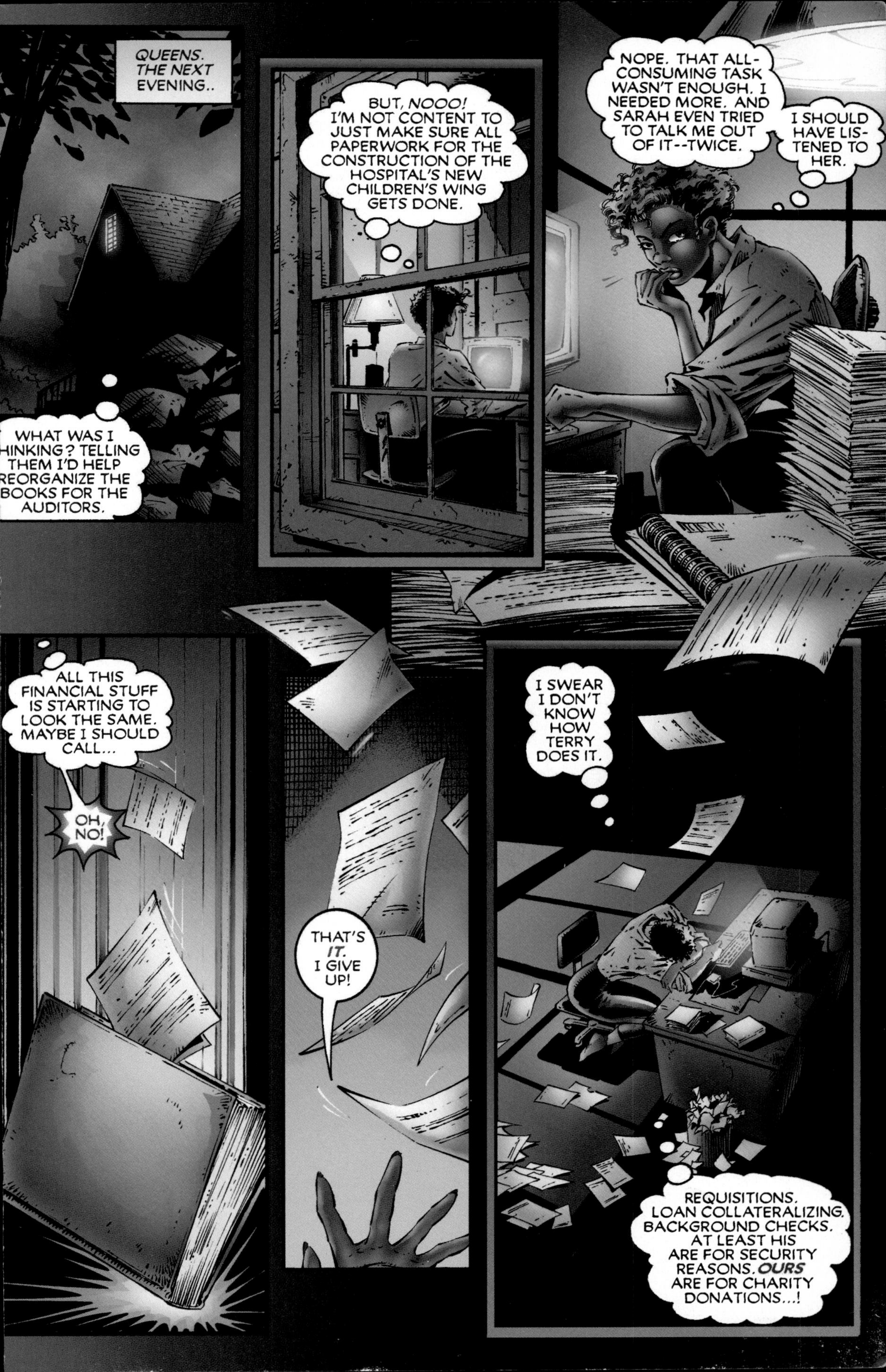
QUEENS. THE NEXT EVENING..
WHAT WAS I THINKING? TELLING THEM I'D HELP REORGANIZE THE BOOKS FOR THE AUDITORS.
BUT, NOOO! I'M NOT CONTENT TO JUST MAKE SURE ALL PAPERWORK FOR THE CONSTRUCTION OF THE HOSPITAL'S NEW CHILDREN'S WING GETS DONE.
NOPE. THAT ALL-CONSUMING TASK WASN'T ENOUGH. I NEEDED MORE. AND SARAH EVEN TRIED TO TALK ME OUT OF IT--TWICE.
I SHOULD HAVE LISTENED TO HER.
ALL THIS FINANCIAL STUFF IS STARTING TO LOOK THE SAME. MAYBE I SHOULD CALL...
OH, NO!
THAT'S IT. I GIVE UP!
I SWEAR I DON'T KNOW HOW TERRY DOES IT.
REQUISITIONS. LOAN COLLATERALIZING. BACKGROUND CHECKS. AT LEAST HIS ARE FOR SECURITY REASONS. OURS ARE FOR CHARITY DONATIONS...!

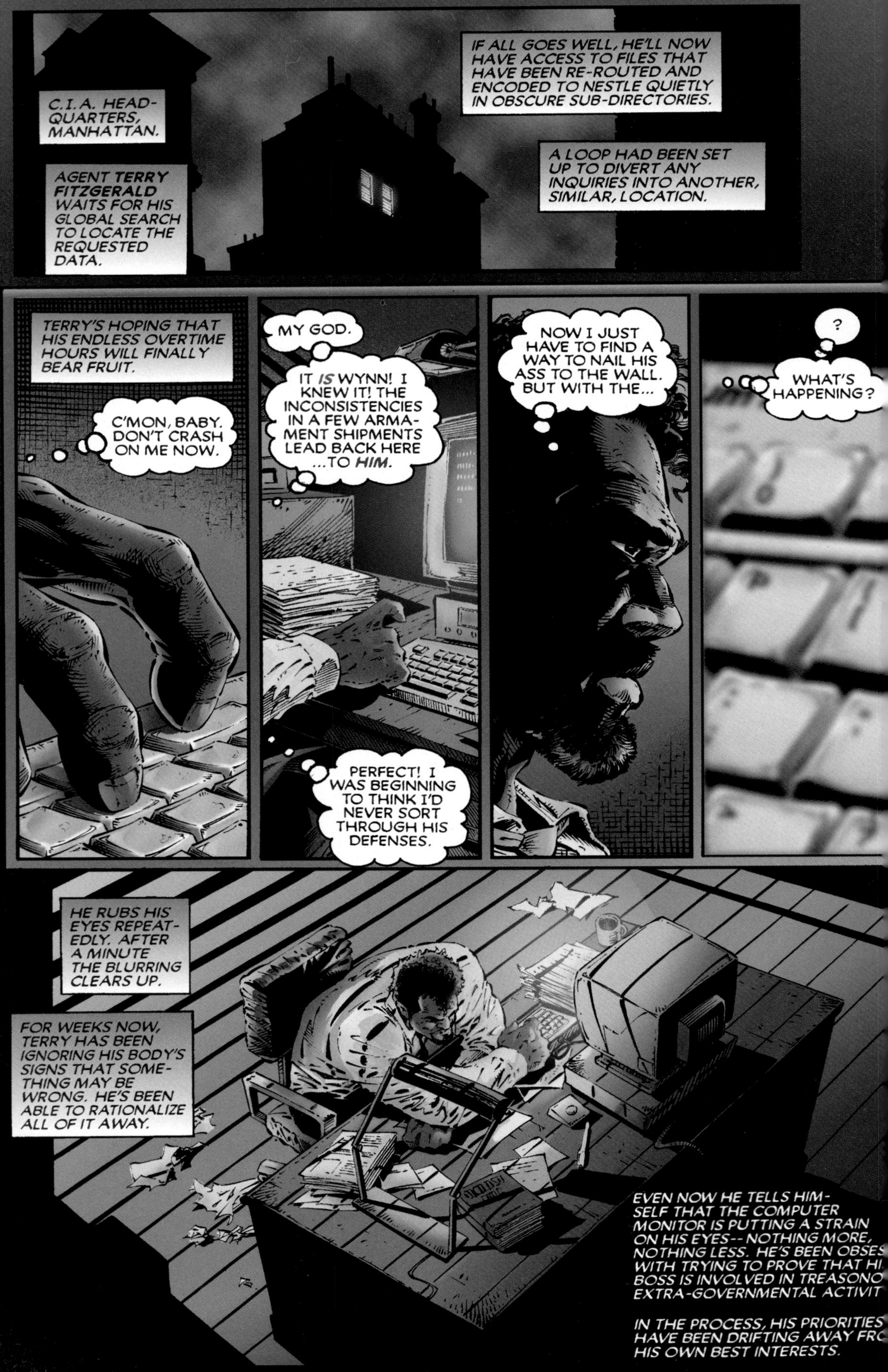

C.I.A. HEAD-QUARTERS, MANHATTAN.
AGENT TERRY FITZGERALD WAITS FOR HIS GLOBAL SEARCH TO LOCATE THE REQUESTED DATA.
IF ALL GOES WELL, HE'LL NOW HAVE ACCESS TO FILES THAT HAVE BEEN RE-ROUTED AND ENCODED TO NESTLE QUIETLY IN OBSCURE SUB-DIRECTORIES.
A LOOP HAD BEEN SET UP TO DIVERT ANY INQUIRIES INTO ANOTHER, SIMILAR, LOCATION.
TERRY'S HOPING THAT HIS ENDLESS OVERTIME HOURS WILL FINALLY BEAR FRUIT.
C'MON, BABY. DON'T CRASH ON ME NOW.
MY GOD.
IT IS WYNN! I KNEW IT! THE INCONSISTENCIES IN A FEW ARMAMENT SHIPMENTS LEAD BACK HERE ...TO HIM.
PERFECT! I WAS BEGINNING TO THINK I'D NEVER SORT THROUGH HIS DEFENSES.
NOW I JUST HAVE TO FIND A WAY TO NAIL HIS ASS TO THE WALL. BUT WITH THE...
?
WHAT'S HAPPENING?
HE RUBS HIS EYES REPEATEDLY. AFTER A MINUTE THE BLURRING CLEARS UP.
FOR WEEKS NOW, TERRY HAS BEEN IGNORING HIS BODY'S SIGNS THAT SOMETHING MAY BE WRONG. HE'S BEEN ABLE TO RATIONALIZE ALL OF IT AWAY.
EVEN NOW HE TELLS HIMSELF THAT THE COMPUTER MONITOR IS PUTTING A STRAIN ON HIS EYES-- NOTHING MORE, NOTHING LESS. HE'S BEEN OBSES WITH TRYING TO PROVE THAT HI BOSS IS INVOLVED IN TREASONO EXTRA-GOVERNMENTAL ACTIVIT
IN THE PROCESS, HIS PRIORITIES HAVE BEEN DRIFTING AWAY FRO HIS OWN BEST INTERESTS.

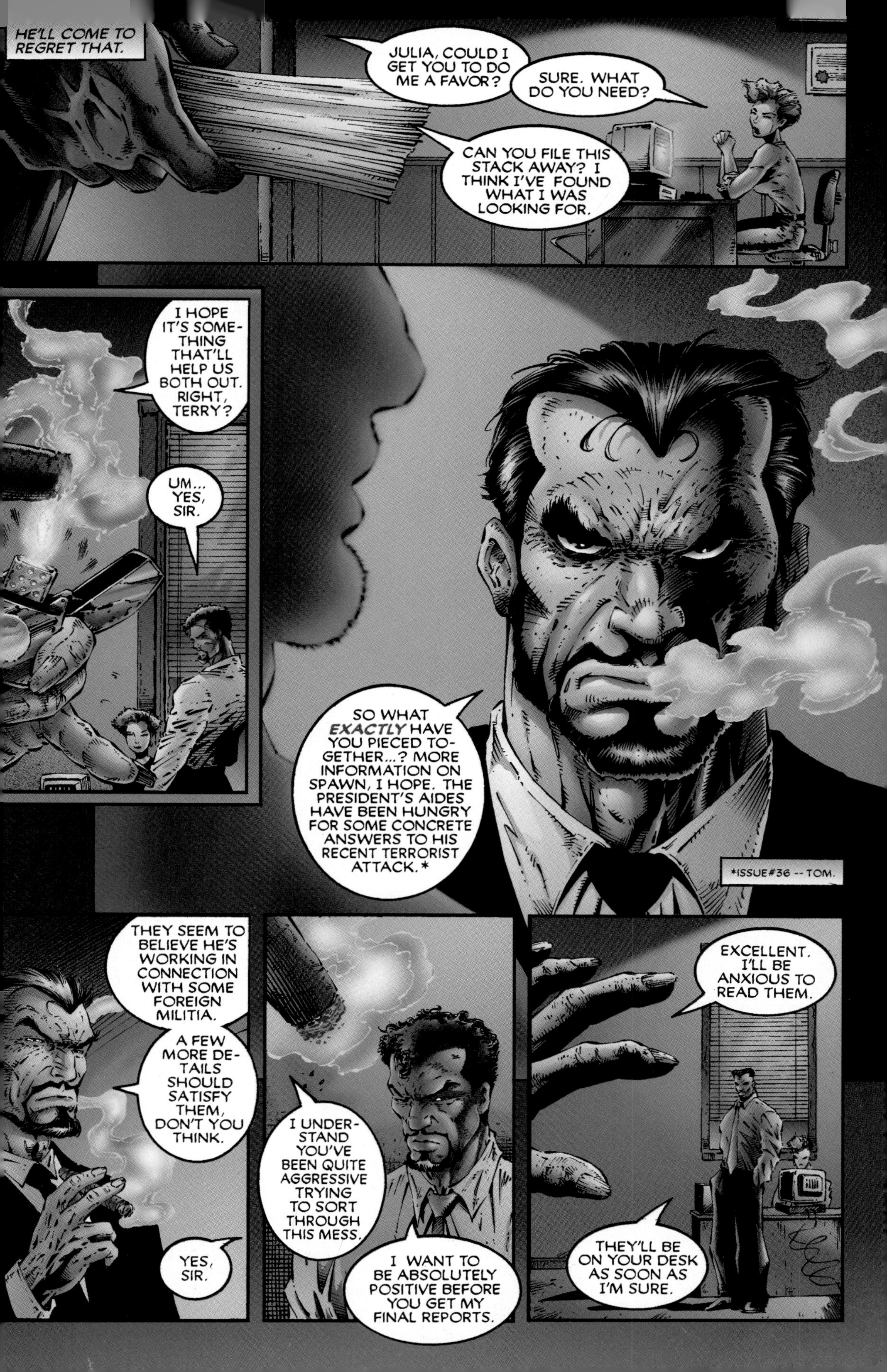
HE'LL COME TO REGRET THAT.
JULIA, COULD I GET YOU TO DO ME A FAVOR?
SURE. WHAT DO YOU NEED?
CAN YOU FILE THIS STACK AWAY? I THINK I'VE FOUND WHAT I WAS LOOKING FOR.
I HOPE IT'S SOMETHING THAT'LL HELP US BOTH OUT. RIGHT, TERRY?
UM... YES, SIR.
SO WHAT EXACTLY HAVE YOU PIECED TOGETHER...? MORE INFORMATION ON SPAWN, I HOPE. THE PRESIDENT'S AIDES HAVE BEEN HUNGRY FOR SOME CONCRETE ANSWERS TO HIS RECENT TERRORIST ATTACK.*
*ISSUE#36 -- TOM.
THEY SEEM TO BELIEVE HE'S WORKING IN CONNECTION WITH SOME FOREIGN MILITIA.
A FEW MORE DETAILS SHOULD SATISFY THEM, DON'T YOU THINK.
YES, SIR.
I UNDERSTAND YOU'VE BEEN QUITE AGGRESSIVE TRYING TO SORT THROUGH THIS MESS.
I WANT TO BE ABSOLUTELY POSITIVE BEFORE YOU GET MY FINAL REPORTS.
EXCELLENT. I'LL BE ANXIOUS TO READ THEM.
THEY'LL BE ON YOUR DESK AS SOON AS I'M SURE.

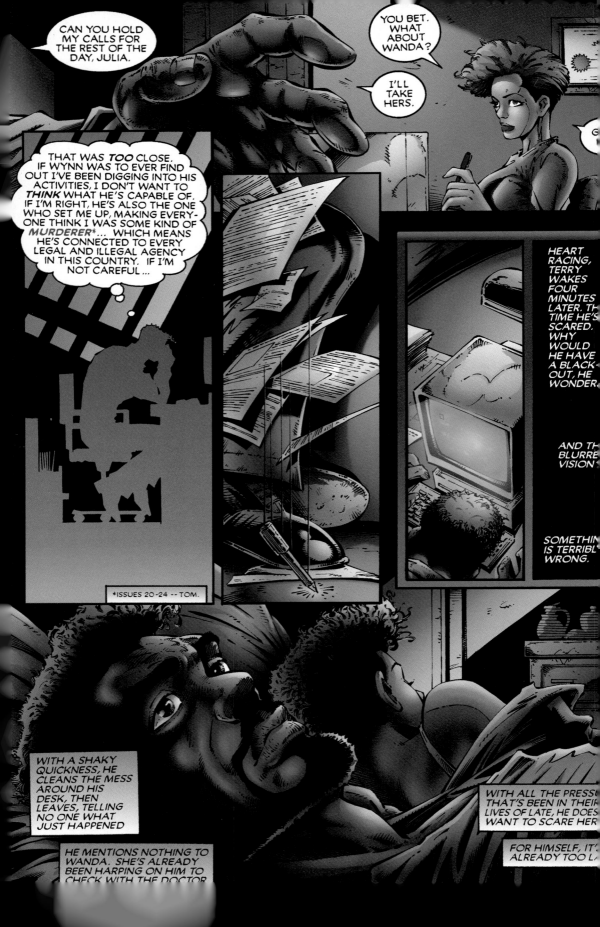

CAN YOU HOLD MY CALLS FOR THE REST OF THE DAY, JULIA.

YOU BET. WHAT ABOUT WANDA?

I'LL TAKE HERS.

THAT WAS *TOO* CLOSE. IF WYNN WAS TO EVER FIND OUT I'VE BEEN DIGGING INTO HIS ACTIVITIES, I DON'T WANT TO *THINK* WHAT HE'S CAPABLE OF. IF I'M RIGHT, HE'S ALSO THE ONE WHO SET ME UP, MAKING EVERY-ONE THINK I WAS SOME KIND OF *MURDERER**... WHICH MEANS HE'S CONNECTED TO EVERY LEGAL AND ILLEGAL AGENCY IN THIS COUNTRY. IF I'M NOT CAREFUL ...

*ISSUES 20-24 -- TOM.

HEART RACING, TERRY WAKES FOUR MINUTES LATER. TH TIME HE'S SCARED. WHY WOULD HE HAVE A BLACK-OUT, HE WONDER

AND TH BLURRE VISION

SOMETHIN IS TERRIBL WRONG.

WITH A SHAKY QUICKNESS, HE CLEANS THE MESS AROUND HIS DESK, THEN LEAVES, TELLING NO ONE WHAT JUST HAPPENED

HE MENTIONS NOTHING TO WANDA. SHE'S ALREADY BEEN HARPING ON HIM TO CHECK WITH THE DOCTOR

WITH ALL THE PRESS THAT'S BEEN IN THEIR LIVES OF LATE, HE DOES WANT TO SCARE HER

FOR HIMSELF, IT' ALREADY TOO L

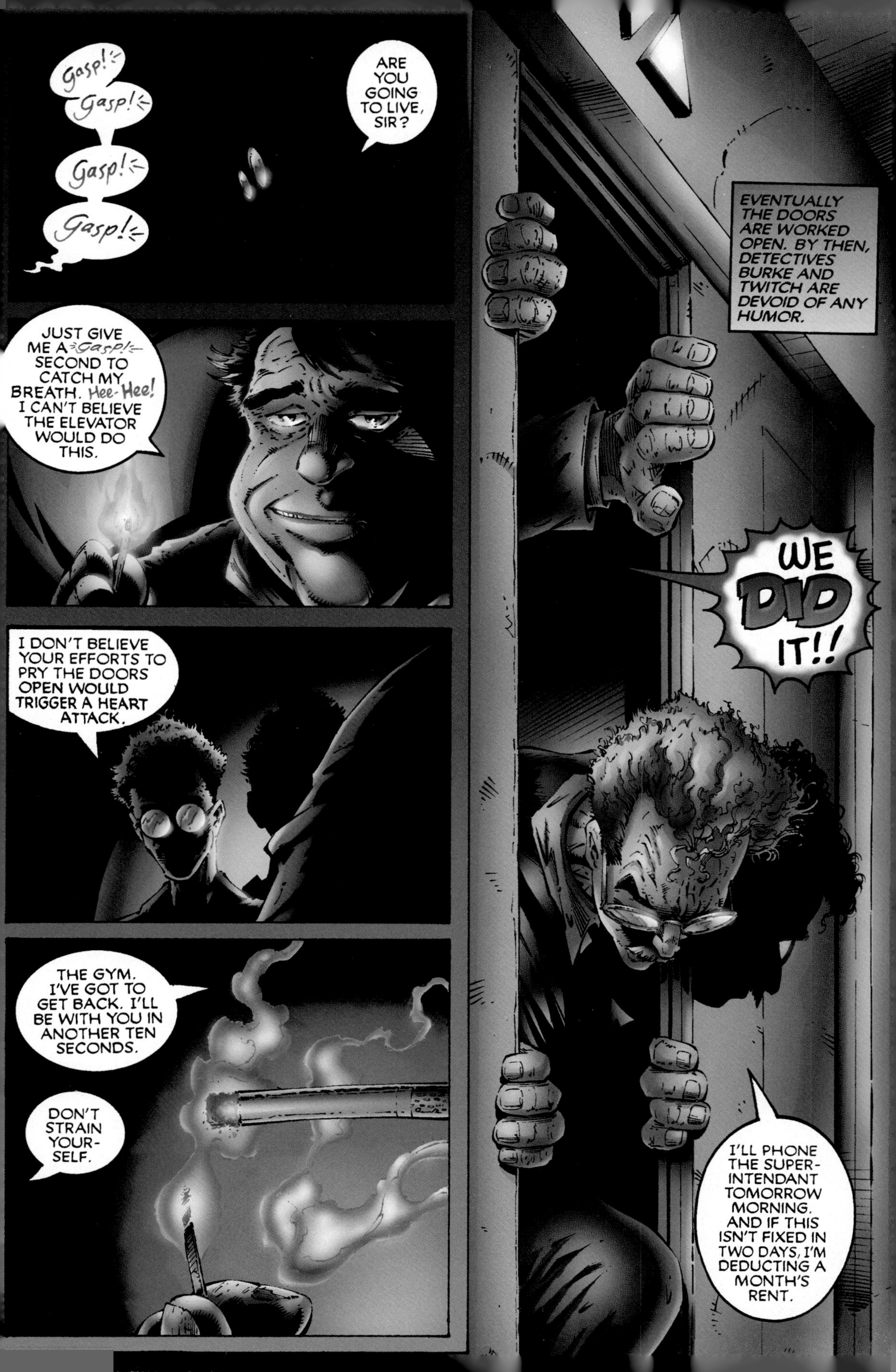
Gasp!
Gasp!
Gasp!
Gasp!
ARE YOU GOING TO LIVE, SIR?
JUST GIVE ME A Gasp! SECOND TO CATCH MY BREATH. Hee-Hee! I CAN'T BELIEVE THE ELEVATOR WOULD DO THIS.
I DON'T BELIEVE YOUR EFFORTS TO PRY THE DOORS OPEN WOULD TRIGGER A HEART ATTACK.
THE GYM. I'VE GOT TO GET BACK. I'LL BE WITH YOU IN ANOTHER TEN SECONDS.
DON'T STRAIN YOUR-SELF.
EVENTUALLY THE DOORS ARE WORKED OPEN. BY THEN, DETECTIVES BURKE AND TWITCH ARE DEVOID OF ANY HUMOR.
WE DID IT!!
I'LL PHONE THE SUPER-INTENDANT TOMORROW MORNING. AND IF THIS ISN'T FIXED IN TWO DAYS, I'M DEDUCTING A MONTH'S RENT.

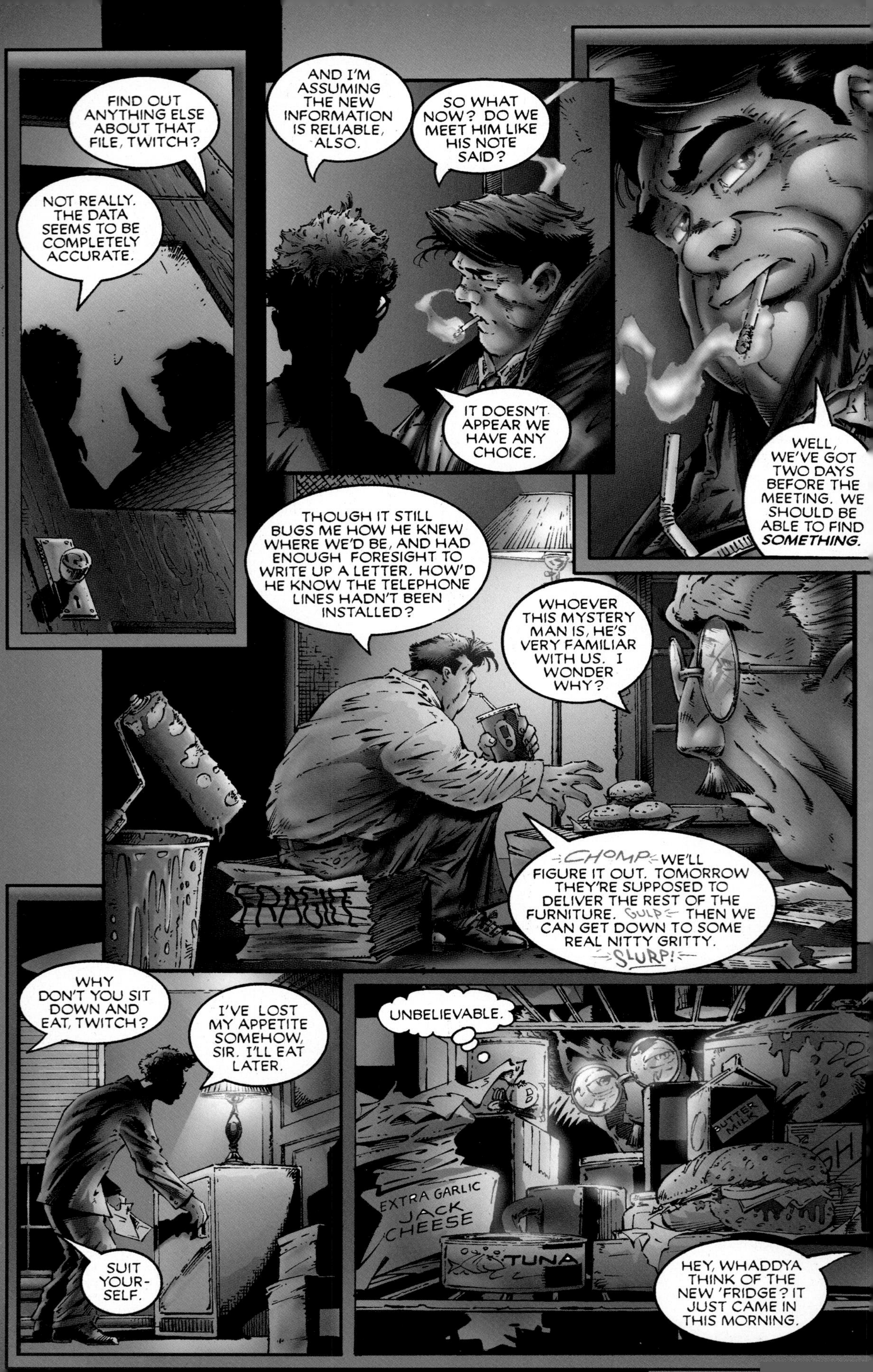

FIND OUT ANYTHING ELSE ABOUT THAT FILE, TWITCH?
NOT REALLY. THE DATA SEEMS TO BE COMPLETELY ACCURATE.
AND I'M ASSUMING THE NEW INFORMATION IS RELIABLE, ALSO.
SO WHAT NOW? DO WE MEET HIM LIKE HIS NOTE SAID?
IT DOESN'T APPEAR WE HAVE ANY CHOICE.
WELL, WE'VE GOT TWO DAYS BEFORE THE MEETING. WE SHOULD BE ABLE TO FIND SOMETHING.
THOUGH IT STILL BUGS ME HOW HE KNEW WHERE WE'D BE, AND HAD ENOUGH FORESIGHT TO WRITE UP A LETTER. HOW'D HE KNOW THE TELEPHONE LINES HADN'T BEEN INSTALLED?
WHOEVER THIS MYSTERY MAN IS, HE'S VERY FAMILIAR WITH US. I WONDER WHY?
FRAGILE
CHOMP WE'LL FIGURE IT OUT. TOMORROW THEY'RE SUPPOSED TO DELIVER THE REST OF THE FURNITURE. GULP THEN WE CAN GET DOWN TO SOME REAL NITTY GRITTY. SLURP!
WHY DON'T YOU SIT DOWN AND EAT, TWITCH?
I'VE LOST MY APPETITE SOMEHOW, SIR. I'LL EAT LATER.
SUIT YOUR-SELF.
UNBELIEVABLE.
BUTTER MILK
EXTRA GARLIC JACK CHEESE
TUNA
HEY, WHADDYA THINK OF THE NEW 'FRIDGE? IT JUST CAME IN THIS MORNING.

IT'S BEEN GOING ON FOR OVER TWENTY MINUTES. AT FIRST THEY CRAWL IN EVERY DIRECTION, CANVASSING AS MUCH OF THE SYMBIOTE'S BEING AS POSSIBLE.

THEN, WHEN THEIR "AURA OF EVIL" HAS BEEN PASSED ON TO THE OUTER SHELL OF THE HELLSPAWN, THEY SLITHER UP TO THE BEING'S HIGHEST POINT.

THEY ARE THE WORMS. THE CARRIERS. GOD'S CREATURES, EVOLVED NOW... SPECIALIZED... TO ABSORB THE SINS OF THE LIVING AND TRANSFER THEM TO THE UNDEAD.

THOUGH HE FIGHTS IT, AL SIMMONS IS A SLAVE TO THIS NEW RITUAL. INTELLECTU-ALLY, HE IS AWARE OF THE PROCESS, BUT HE CANNOT PHYSICALLY CON-TROL ANY OF IT.

THE SYMBIOTE MUST FEED ITSELF.

FORTUNATELY, IT WON'T MATTER. THE CEREMONY WILL CONCLUDE IN ANOTHER FEW MINUTES.

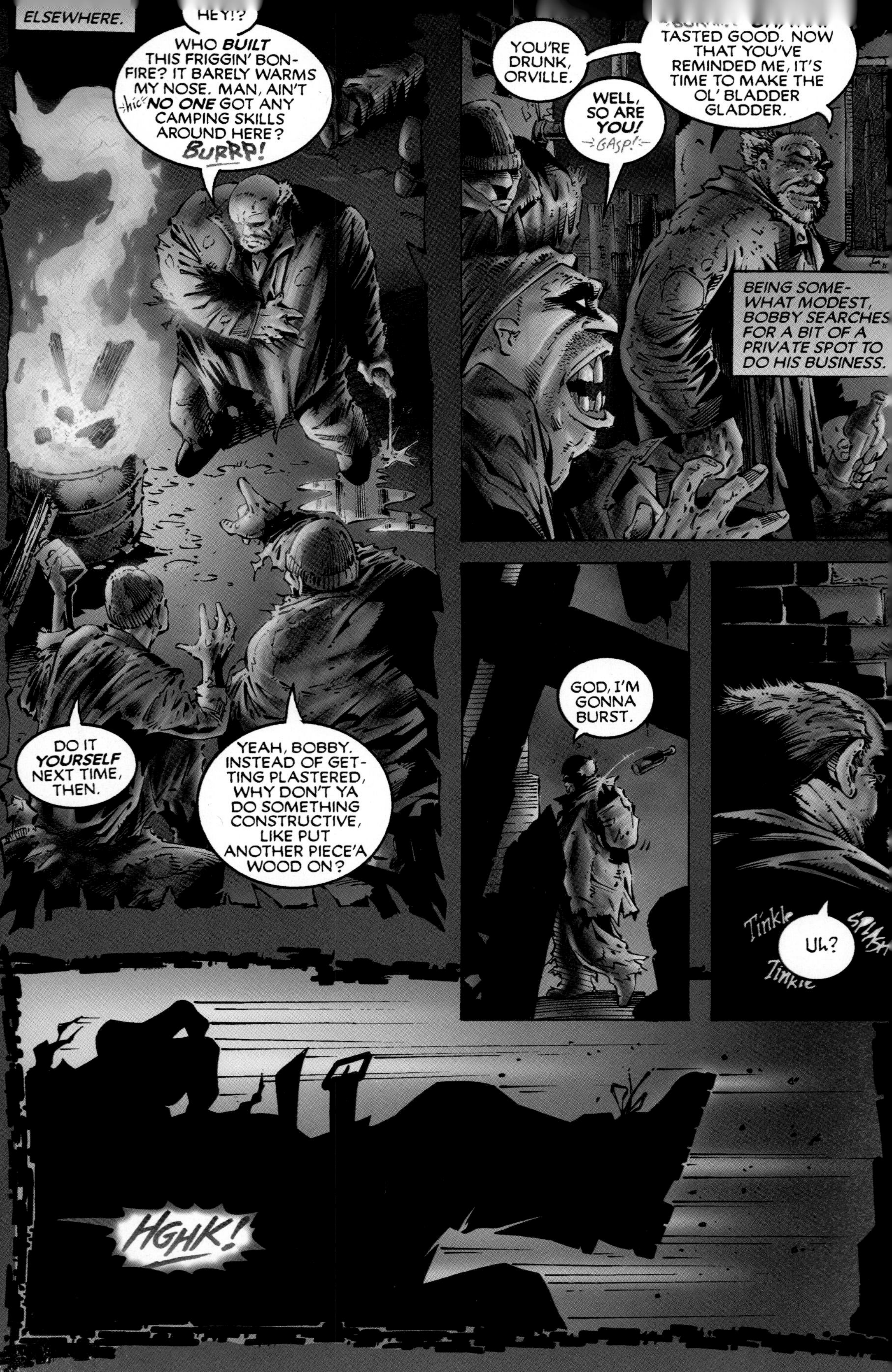
ELSEWHERE.
HEY!? WHO BUILT THIS FRIGGIN' BON-FIRE? IT BARELY WARMS MY NOSE. MAN, AIN'T -hic- NO ONE GOT ANY CAMPING SKILLS AROUND HERE? BURRP!
DO IT YOURSELF NEXT TIME, THEN.
YEAH, BOBBY. INSTEAD OF GET-TING PLASTERED, WHY DON'T YA DO SOMETHING CONSTRUCTIVE, LIKE PUT ANOTHER PIECE'A WOOD ON?
YOU'RE DRUNK, ORVILLE.
TASTED GOOD. NOW THAT YOU'VE REMINDED ME, IT'S TIME TO MAKE THE OL' BLADDER GLADDER.
WELL, SO ARE YOU! -GASP!-
BEING SOME-WHAT MODEST, BOBBY SEARCHES FOR A BIT OF A PRIVATE SPOT TO DO HIS BUSINESS.
GOD, I'M GONNA BURST.
Tinkle
Uh?
Tinkle
HGHK!

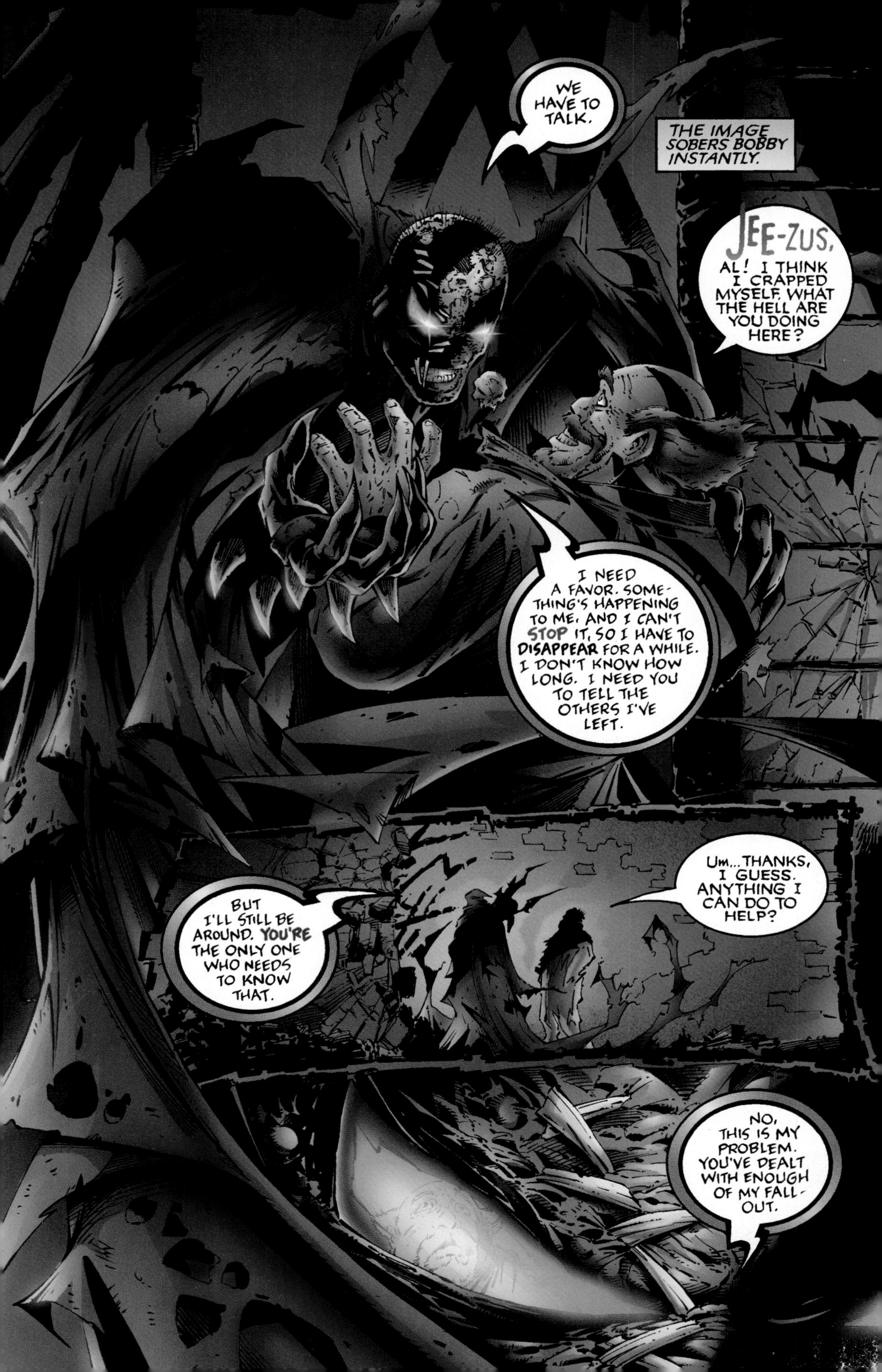
WE HAVE TO TALK.
THE IMAGE SOBERS BOBBY INSTANTLY.
JEE-ZUS, AL! I THINK I CRAPPED MYSELF. WHAT THE HELL ARE YOU DOING HERE?
I NEED A FAVOR. SOMETHING'S HAPPENING TO ME, AND I CAN'T STOP IT, SO I HAVE TO DISAPPEAR FOR A WHILE. I DON'T KNOW HOW LONG. I NEED YOU TO TELL THE OTHERS I'VE LEFT.
BUT I'LL STILL BE AROUND. YOU'RE THE ONLY ONE WHO NEEDS TO KNOW THAT.
Um... THANKS, I GUESS. ANYTHING I CAN DO TO HELP?
NO, THIS IS MY PROBLEM. YOU'VE DEALT WITH ENOUGH OF MY FALL-OUT.

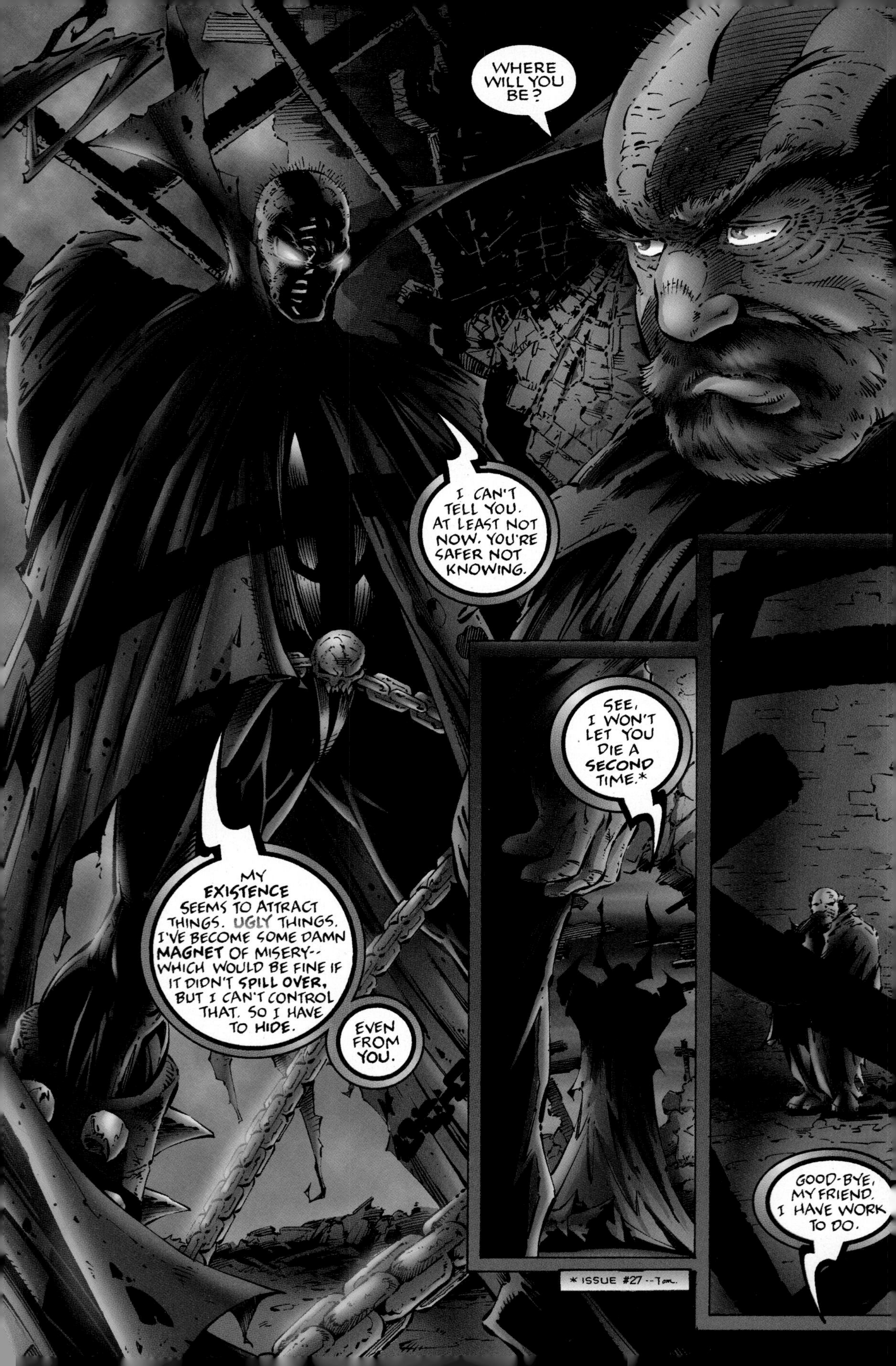
WHERE WILL YOU BE?
I CAN'T TELL YOU. AT LEAST NOT NOW. YOU'RE SAFER NOT KNOWING.
MY EXISTENCE SEEMS TO ATTRACT THINGS. UGLY THINGS. I'VE BECOME SOME DAMN MAGNET OF MISERY-- WHICH WOULD BE FINE IF IT DIDN'T SPILL OVER, BUT I CAN'T CONTROL THAT. SO I HAVE TO HIDE.
EVEN FROM YOU.
SEE, I WON'T LET YOU DIE A SECOND TIME.*
* ISSUE #27 --Tom.
GOOD-BYE, MY FRIEND. I HAVE WORK TO DO.

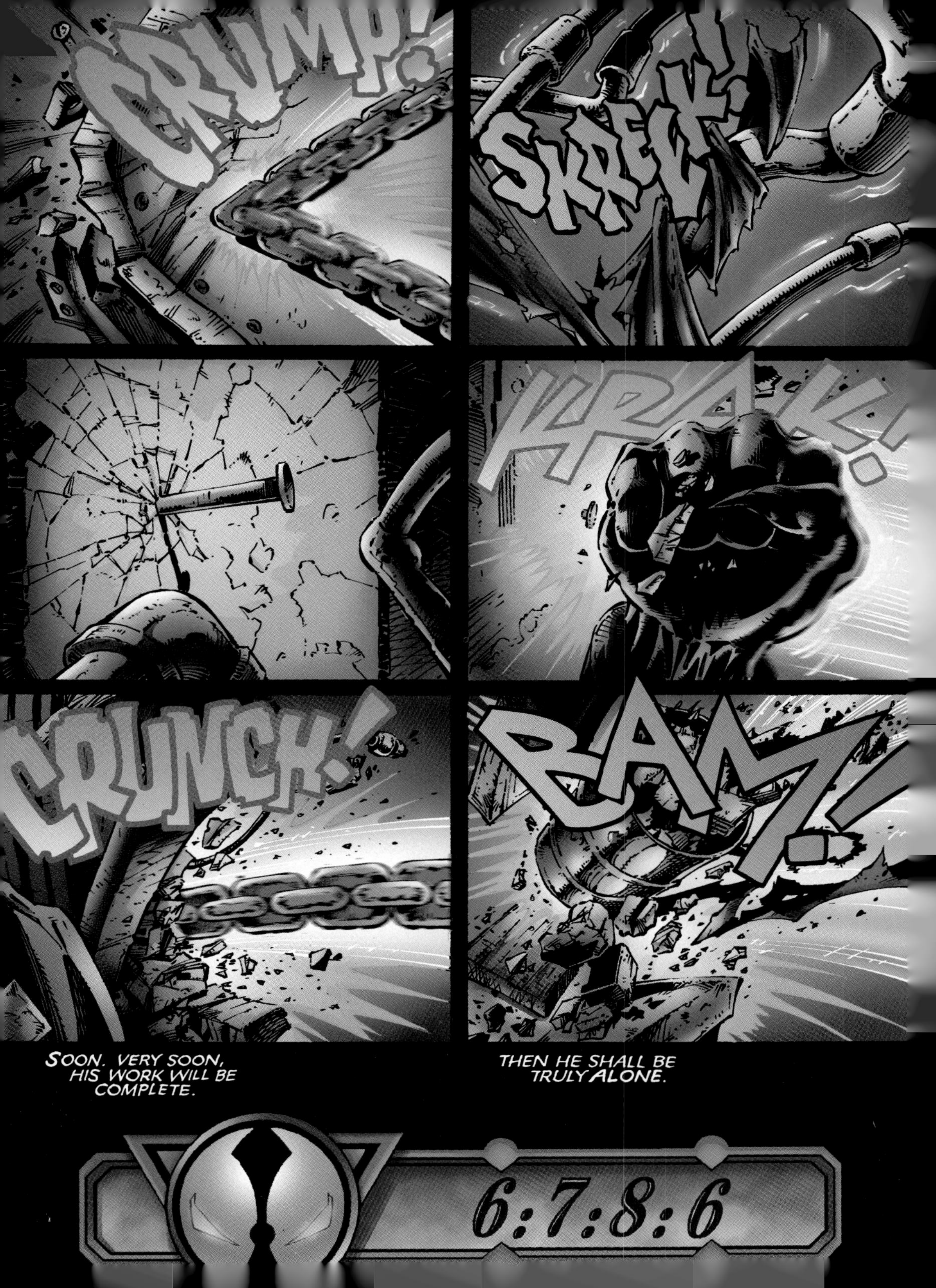
CRUMP!
SKRECK!
KRAK!
CRUNCH!
BAM!
SOON. VERY SOON, HIS WORK WILL BE COMPLETE.
THEN HE SHALL BE TRULY ALONE.
6:7:8:6

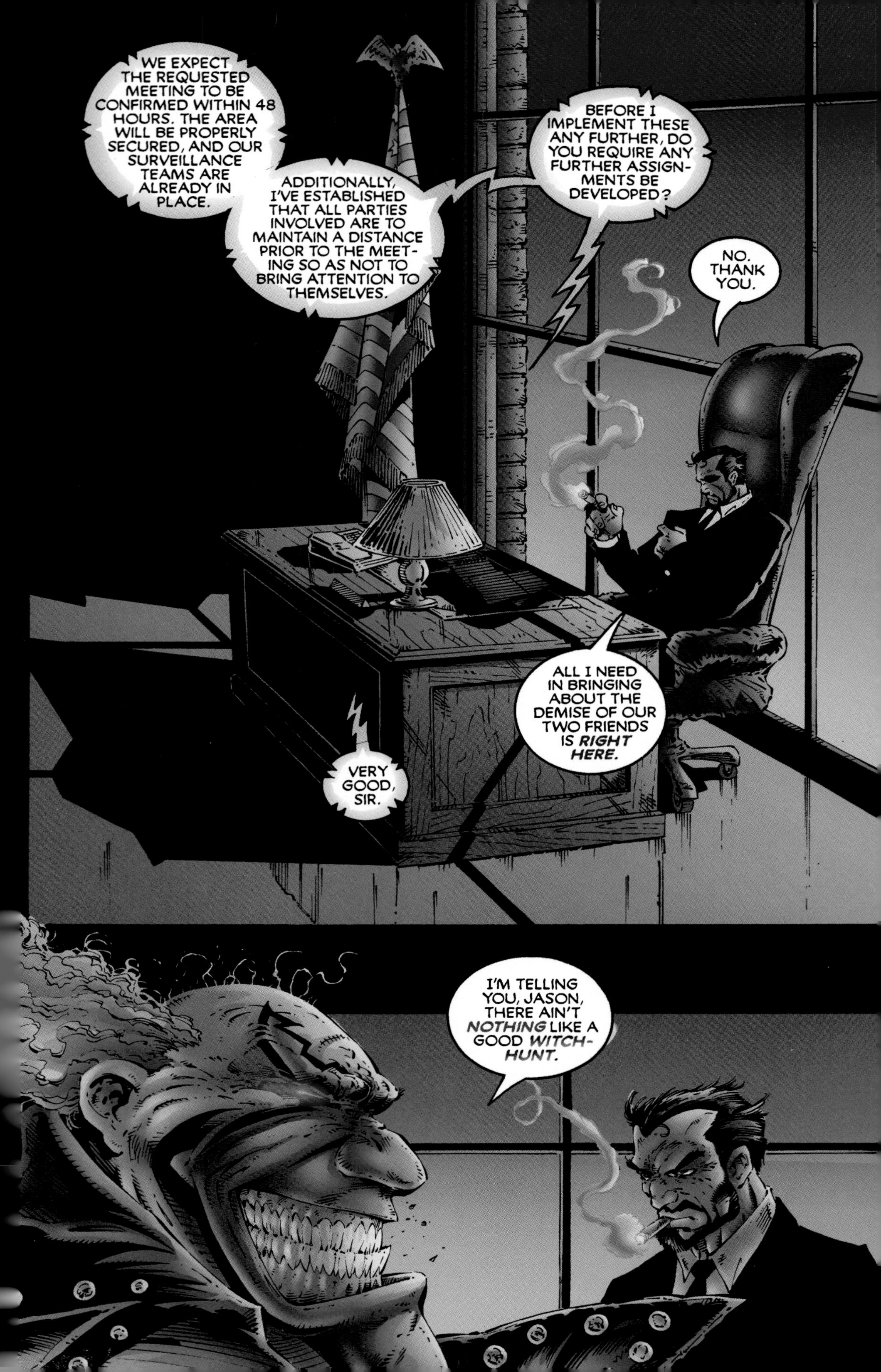
WE EXPECT THE REQUESTED MEETING TO BE CONFIRMED WITHIN 48 HOURS. THE AREA WILL BE PROPERLY SECURED, AND OUR SURVEILLANCE TEAMS ARE ALREADY IN PLACE.
ADDITIONALLY, I'VE ESTABLISHED THAT ALL PARTIES INVOLVED ARE TO MAINTAIN A DISTANCE PRIOR TO THE MEETING SO AS NOT TO BRING ATTENTION TO THEMSELVES.
BEFORE I IMPLEMENT THESE ANY FURTHER, DO YOU REQUIRE ANY FURTHER ASSIGNMENTS BE DEVELOPED?
NO. THANK YOU.
ALL I NEED IN BRINGING ABOUT THE DEMISE OF OUR TWO FRIENDS IS *RIGHT HERE.*
VERY GOOD, SIR.
I'M TELLING YOU, JASON, THERE AIN'T *NOTHING* LIKE A GOOD *WITCH-HUNT.*

Dusk. The triumph of darkness over the retreating light. The passing of light's influence over the land. When the balance between good and evil begins its shift.

–HELTER SKELTER

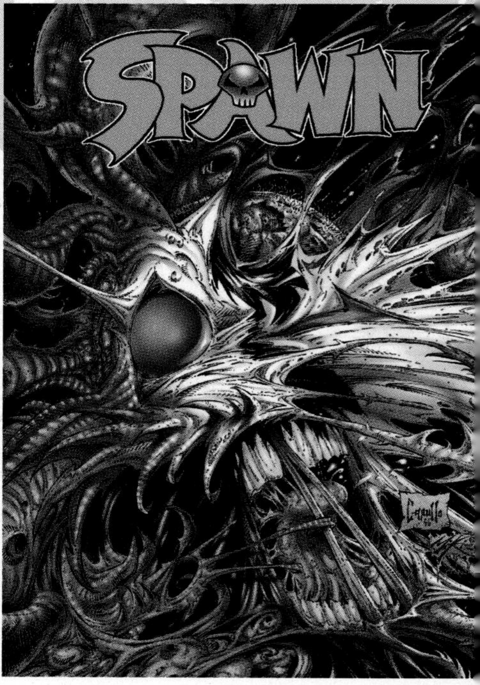
SPAWN

FORTY-NINE

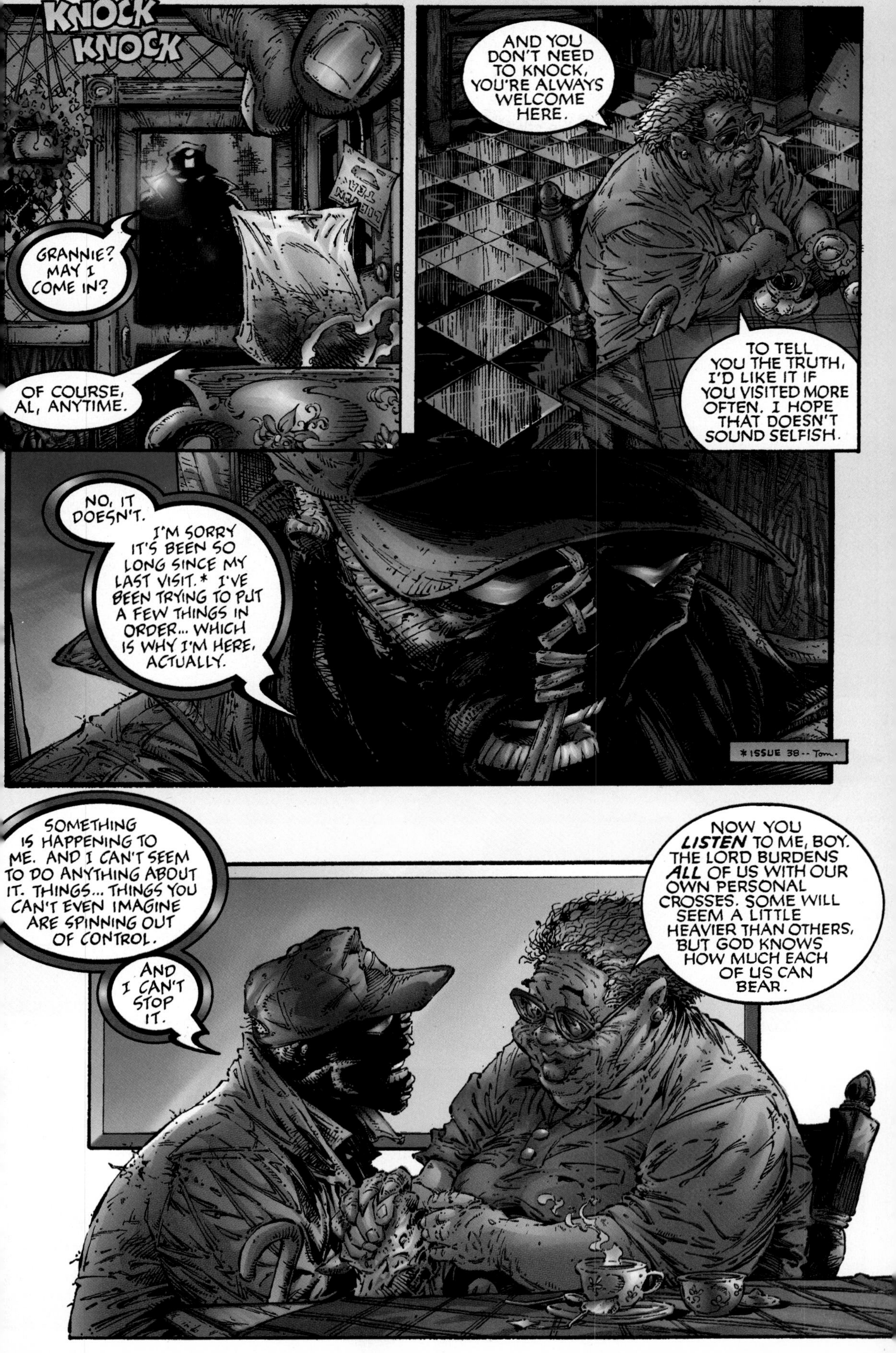
KNOCK KNOCK
GRANNIE? MAY I COME IN?
OF COURSE, AL, ANYTIME.
AND YOU DON'T NEED TO KNOCK, YOU'RE ALWAYS WELCOME HERE.
TO TELL YOU THE TRUTH, I'D LIKE IT IF YOU VISITED MORE OFTEN. I HOPE THAT DOESN'T SOUND SELFISH.
NO, IT DOESN'T.
I'M SORRY IT'S BEEN SO LONG SINCE MY LAST VISIT.* I'VE BEEN TRYING TO PUT A FEW THINGS IN ORDER... WHICH IS WHY I'M HERE, ACTUALLY.
*ISSUE 38--Tom.
SOMETHING IS HAPPENING TO ME. AND I CAN'T SEEM TO DO ANYTHING ABOUT IT. THINGS... THINGS YOU CAN'T EVEN IMAGINE ARE SPINNING OUT OF CONTROL.
AND I CAN'T STOP IT.
NOW YOU LISTEN TO ME, BOY. THE LORD BURDENS ALL OF US WITH OUR OWN PERSONAL CROSSES. SOME WILL SEEM A LITTLE HEAVIER THAN OTHERS, BUT GOD KNOWS HOW MUCH EACH OF US CAN BEAR.

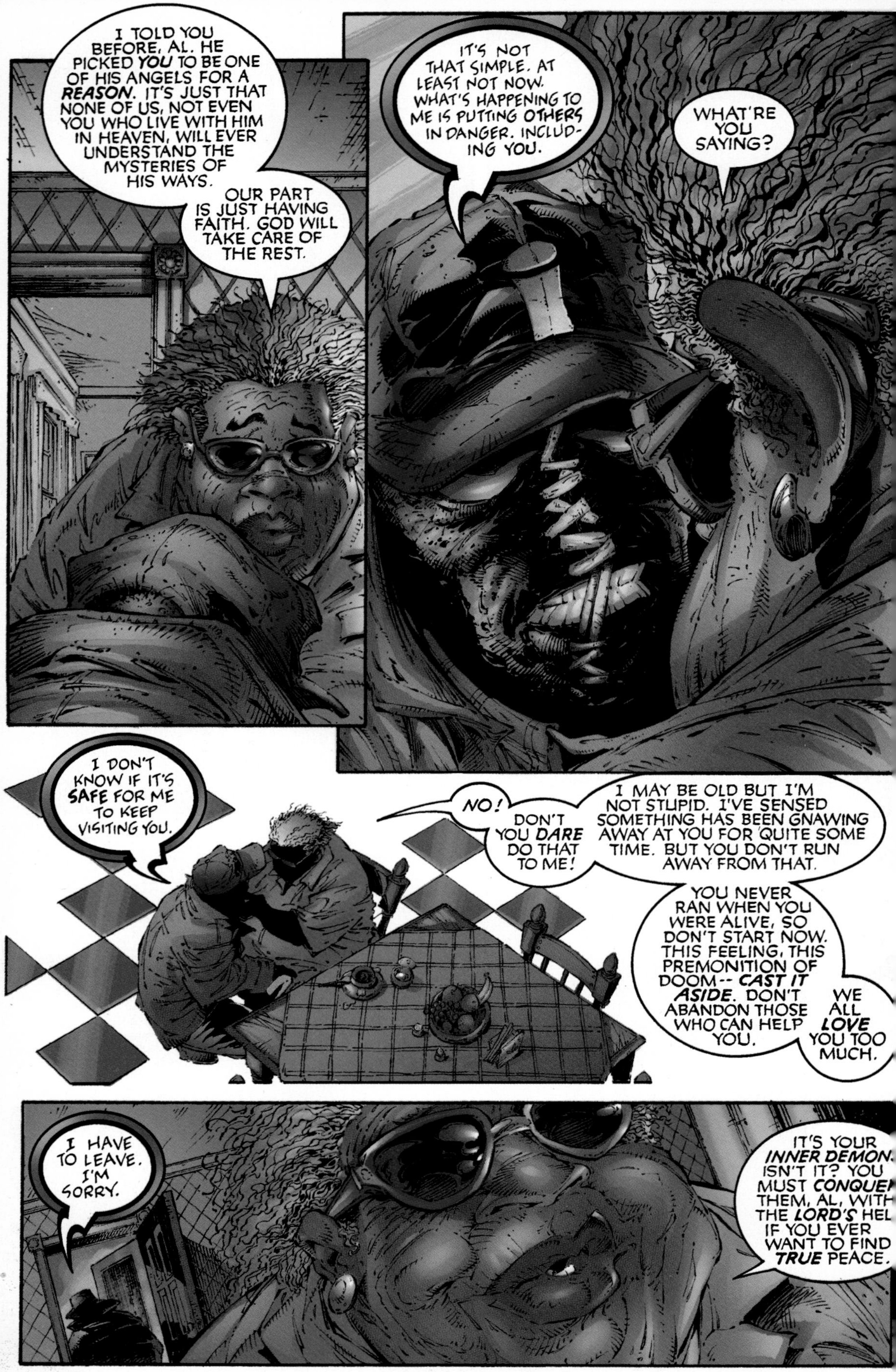
I TOLD YOU BEFORE, AL. HE PICKED YOU TO BE ONE OF HIS ANGELS FOR A REASON. IT'S JUST THAT NONE OF US, NOT EVEN YOU WHO LIVE WITH HIM IN HEAVEN, WILL EVER UNDERSTAND THE MYSTERIES OF HIS WAYS.
OUR PART IS JUST HAVING FAITH. GOD WILL TAKE CARE OF THE REST.
IT'S NOT THAT SIMPLE. AT LEAST NOT NOW. WHAT'S HAPPENING TO ME IS PUTTING OTHERS IN DANGER. INCLUD-ING YOU.
WHAT'RE YOU SAYING?
I DON'T KNOW IF IT'S SAFE FOR ME TO KEEP VISITING YOU.
NO!
DON'T YOU DARE DO THAT TO ME!
I MAY BE OLD BUT I'M NOT STUPID. I'VE SENSED SOMETHING HAS BEEN GNAWING AWAY AT YOU FOR QUITE SOME TIME. BUT YOU DON'T RUN AWAY FROM THAT.
YOU NEVER RAN WHEN YOU WERE ALIVE, SO DON'T START NOW. THIS FEELING, THIS PREMONITION OF DOOM-- CAST IT ASIDE. DON'T ABANDON THOSE WHO CAN HELP YOU.
WE ALL LOVE YOU TOO MUCH.
I HAVE TO LEAVE. I'M SORRY.
IT'S YOUR INNER DEMON ISN'T IT? YOU MUST CONQUE THEM, AL, WITH THE LORD'S HEL IF YOU EVER WANT TO FIND TRUE PEACE.

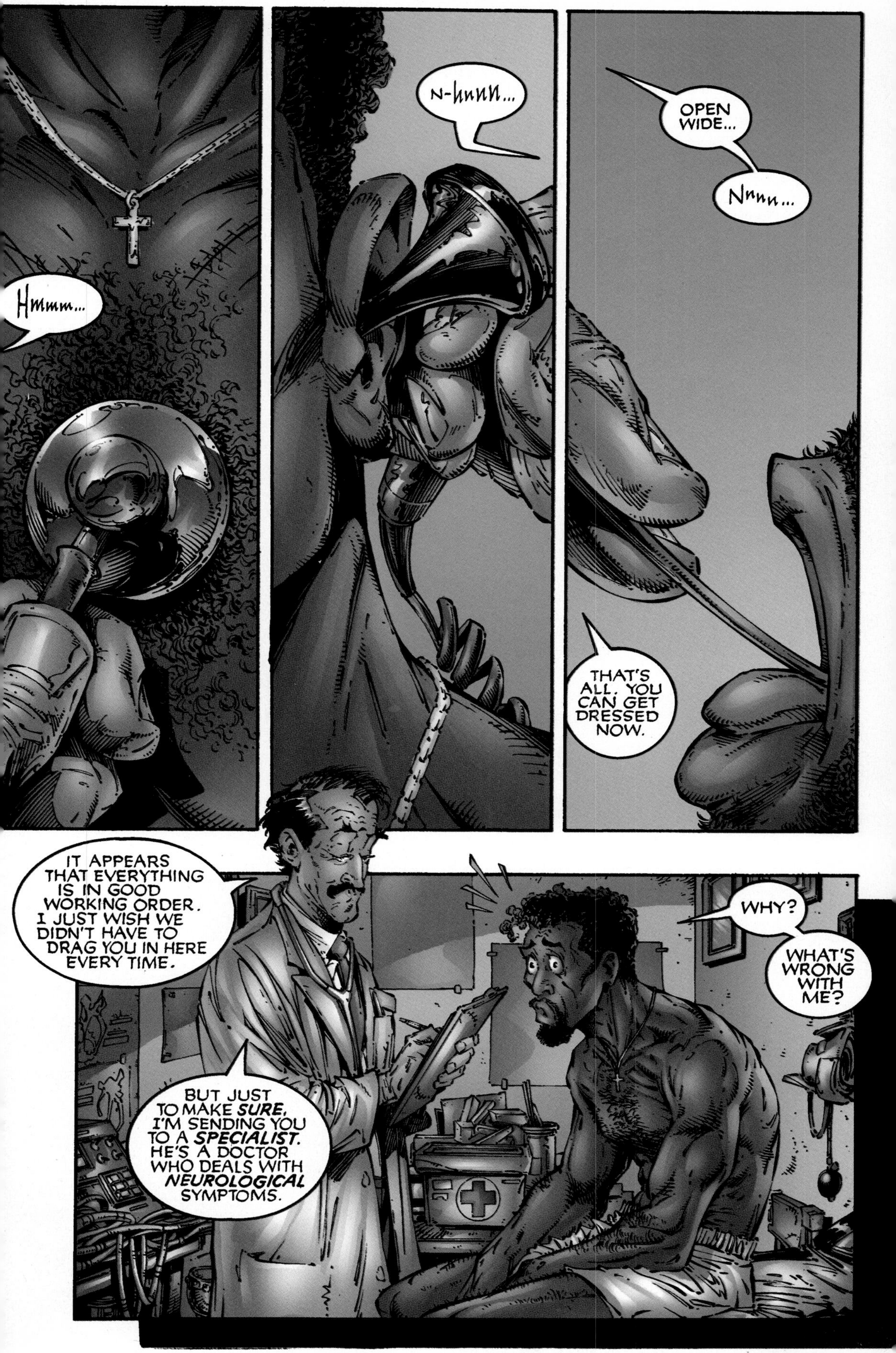
Hmmm...
N-hnnn...
OPEN WIDE...
Nnnn...
THAT'S ALL. YOU CAN GET DRESSED NOW.
IT APPEARS THAT EVERYTHING IS IN GOOD WORKING ORDER. I JUST WISH WE DIDN'T HAVE TO DRAG YOU IN HERE EVERY TIME.
WHY?
WHAT'S WRONG WITH ME?
BUT JUST TO MAKE SURE, I'M SENDING YOU TO A SPECIALIST. HE'S A DOCTOR WHO DEALS WITH NEUROLOGICAL SYMPTOMS.

NOTHING, I HOPE... BUT YOUR FAINTING SPELL TELLS ME THAT SOMETHING WENT WRONG. *

I JUST LIKE TO BE CERTAIN I HAVEN'T OVERLOOKED ANYTHING.

* LAST ISSUE -- Tom.

OH, NOW DON'T LOOK SO WORRIED.

THE DOCTOR WILL JUST RUN A FEW *TESTS*, POSSIBLY A C.T. SCAN, JUST TO EASE *ALL* OUR MINDS. I KNOW YOU'VE BEEN UNDER A GREAT DEAL OF PRESSURE LATELY... ON *TOP* OF THAT NASTY COUGH YOU'VE HAD... BUT US MEDICAL GEEKS LIKE TO KNOW WHY PEOPLE BLACK OUT FOR NO REASON.

IT HAPPENS TO MOST PEOPLE AT LEAST ONCE IN THEIR LIVES. WE JUST NEVER KNOW *WHY*.

WHAT CAN I SAY, WE'RE A CURIOUS LO SO I'LL SCHEDULE AN APPOIN MENT...?

UH... YEAH, SURE. IF YOU THINK IT'S BEST.

COFF

COFF

COFF

OUT IN THE PARKING LOT, TERRY'S CHEST BEGINS TO TIGHTEN AS HIS MIND SWIRLS WITH FABRICATED IMAGES AND THOUGHTS.

IT TRIGGERS A SLIGHT COUGHING FIT.

HE CURSES HIMSELF FOR NOT DOING SOMETHING EARLIER.

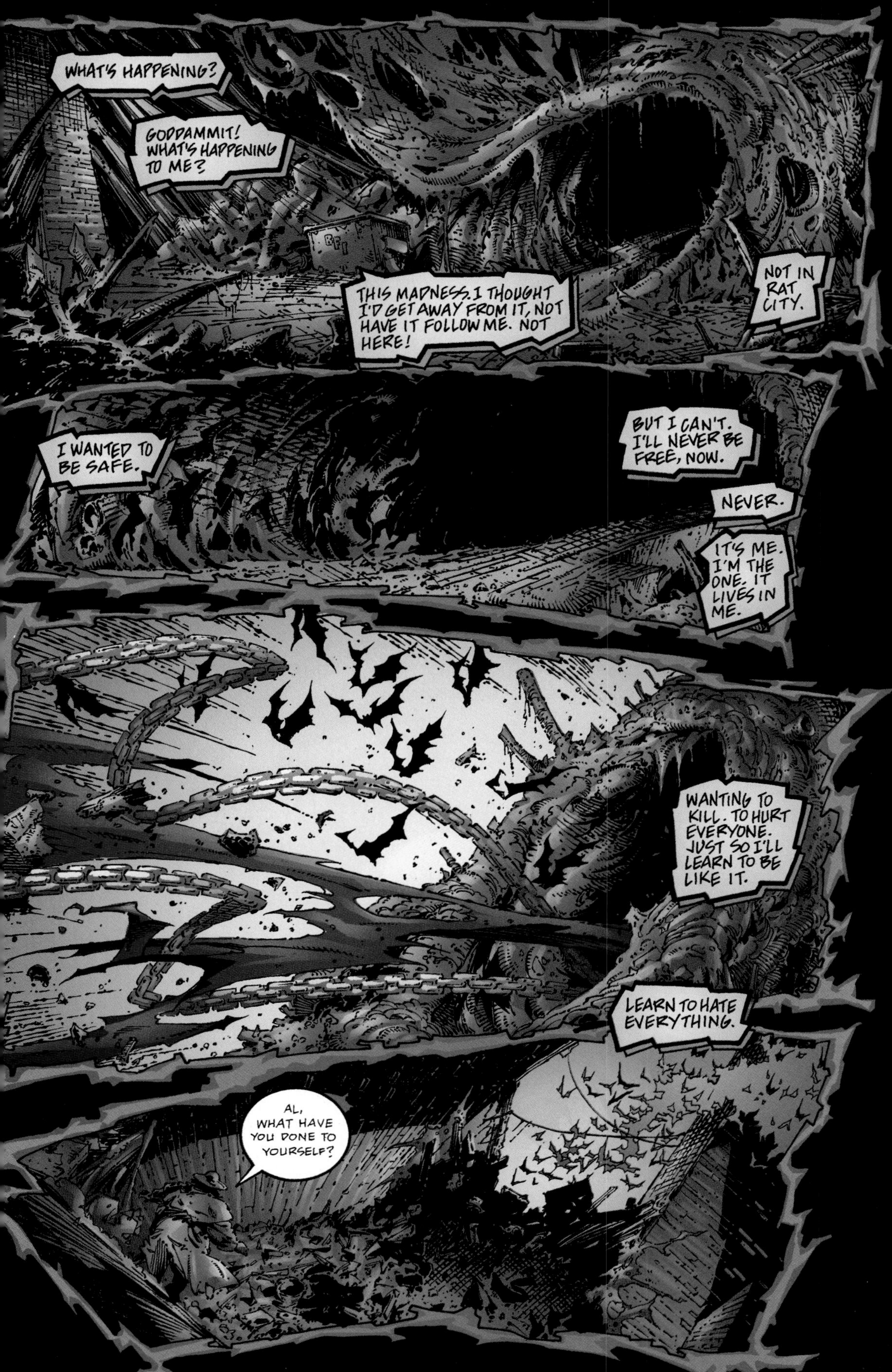
WHAT'S HAPPENING?
GODDAMMIT! WHAT'S HAPPENING TO ME?
THIS MADNESS. I THOUGHT I'D GET AWAY FROM IT, NOT HAVE IT FOLLOW ME. NOT HERE!
NOT IN RAT CITY.
I WANTED TO BE SAFE.
BUT I CAN'T. I'LL NEVER BE FREE, NOW.
NEVER.
IT'S ME. I'M THE ONE. IT LIVES IN ME.
WANTING TO KILL. TO HURT EVERYONE. JUST SO I'LL LEARN TO BE LIKE IT.
LEARN TO HATE EVERYTHING.
AL, WHAT HAVE YOU DONE TO YOURSELF?

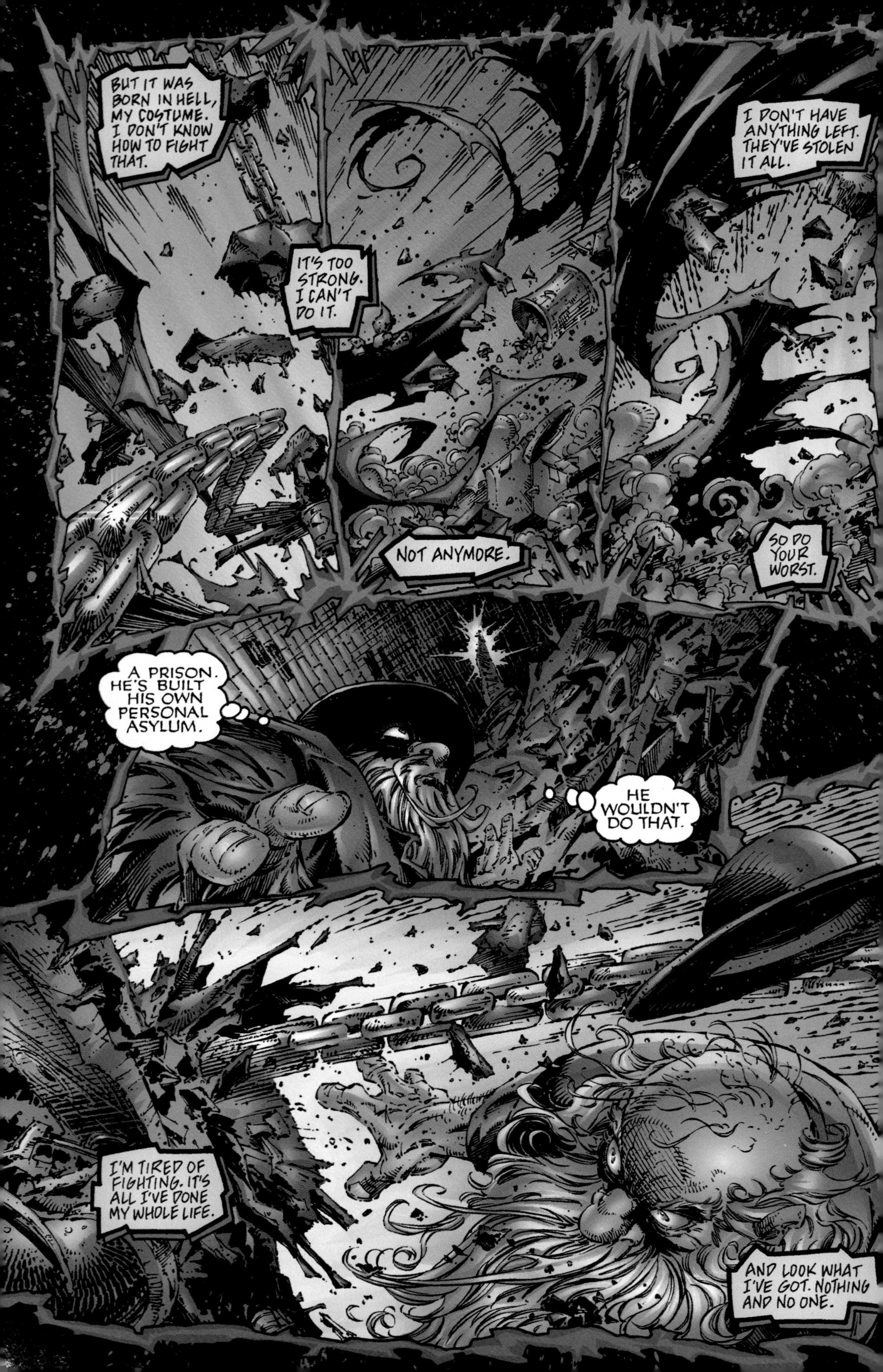
BUT IT WAS BORN IN HELL, MY COSTUME. I DON'T KNOW HOW TO FIGHT THAT.
IT'S TOO STRONG. I CAN'T DO IT.
I DON'T HAVE ANYTHING LEFT. THEY'VE STOLEN IT ALL.
NOT ANYMORE.
SO DO YOUR WORST.
A PRISON. HE'S BUILT HIS OWN PERSONAL ASYLUM.
HE WOULDN'T DO THAT.
I'M TIRED OF FIGHTING. IT'S ALL I'VE DONE MY WHOLE LIFE.
AND LOOK WHAT I'VE GOT. NOTHING AND NO ONE.

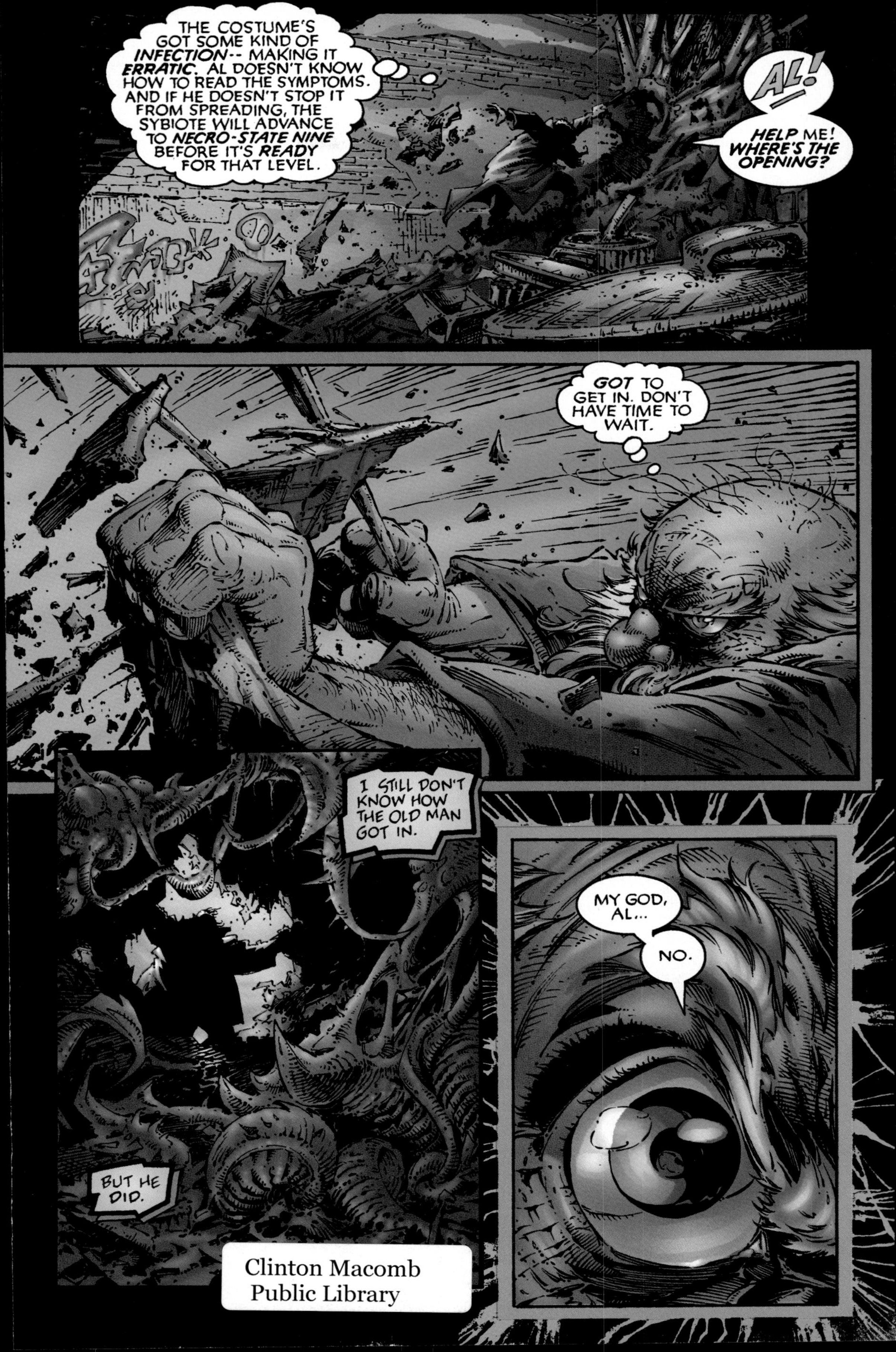
THE COSTUME'S GOT SOME KIND OF INFECTION-- MAKING IT ERRATIC. AL DOESN'T KNOW HOW TO READ THE SYMPTOMS. AND IF HE DOESN'T STOP IT FROM SPREADING, THE SYBIOTE WILL ADVANCE TO NECRO-STATE NINE BEFORE IT'S READY FOR THAT LEVEL.
AL!
HELP ME! WHERE'S THE OPENING?
GOT TO GET IN. DON'T HAVE TIME TO WAIT.
I STILL DON'T KNOW HOW THE OLD MAN GOT IN.
BUT HE DID.
MY GOD, AL...
NO.

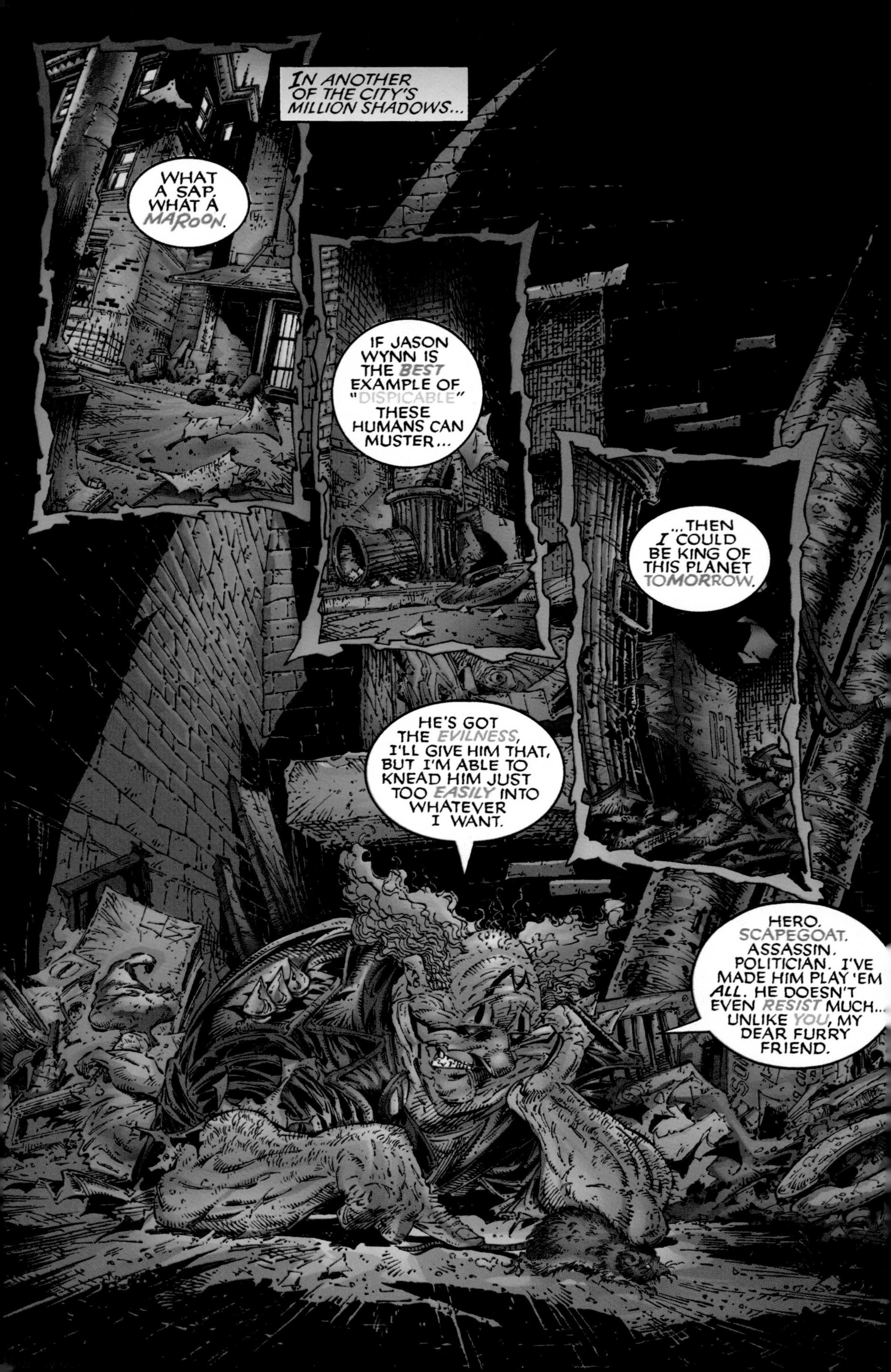
IN ANOTHER OF THE CITY'S MILLION SHADOWS...
WHAT A SAP. WHAT A MAROON.
IF JASON WYNN IS THE BEST EXAMPLE OF "DISPICABLE" THESE HUMANS CAN MUSTER...
...THEN I COULD BE KING OF THIS PLANET TOMORROW.
HE'S GOT THE EVILNESS, I'LL GIVE HIM THAT, BUT I'M ABLE TO KNEAD HIM JUST TOO EASILY INTO WHATEVER I WANT.
HERO. SCAPEGOAT. ASSASSIN. POLITICIAN. I'VE MADE HIM PLAY 'EM ALL. HE DOESN'T EVEN RESIST MUCH... UNLIKE YOU, MY DEAR FURRY FRIEND.

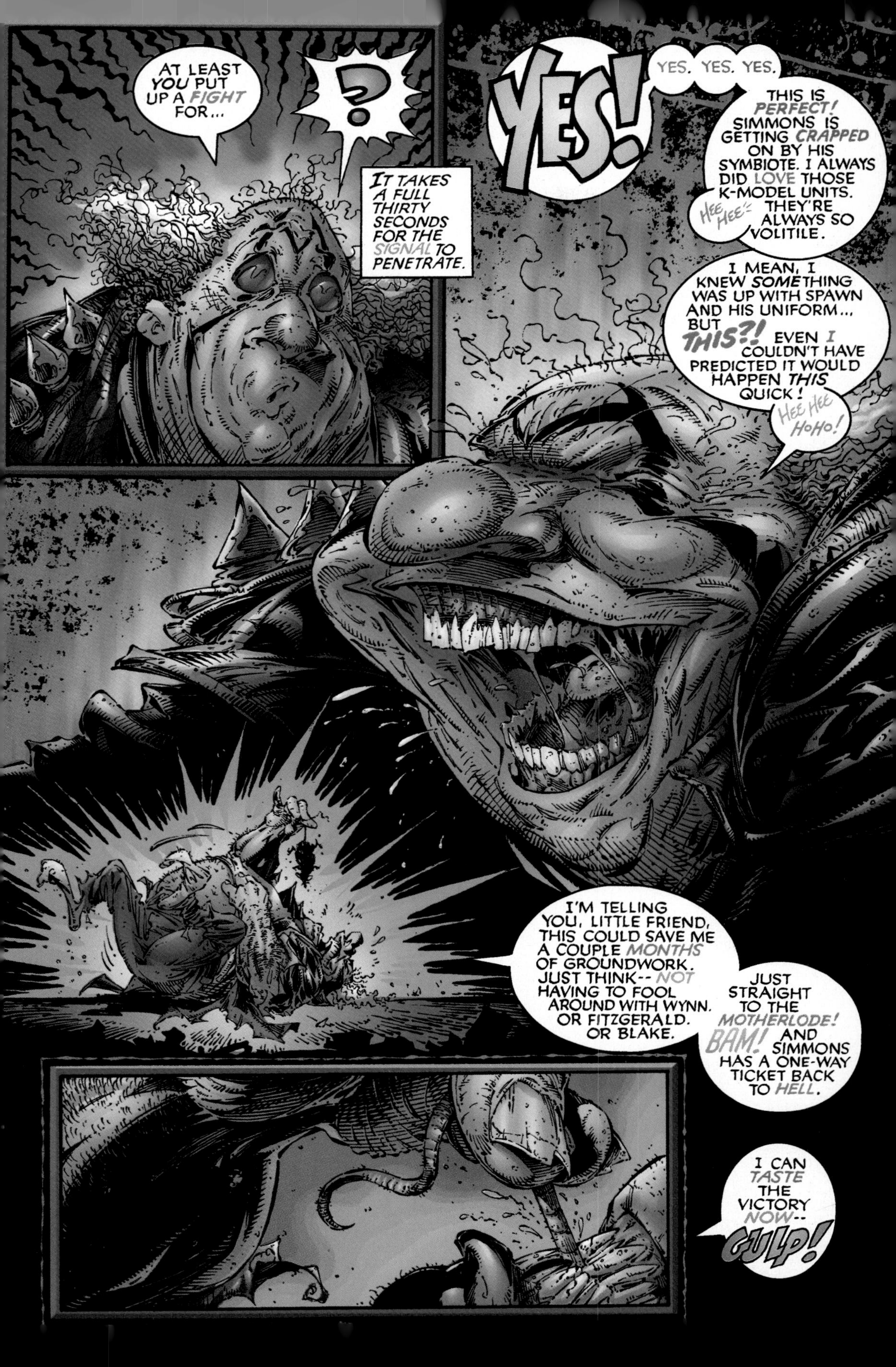

AT LEAST YOU PUT UP A FIGHT FOR...
?
IT TAKES A FULL THIRTY SECONDS FOR THE SIGNAL TO PENETRATE.
YES!
YES. YES. YES.
THIS IS PERFECT! SIMMONS IS GETTING CRAPPED ON BY HIS SYMBIOTE. I ALWAYS DID LOVE THOSE K-MODEL UNITS. HEE HEE THEY'RE ALWAYS SO VOLITILE.
I MEAN, I KNEW SOMETHING WAS UP WITH SPAWN AND HIS UNIFORM..., BUT THIS?! EVEN I COULDN'T HAVE PREDICTED IT WOULD HAPPEN THIS QUICK! HEE HEE HOHO!
I'M TELLING YOU, LITTLE FRIEND, THIS COULD SAVE ME A COUPLE MONTHS OF GROUNDWORK. JUST THINK-- NOT HAVING TO FOOL AROUND WITH WYNN. OR FITZGERALD. OR BLAKE.
JUST STRAIGHT TO THE MOTHERLODE! BAM! AND SIMMONS HAS A ONE-WAY TICKET BACK TO HELL.
I CAN TASTE THE VICTORY NOW-- GULP!

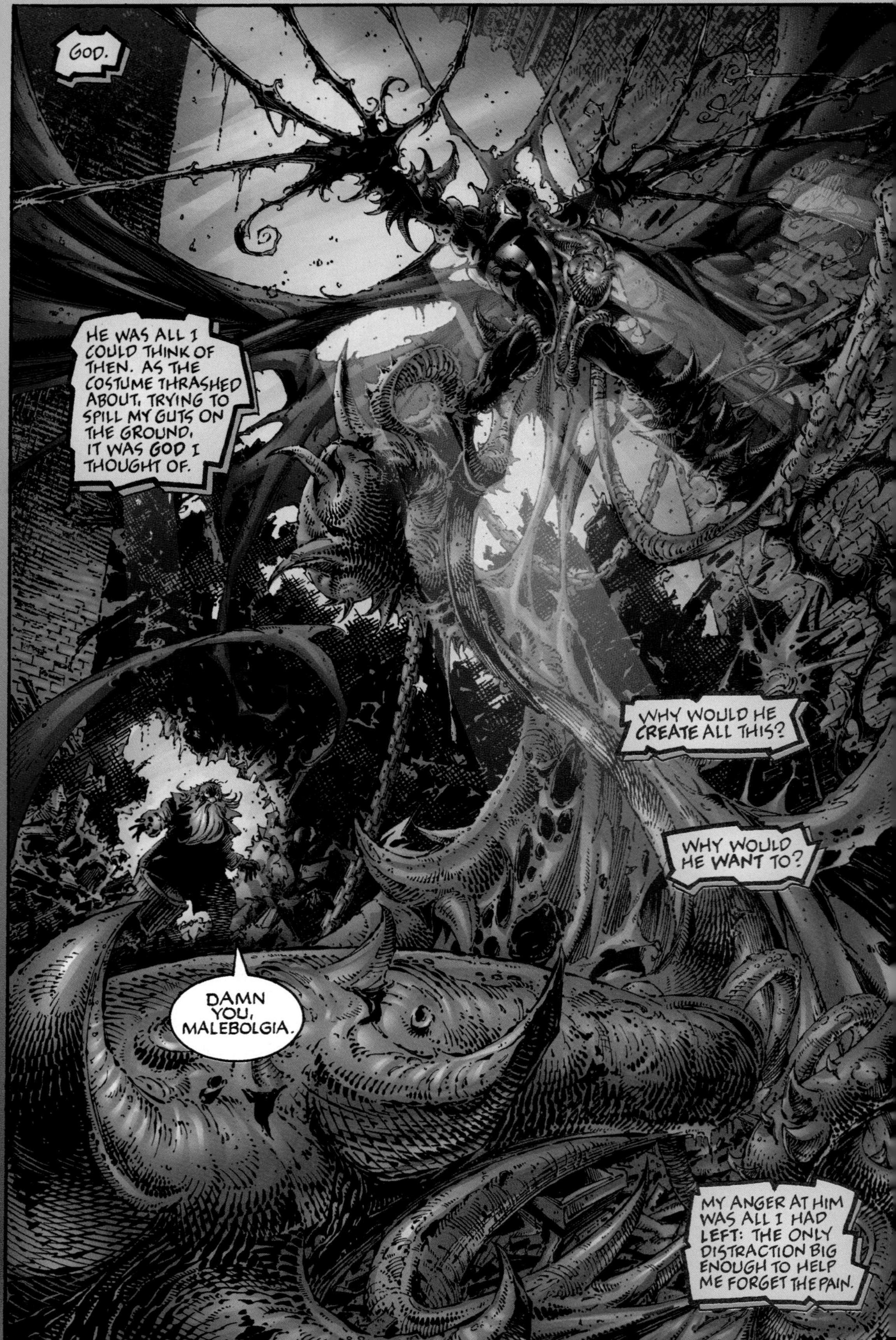
GOD.
HE WAS ALL I COULD THINK OF THEN. AS THE COSTUME THRASHED ABOUT, TRYING TO SPILL MY GUTS ON THE GROUND, IT WAS GOD I THOUGHT OF.
WHY WOULD HE CREATE ALL THIS?
WHY WOULD HE WANT TO?
DAMN YOU, MALEBOLGIA.
MY ANGER AT HIM WAS ALL I HAD LEFT: THE ONLY DISTRACTION BIG ENOUGH TO HELP ME FORGET THE PAIN.

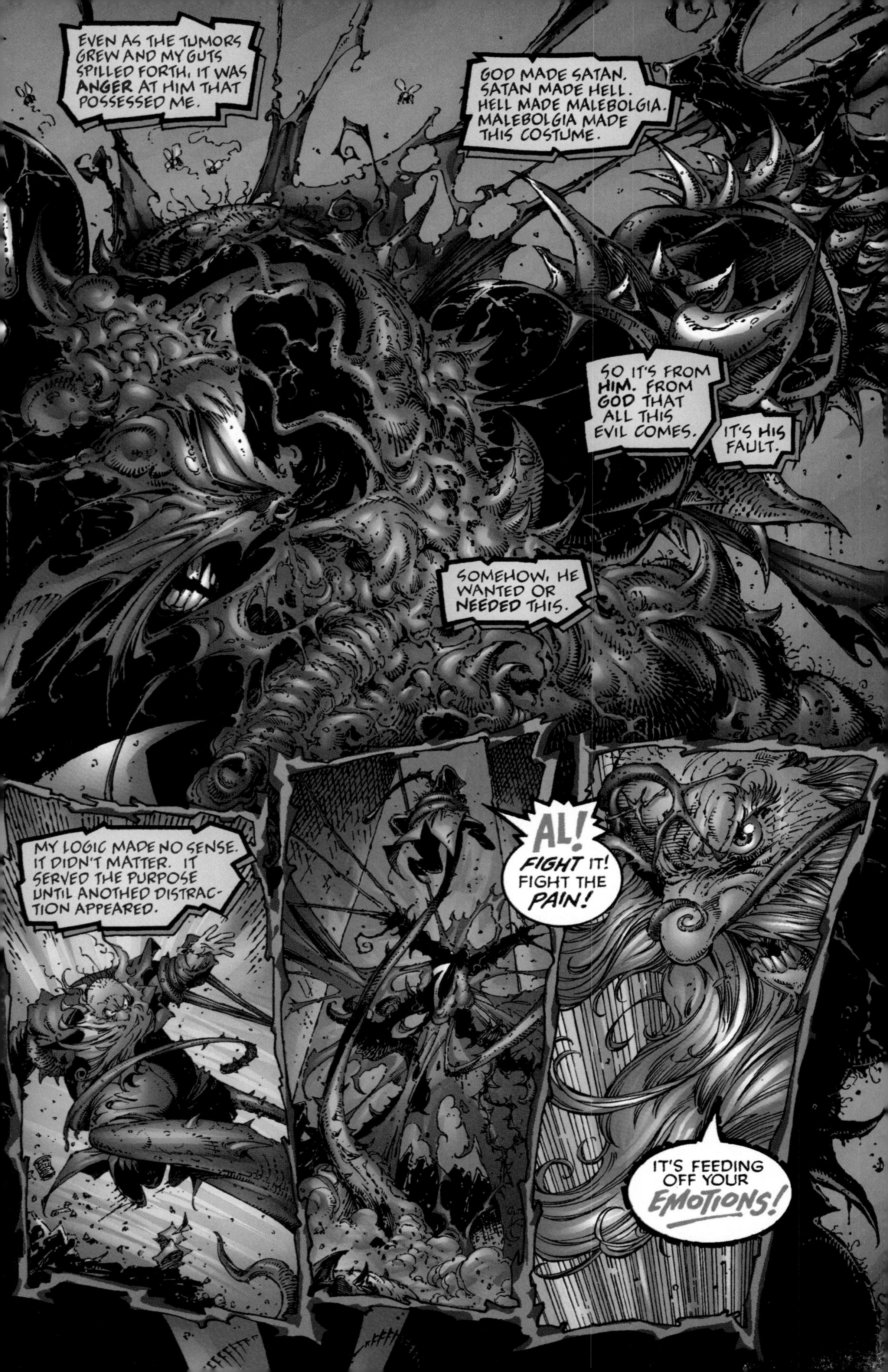
EVEN AS THE TUMORS GREW AND MY GUTS SPILLED FORTH, IT WAS ANGER AT HIM THAT POSSESSED ME.
GOD MADE SATAN. SATAN MADE HELL. HELL MADE MALEBOLGIA. MALEBOLGIA MADE THIS COSTUME.
SO IT'S FROM HIM. FROM GOD THAT ALL THIS EVIL COMES.
IT'S HIS FAULT.
SOMEHOW, HE WANTED OR NEEDED THIS.
MY LOGIC MADE NO SENSE. IT DIDN'T MATTER. IT SERVED THE PURPOSE UNTIL ANOTHED DISTRACTION APPEARED.
AL! FIGHT IT! FIGHT THE PAIN!
IT'S FEEDING OFF YOUR EMOTIONS!

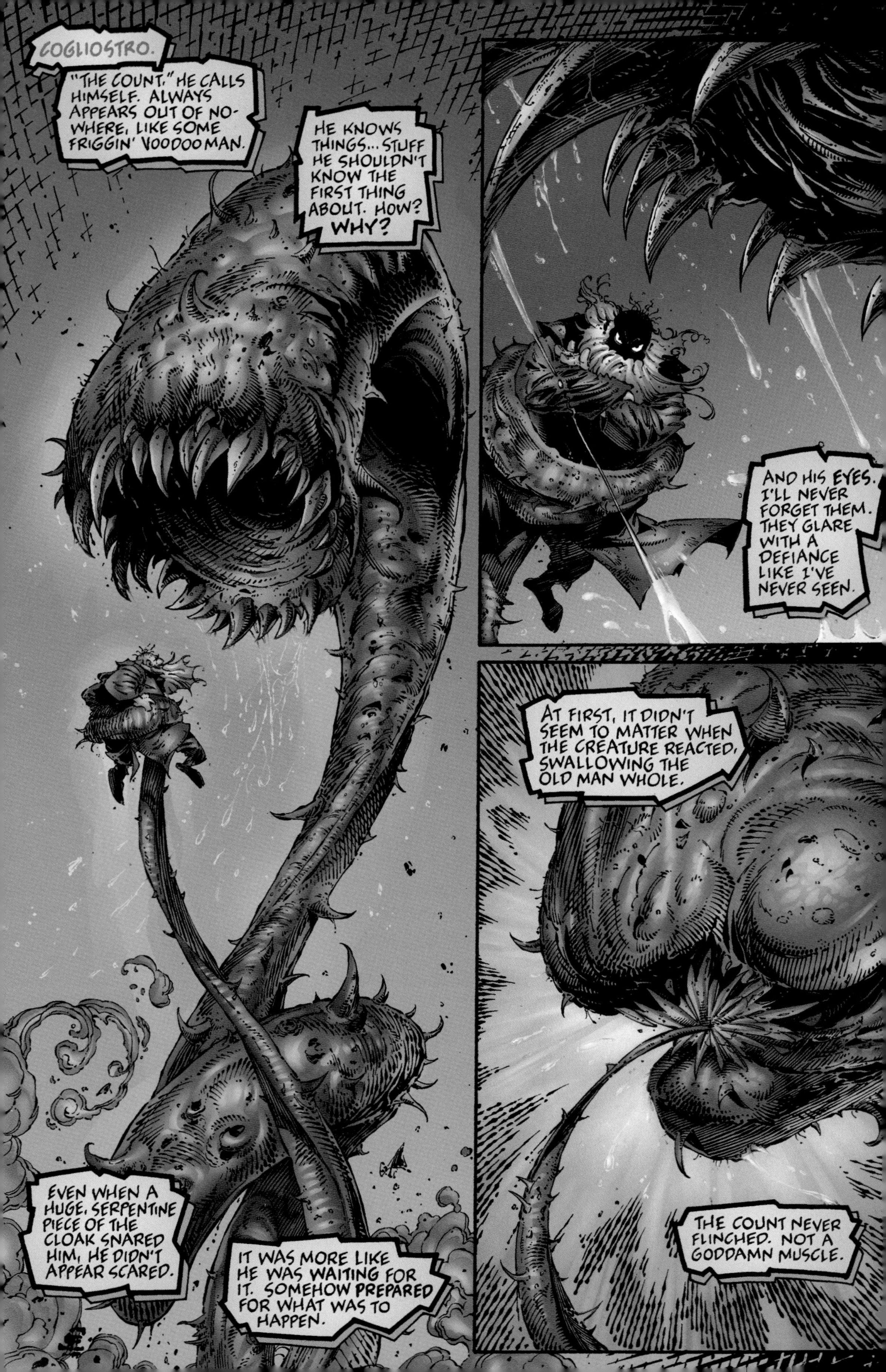
COGLIOSTRO.
"THE COUNT," HE CALLS HIMSELF. ALWAYS APPEARS OUT OF NOWHERE, LIKE SOME FRIGGIN' VOODOO MAN.
HE KNOWS THINGS... STUFF HE SHOULDN'T KNOW THE FIRST THING ABOUT. HOW? WHY?
AND HIS EYES. I'LL NEVER FORGET THEM. THEY GLARE WITH A DEFIANCE LIKE I'VE NEVER SEEN.
EVEN WHEN A HUGE, SERPENTINE PIECE OF THE CLOAK SNARED HIM, HE DIDN'T APPEAR SCARED.
IT WAS MORE LIKE HE WAS WAITING FOR IT. SOMEHOW PREPARED FOR WHAT WAS TO HAPPEN.
AT FIRST, IT DIDN'T SEEM TO MATTER WHEN THE CREATURE REACTED, SWALLOWING THE OLD MAN WHOLE.
THE COUNT NEVER FLINCHED. NOT A GODDAMN MUSCLE.

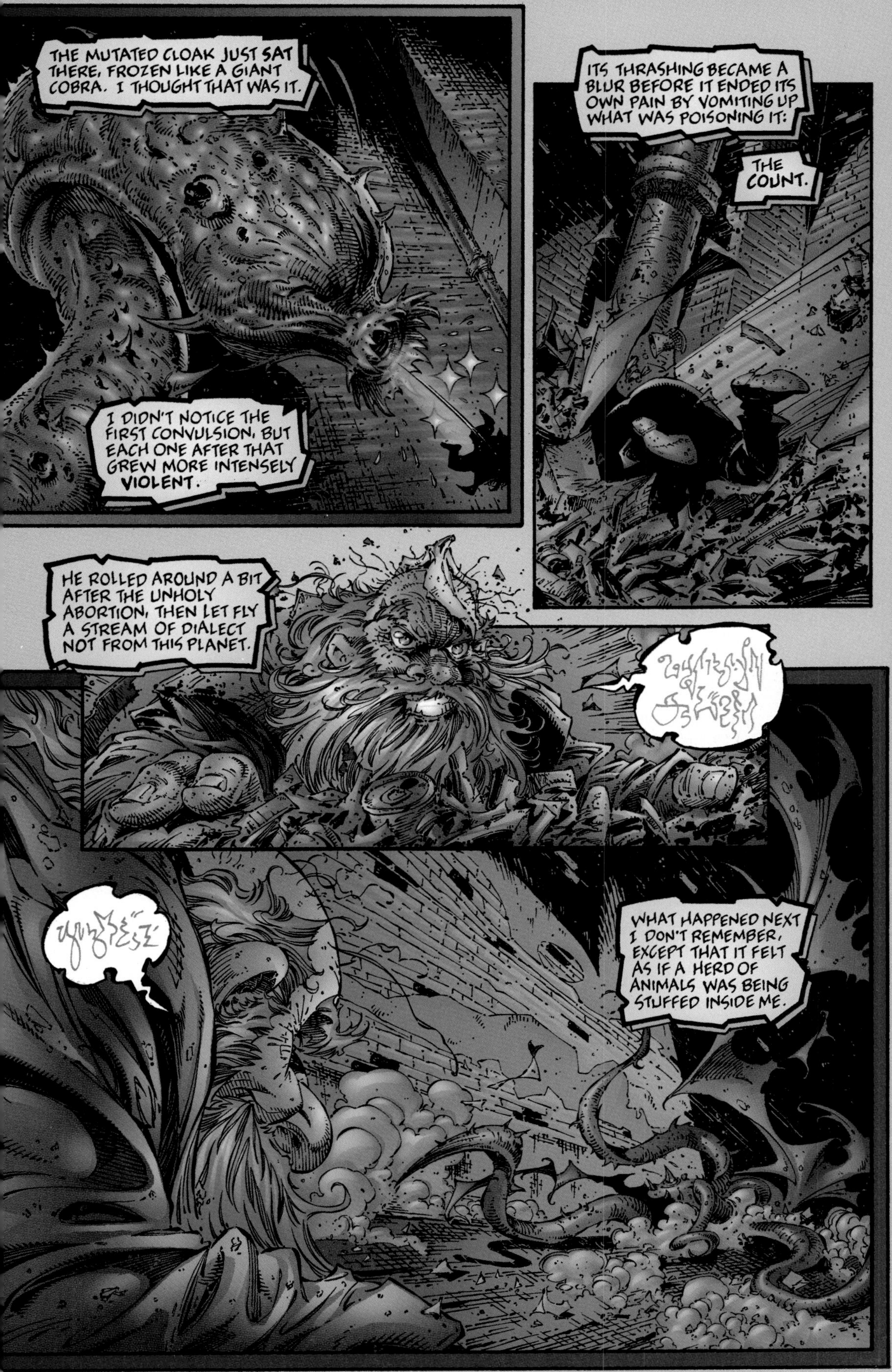
THE MUTATED CLOAK JUST SAT THERE, FROZEN LIKE A GIANT COBRA. I THOUGHT THAT WAS IT.
I DIDN'T NOTICE THE FIRST CONVULSION, BUT EACH ONE AFTER THAT GREW MORE INTENSELY VIOLENT.
ITS THRASHING BECAME A BLUR BEFORE IT ENDED ITS OWN PAIN BY VOMITING UP WHAT WAS POISONING IT:
THE COUNT.
HE ROLLED AROUND A BIT AFTER THE UNHOLY ABORTION, THEN LET FLY A STREAM OF DIALECT NOT FROM THIS PLANET.
WHAT HAPPENED NEXT I DON'T REMEMBER, EXCEPT THAT IT FELT AS IF A HERD OF ANIMALS WAS BEING STUFFED INSIDE ME.

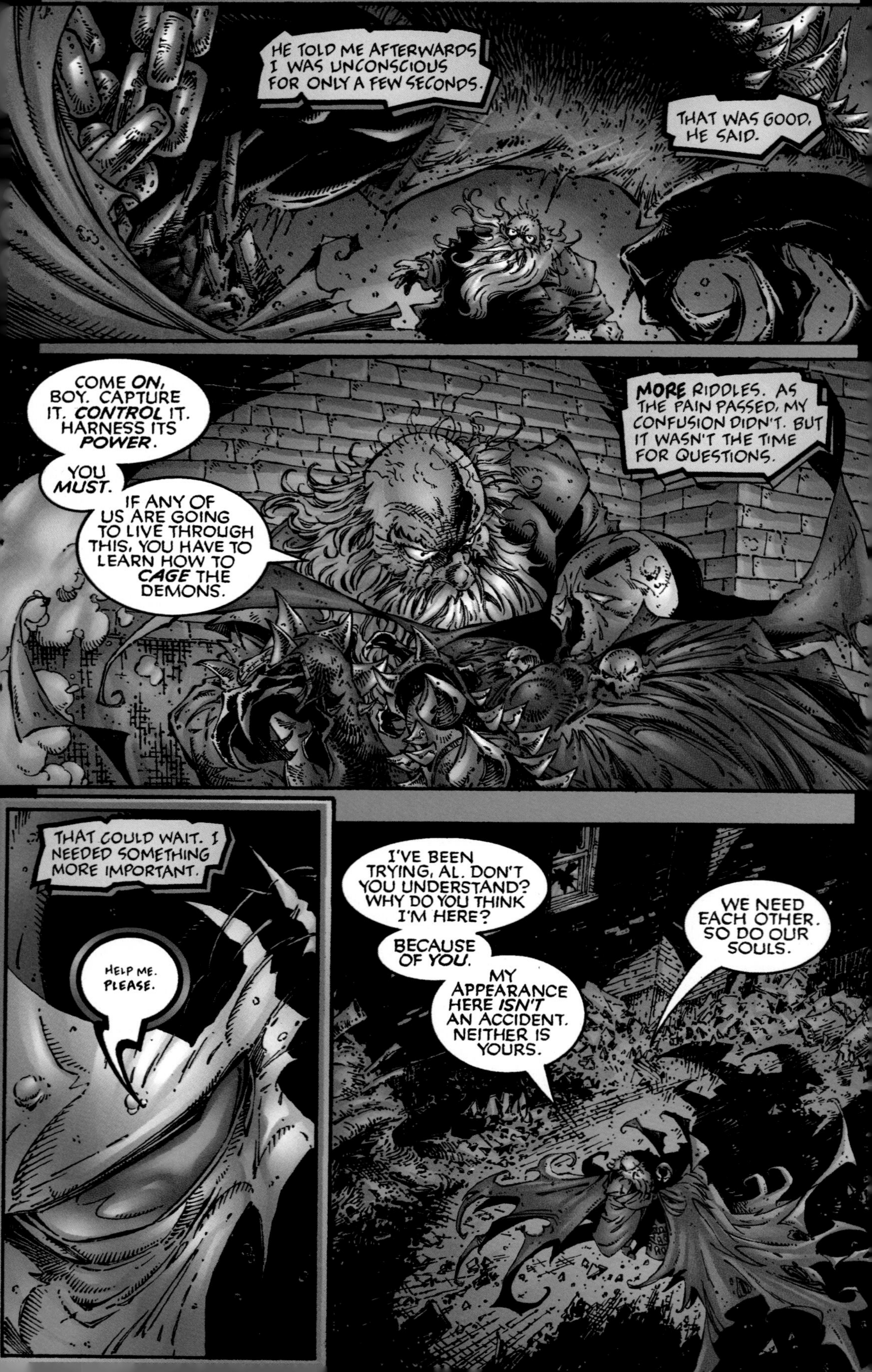
HE TOLD ME AFTERWARDS I WAS UNCONSCIOUS FOR ONLY A FEW SECONDS.
THAT WAS GOOD, HE SAID.
COME ON, BOY. CAPTURE IT. CONTROL IT. HARNESS ITS POWER.
YOU MUST.
IF ANY OF US ARE GOING TO LIVE THROUGH THIS, YOU HAVE TO LEARN HOW TO CAGE THE DEMONS.
MORE RIDDLES. AS THE PAIN PASSED, MY CONFUSION DIDN'T. BUT IT WASN'T THE TIME FOR QUESTIONS.
THAT COULD WAIT. I NEEDED SOMETHING MORE IMPORTANT.
HELP ME. PLEASE.
I'VE BEEN TRYING, AL. DON'T YOU UNDERSTAND? WHY DO YOU THINK I'M HERE?
BECAUSE OF YOU.
MY APPEARANCE HERE ISN'T AN ACCIDENT. NEITHER IS YOURS.
WE NEED EACH OTHER. SO DO OUR SOULS.

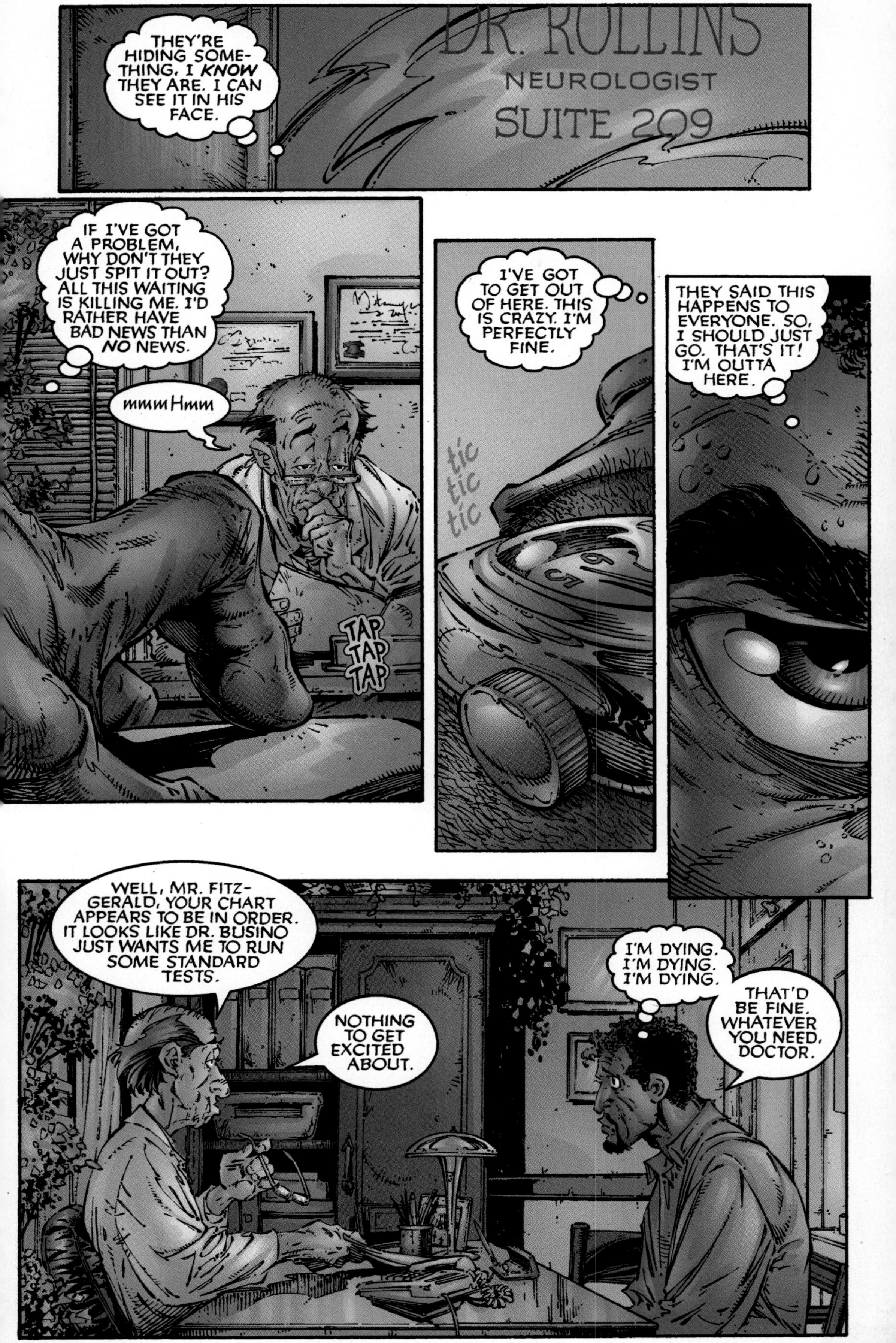

DR. ROLLINS
NEUROLOGIST
SUITE 209
THEY'RE HIDING SOMETHING. I KNOW THEY ARE. I CAN SEE IT IN HIS FACE.
IF I'VE GOT A PROBLEM, WHY DON'T THEY JUST SPIT IT OUT? ALL THIS WAITING IS KILLING ME. I'D RATHER HAVE BAD NEWS THAN NO NEWS.
mmm Hmm
TAP TAP TAP
I'VE GOT TO GET OUT OF HERE. THIS IS CRAZY. I'M PERFECTLY FINE.
tic tic tic
THEY SAID THIS HAPPENS TO EVERYONE. SO, I SHOULD JUST GO. THAT'S IT! I'M OUTTA HERE.
WELL, MR. FITZ-GERALD, YOUR CHART APPEARS TO BE IN ORDER. IT LOOKS LIKE DR. BUSINO JUST WANTS ME TO RUN SOME STANDARD TESTS.
NOTHING TO GET EXCITED ABOUT.
I'M DYING. I'M DYING. I'M DYING.
THAT'D BE FINE. WHATEVER YOU NEED, DOCTOR.

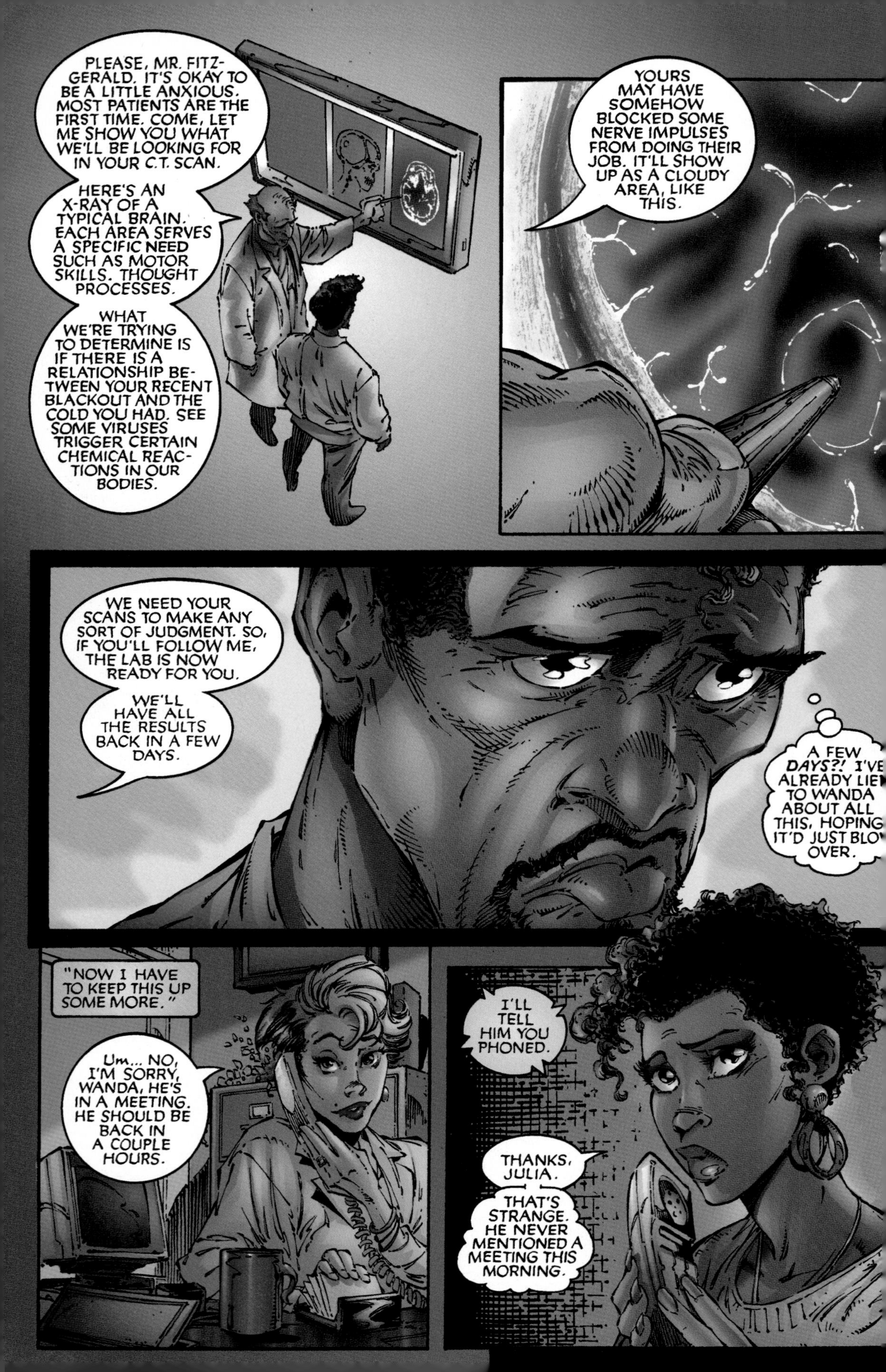
PLEASE, MR. FITZGERALD. IT'S OKAY TO BE A LITTLE ANXIOUS. MOST PATIENTS ARE THE FIRST TIME. COME, LET ME SHOW YOU WHAT WE'LL BE LOOKING FOR IN YOUR C.T. SCAN.
HERE'S AN X-RAY OF A TYPICAL BRAIN. EACH AREA SERVES A SPECIFIC NEED SUCH AS MOTOR SKILLS. THOUGHT PROCESSES.
WHAT WE'RE TRYING TO DETERMINE IS IF THERE IS A RELATIONSHIP BETWEEN YOUR RECENT BLACKOUT AND THE COLD YOU HAD. SEE SOME VIRUSES TRIGGER CERTAIN CHEMICAL REACTIONS IN OUR BODIES.
YOURS MAY HAVE SOMEHOW BLOCKED SOME NERVE IMPULSES FROM DOING THEIR JOB. IT'LL SHOW UP AS A CLOUDY AREA, LIKE THIS.
WE NEED YOUR SCANS TO MAKE ANY SORT OF JUDGMENT. SO, IF YOU'LL FOLLOW ME, THE LAB IS NOW READY FOR YOU.
WE'LL HAVE ALL THE RESULTS BACK IN A FEW DAYS.
A FEW DAYS?! I'VE ALREADY LIE TO WANDA ABOUT ALL THIS, HOPING IT'D JUST BLO OVER.
"NOW I HAVE TO KEEP THIS UP SOME MORE."
Um... NO, I'M SORRY, WANDA, HE'S IN A MEETING. HE SHOULD BE BACK IN A COUPLE HOURS.
I'LL TELL HIM YOU PHONED.
THANKS, JULIA.
THAT'S STRANGE. HE NEVER MENTIONED A MEETING THIS MORNING.

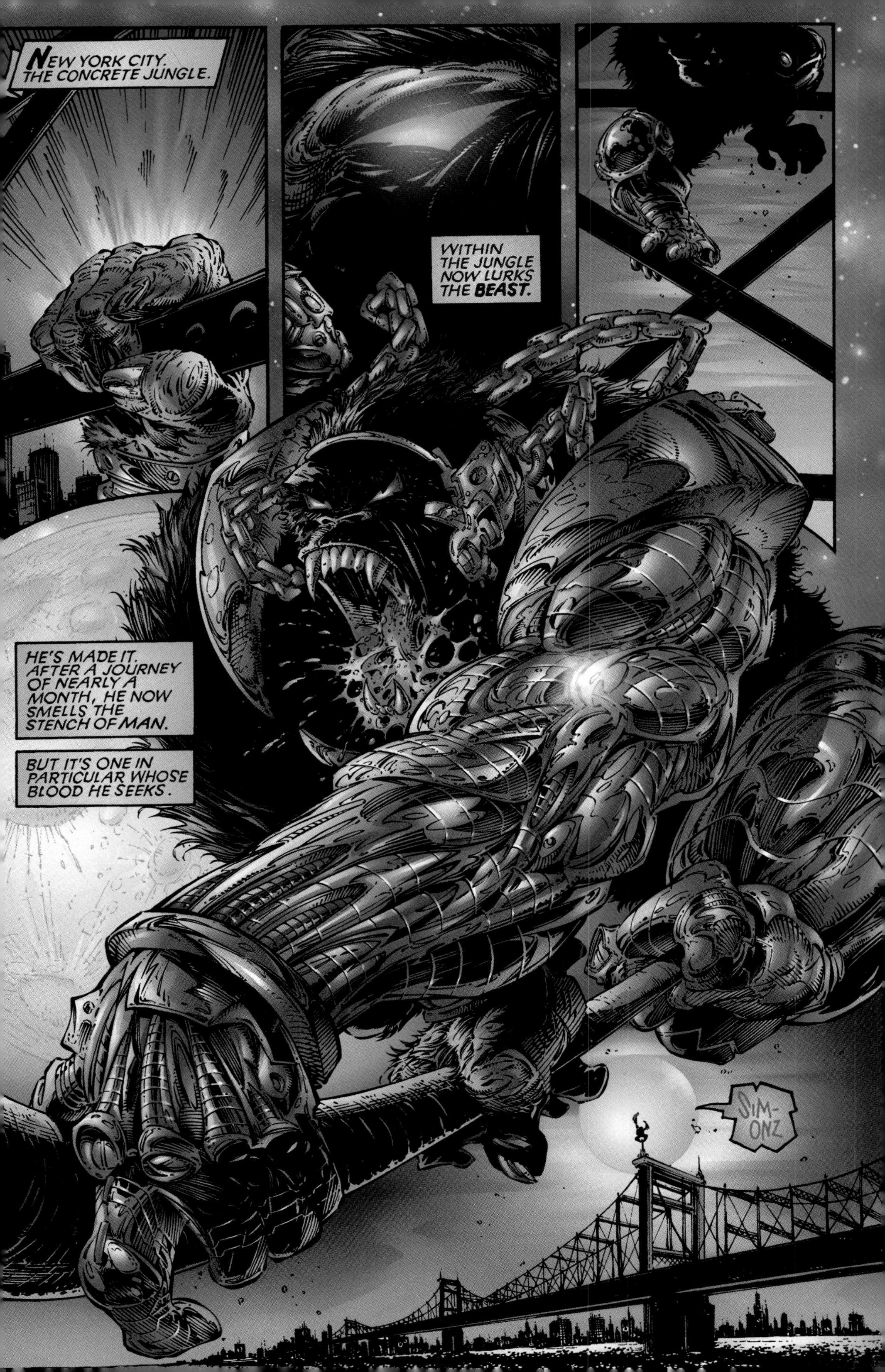
NEW YORK CITY. THE CONCRETE JUNGLE.
WITHIN THE JUNGLE NOW LURKS THE BEAST.
HE'S MADE IT. AFTER A JOURNEY OF NEARLY A MONTH, HE NOW SMELLS THE STENCH OF MAN.
BUT IT'S ONE IN PARTICULAR WHOSE BLOOD HE SEEKS.
SIM-ONZ

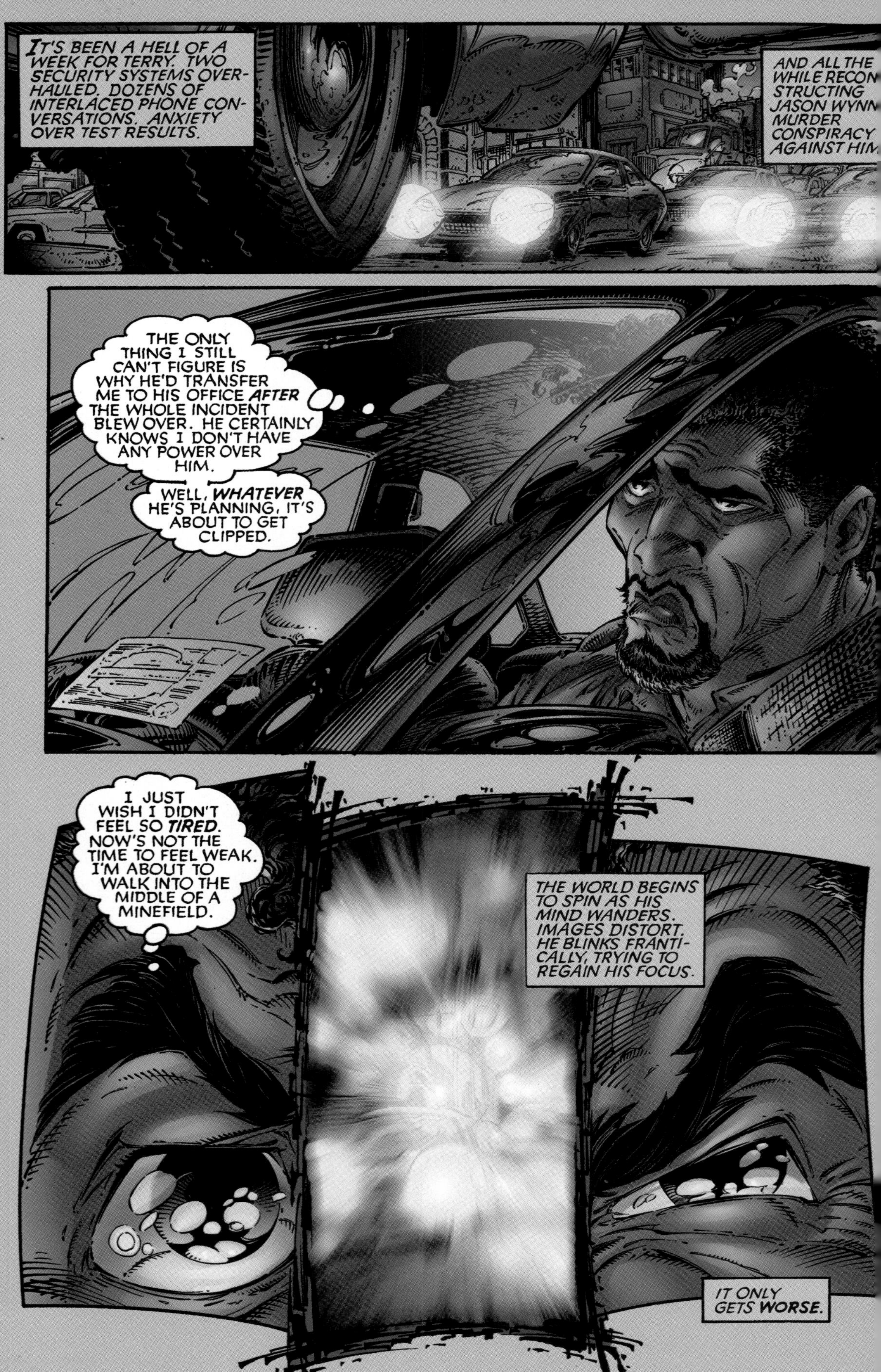
IT'S BEEN A HELL OF A WEEK FOR TERRY. TWO SECURITY SYSTEMS OVER-HAULED. DOZENS OF INTERLACED PHONE CON-VERSATIONS. ANXIETY OVER TEST RESULTS.
AND ALL THE WHILE RECON STRUCTING JASON WYNN MURDER CONSPIRACY AGAINST HIM
THE ONLY THING I STILL CAN'T FIGURE IS WHY HE'D TRANSFER ME TO HIS OFFICE AFTER THE WHOLE INCIDENT BLEW OVER. HE CERTAINLY KNOWS I DON'T HAVE ANY POWER OVER HIM.
WELL, WHATEVER HE'S PLANNING, IT'S ABOUT TO GET CLIPPED.
I JUST WISH I DIDN'T FEEL SO TIRED. NOW'S NOT THE TIME TO FEEL WEAK. I'M ABOUT TO WALK INTO THE MIDDLE OF A MINEFIELD.
THE WORLD BEGINS TO SPIN AS HIS MIND WANDERS. IMAGES DISTORT. HE BLINKS FRANTI-CALLY, TRYING TO REGAIN HIS FOCUS.
IT ONLY GETS WORSE.

THEN IT STOPS.
LEAVING HIM IN TOTAL DARKNESS.
HONNNNNK
CRASH!
SCREE
HONK HONK
THE CAR JERKS AS HE SLUMPS ACROSS THE STEERING WHEEL.
IT'S HIS SECOND BLACKOUT IN SEVEN DAYS.
HRONKK
LEAVING HIM COMPLETELY AT THE MERCY OF OTHERS.
HOLY SH...!!

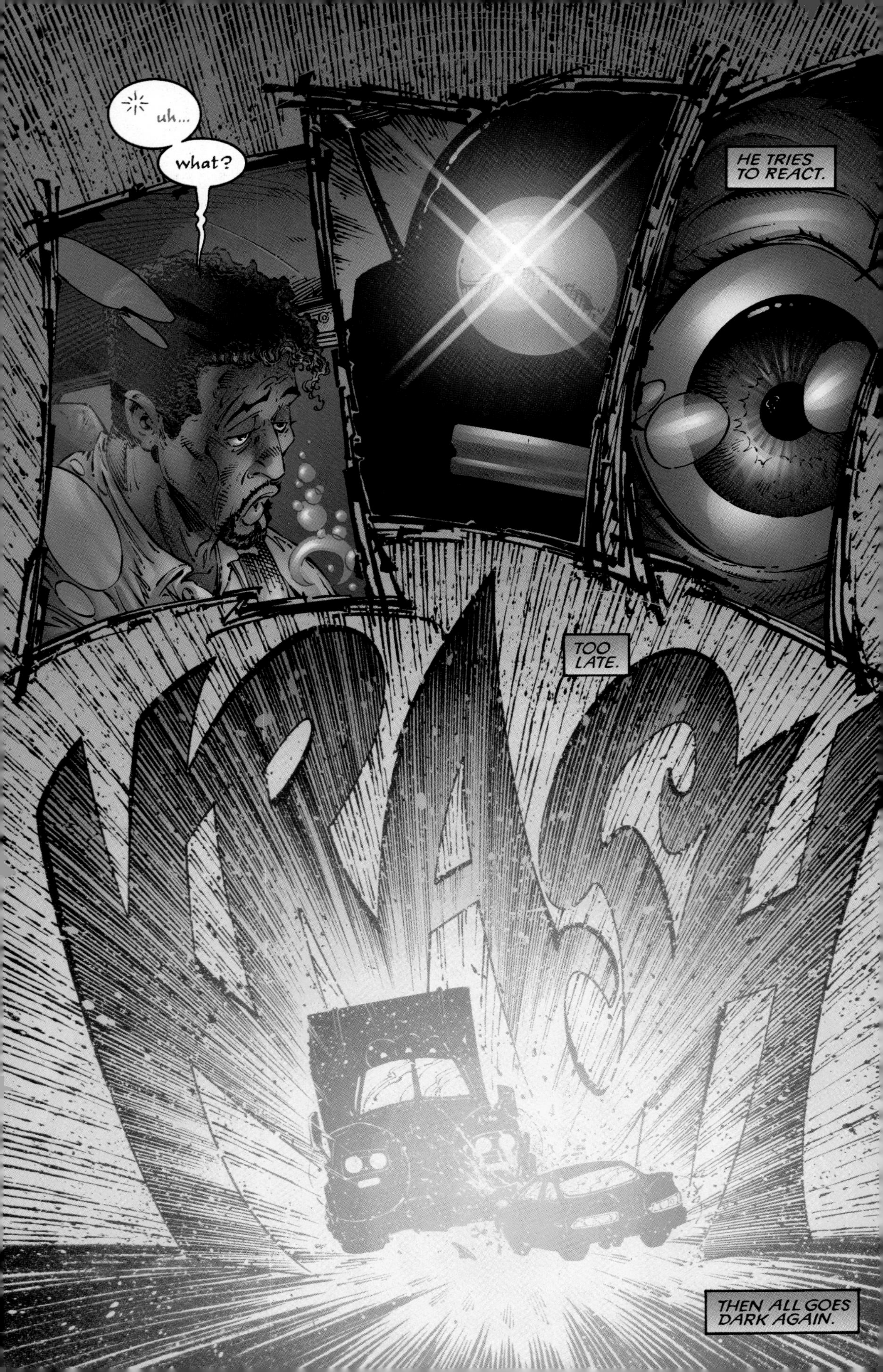

uh...
what?
HE TRIES TO REACT.
TOO LATE.
THEN ALL GOES DARK AGAIN.

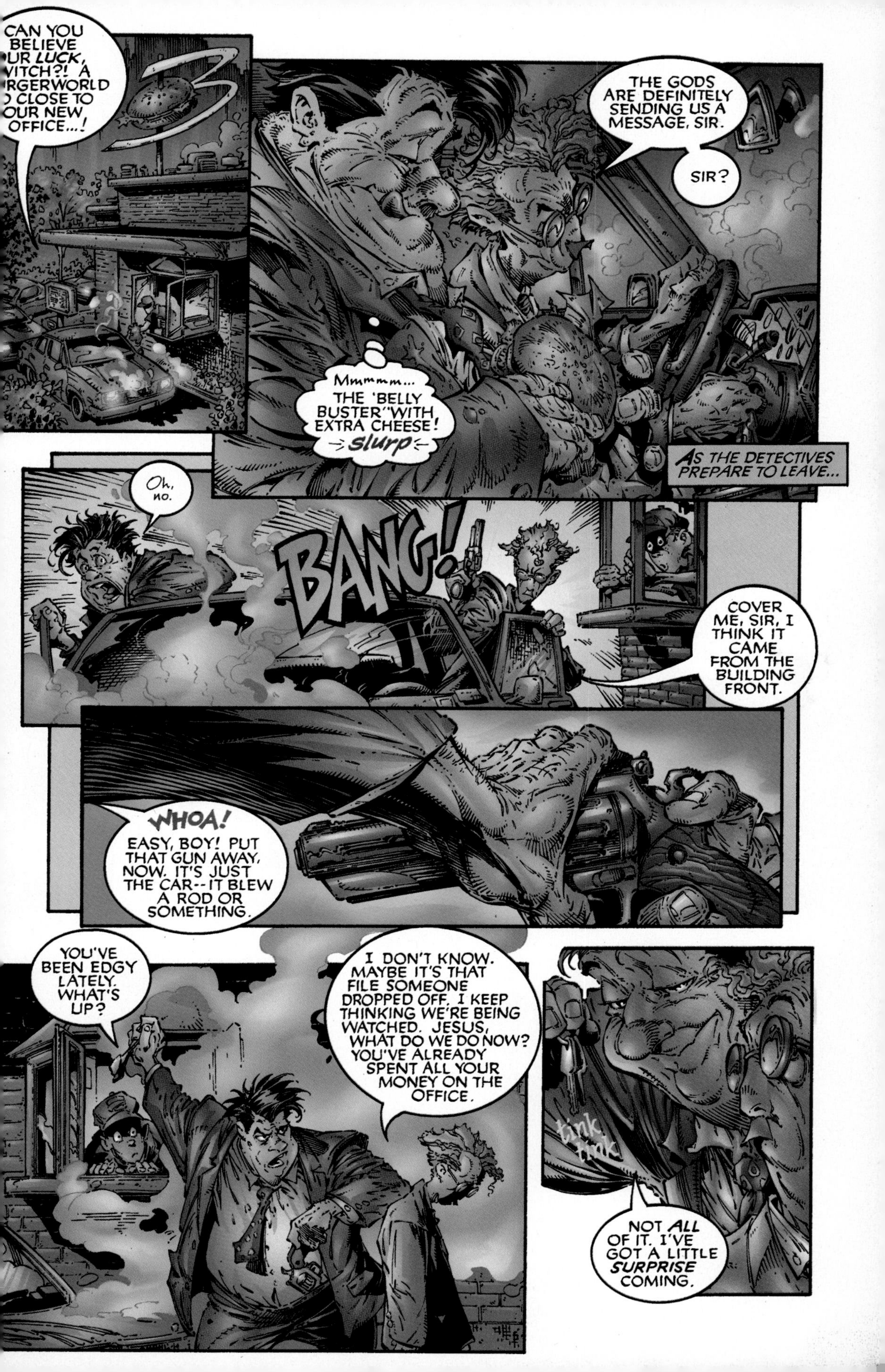
CAN YOU BELIEVE OUR LUCK, WITCH?! A BURGERWORLD SO CLOSE TO OUR NEW OFFICE...!
THE GODS ARE DEFINITELY SENDING US A MESSAGE, SIR.
SIR?
Mmmmm... THE 'BELLY BUSTER" WITH EXTRA CHEESE!
slurp
AS THE DETECTIVES PREPARE TO LEAVE...
Oh, no.
BANG!
COVER ME, SIR, I THINK IT CAME FROM THE BUILDING FRONT.
WHOA! EASY, BOY! PUT THAT GUN AWAY, NOW. IT'S JUST THE CAR--IT BLEW A ROD OR SOMETHING.
YOU'VE BEEN EDGY LATELY. WHAT'S UP?
I DON'T KNOW. MAYBE IT'S THAT FILE SOMEONE DROPPED OFF. I KEEP THINKING WE'RE BEING WATCHED. JESUS, WHAT DO WE DO NOW? YOU'VE ALREADY SPENT ALL YOUR MONEY ON THE OFFICE.
tink tink
NOT ALL OF IT. I'VE GOT A LITTLE SURPRISE COMING.

BRIING

BRIING

HELLO?

THIS IS SGT. FRITSCH OF THE NEW YORK CITY POLICE, MA'AM. ARE YOU WANDA BLAKE, TERRY FITZGERALD'S WIFE?

YES. WHY? WHAT'S WRONG?

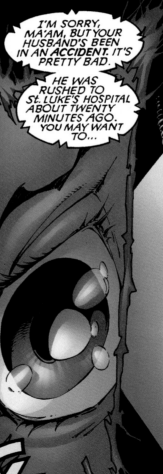

I'M SORRY, MA'AM, BUT YOUR HUSBAND'S BEEN IN AN ACCIDENT. IT'S PRETTY BAD.

HE WAS RUSHED TO St. LUKE'S HOSPITAL ABOUT TWENTY MINUTES AGO. YOU MAY WANT TO...

CLUNK

HELLO?

HELLO? MA'AM?

clatter

Then and only then will the undead finally die.

–WARRIORS

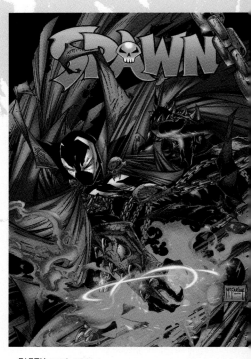

FIFTY part-one

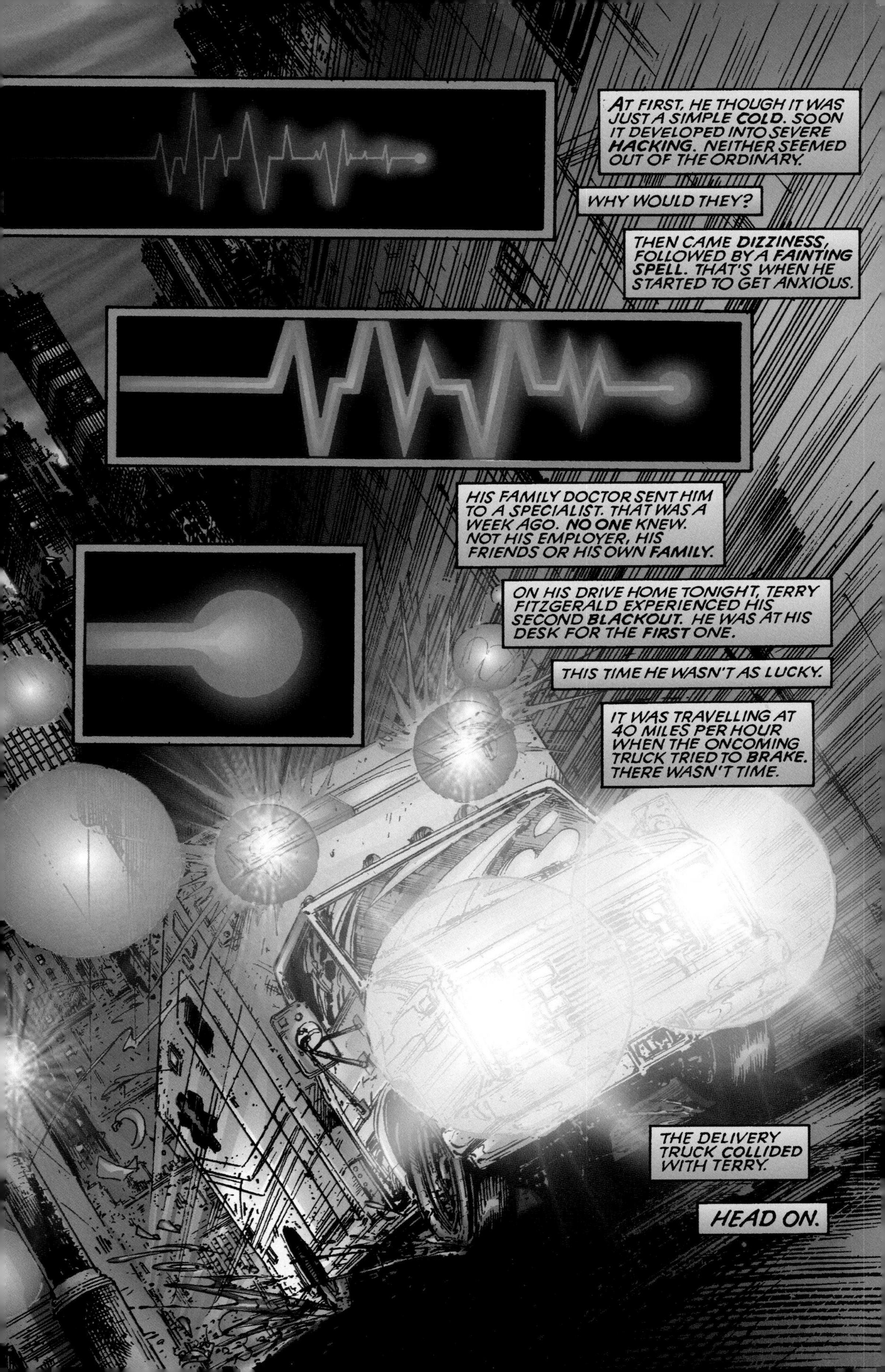
AT FIRST, HE THOUGH IT WAS JUST A SIMPLE COLD. SOON IT DEVELOPED INTO SEVERE HACKING. NEITHER SEEMED OUT OF THE ORDINARY.
WHY WOULD THEY?
THEN CAME DIZZINESS, FOLLOWED BY A FAINTING SPELL. THAT'S WHEN HE STARTED TO GET ANXIOUS.
HIS FAMILY DOCTOR SENT HIM TO A SPECIALIST. THAT WAS A WEEK AGO. NO ONE KNEW. NOT HIS EMPLOYER, HIS FRIENDS OR HIS OWN FAMILY.
ON HIS DRIVE HOME TONIGHT, TERRY FITZGERALD EXPERIENCED HIS SECOND BLACKOUT. HE WAS AT HIS DESK FOR THE FIRST ONE.
THIS TIME HE WASN'T AS LUCKY.
IT WAS TRAVELLING AT 40 MILES PER HOUR WHEN THE ONCOMING TRUCK TRIED TO BRAKE. THERE WASN'T TIME.
THE DELIVERY TRUCK COLLIDED WITH TERRY.
HEAD ON.

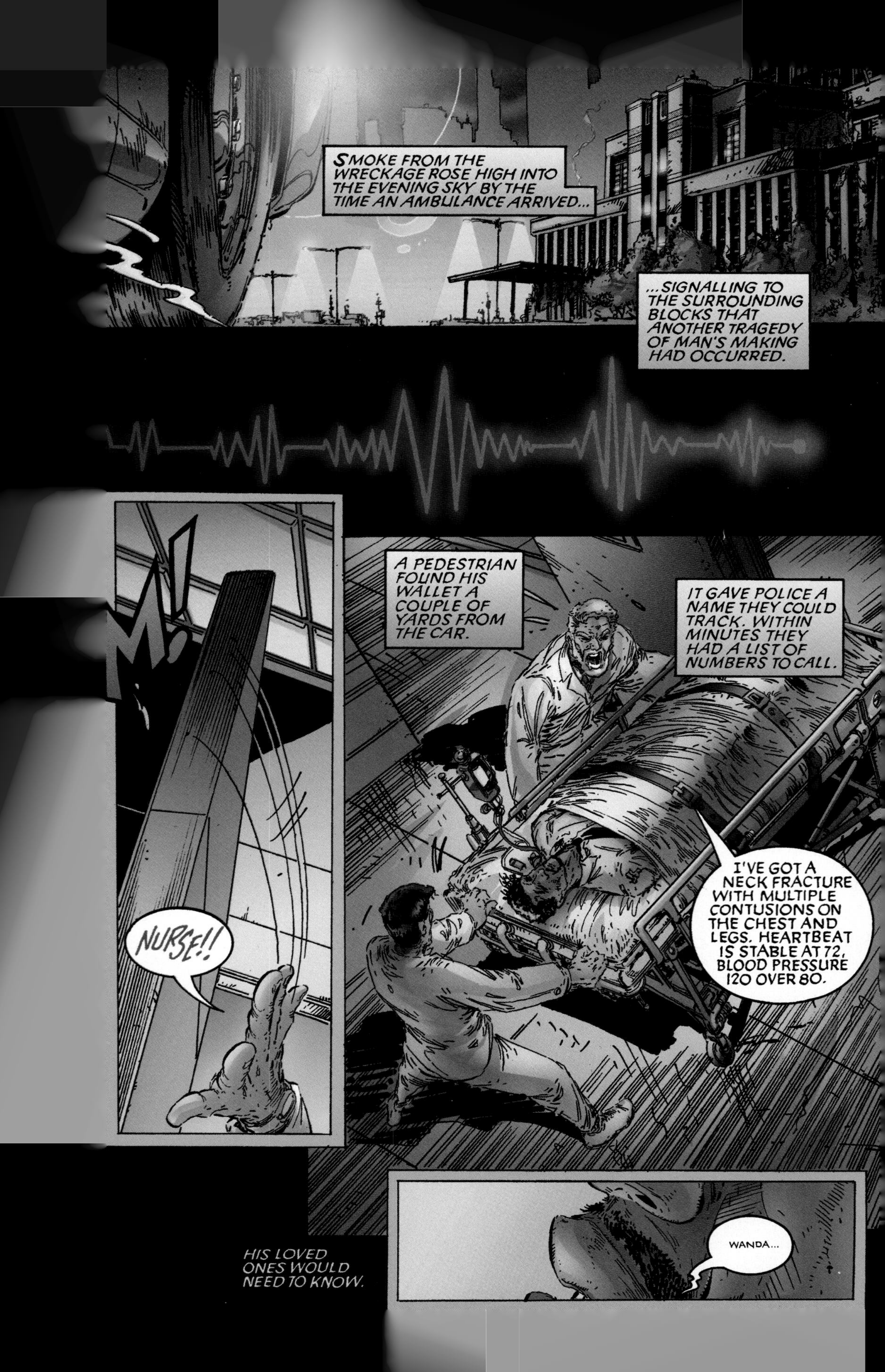
SMOKE FROM THE WRECKAGE ROSE HIGH INTO THE EVENING SKY BY THE TIME AN AMBULANCE ARRIVED...
...SIGNALLING TO THE SURROUNDING BLOCKS THAT ANOTHER TRAGEDY OF MAN'S MAKING HAD OCCURRED.
NURSE!!
A PEDESTRIAN FOUND HIS WALLET A COUPLE OF YARDS FROM THE CAR.
IT GAVE POLICE A NAME THEY COULD TRACK. WITHIN MINUTES THEY HAD A LIST OF NUMBERS TO CALL.
I'VE GOT A NECK FRACTURE WITH MULTIPLE CONTUSIONS ON THE CHEST AND LEGS. HEARTBEAT IS STABLE AT 72, BLOOD PRESSURE 120 OVER 80.
HIS LOVED ONES WOULD NEED TO KNOW.
WANDA...

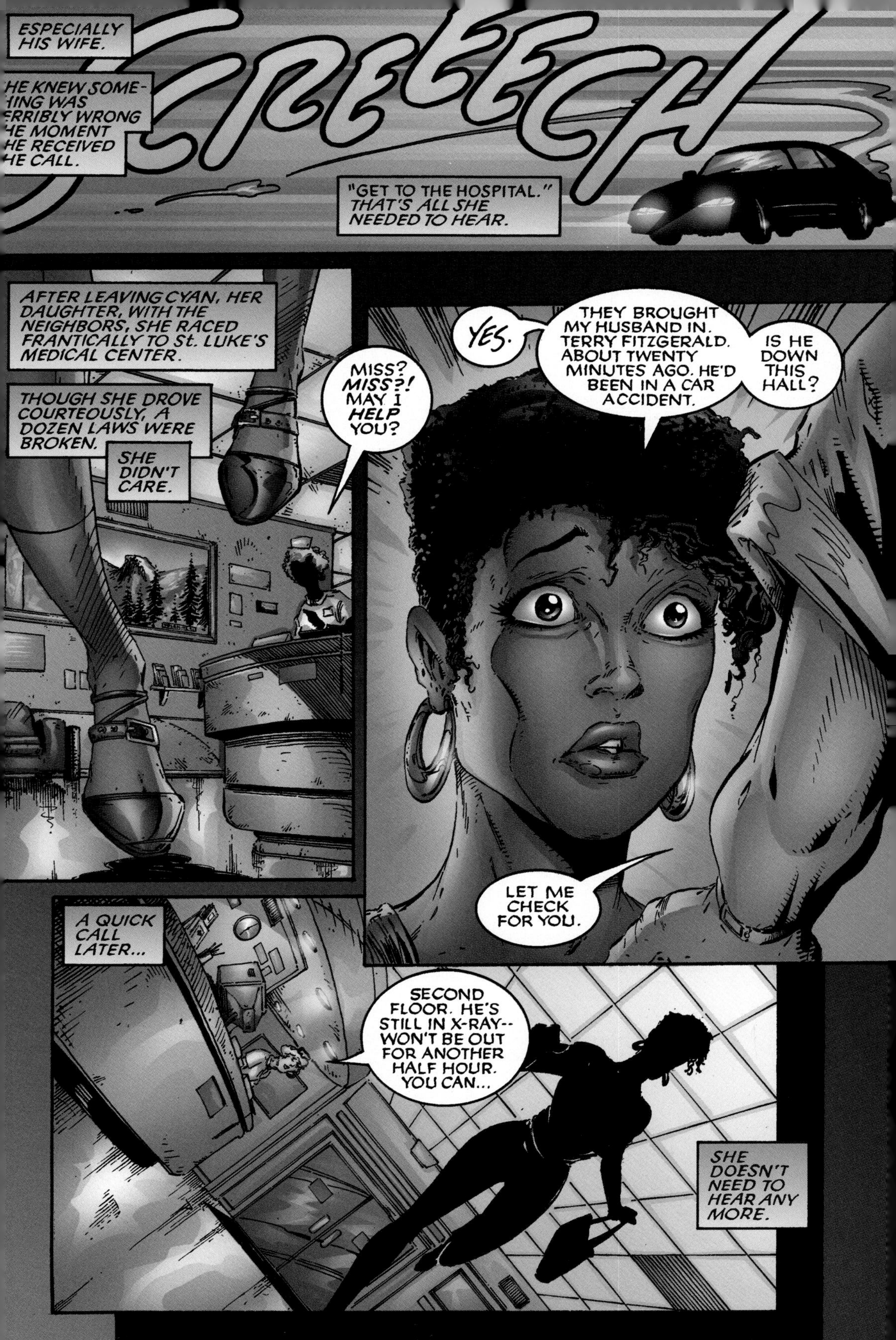
ESPECIALLY HIS WIFE.
SCREECH
HE KNEW SOME-
HING WAS
ERRIBLY WRONG
HE MOMENT
HE RECEIVED
HE CALL.
"GET TO THE HOSPITAL." THAT'S ALL SHE NEEDED TO HEAR.
AFTER LEAVING CYAN, HER DAUGHTER, WITH THE NEIGHBORS, SHE RACED FRANTICALLY TO St. LUKE'S MEDICAL CENTER.
THOUGH SHE DROVE COURTEOUSLY, A DOZEN LAWS WERE BROKEN.
SHE DIDN'T CARE.
MISS? MISS?! MAY I HELP YOU?
YES.
THEY BROUGHT MY HUSBAND IN. TERRY FITZGERALD. ABOUT TWENTY MINUTES AGO. HE'D BEEN IN A CAR ACCIDENT.
IS HE DOWN THIS HALL?
LET ME CHECK FOR YOU.
A QUICK CALL LATER...
SECOND FLOOR. HE'S STILL IN X-RAY-- WON'T BE OUT FOR ANOTHER HALF HOUR. YOU CAN...
SHE DOESN'T NEED TO HEAR ANY MORE.

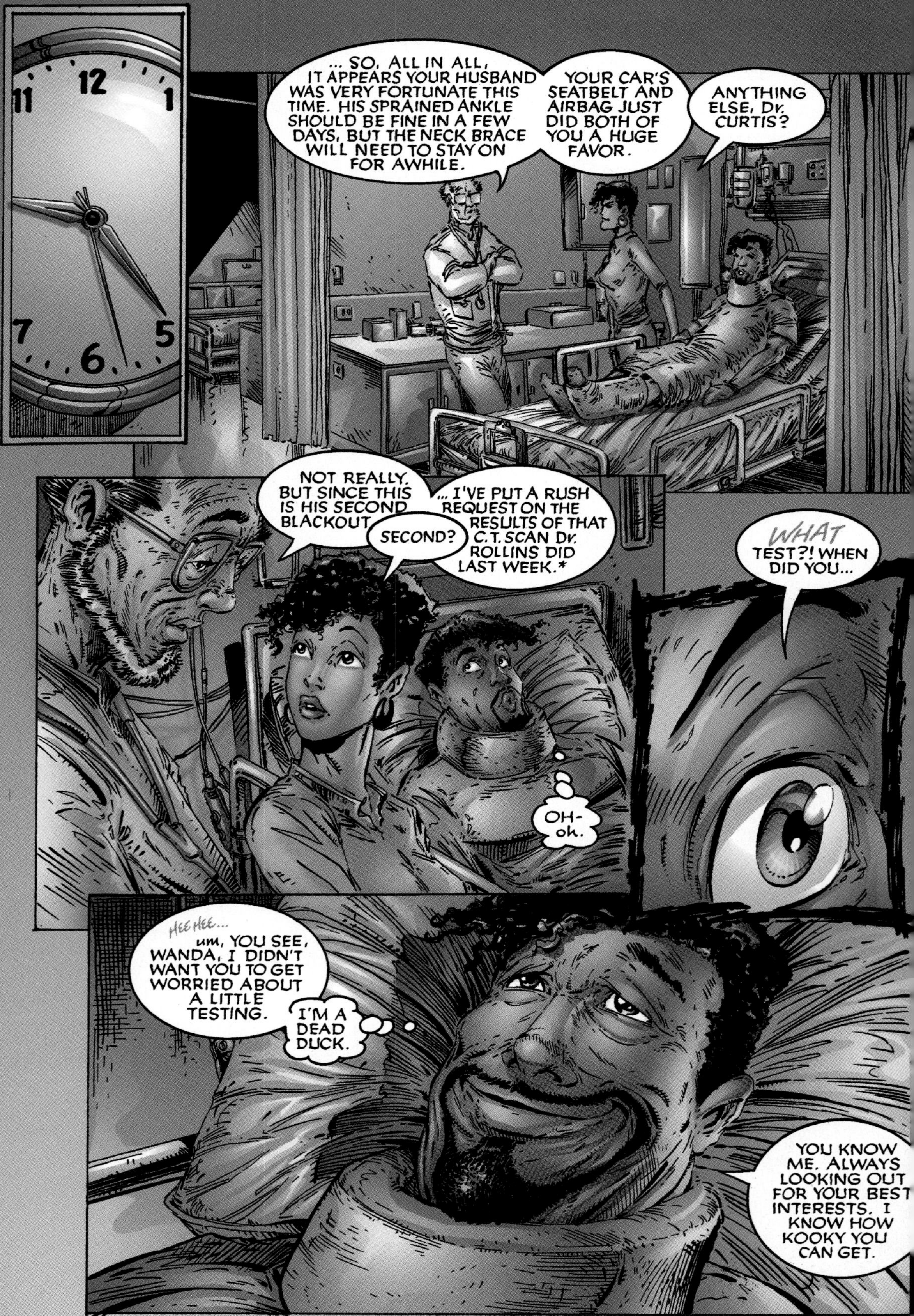

... SO, ALL IN ALL, IT APPEARS YOUR HUSBAND WAS VERY FORTUNATE THIS TIME. HIS SPRAINED ANKLE SHOULD BE FINE IN A FEW DAYS, BUT THE NECK BRACE WILL NEED TO STAY ON FOR AWHILE.
YOUR CAR'S SEATBELT AND AIRBAG JUST DID BOTH OF YOU A HUGE FAVOR.
ANYTHING ELSE, Dr. CURTIS?
NOT REALLY. BUT SINCE THIS IS HIS SECOND BLACKOUT
... I'VE PUT A RUSH REQUEST ON THE RESULTS OF THAT C.T. SCAN Dr. ROLLINS DID LAST WEEK.*
SECOND?
OH-oh.
WHAT TEST?! WHEN DID YOU...
HEE HEE... um, YOU SEE, WANDA, I DIDN'T WANT YOU TO GET WORRIED ABOUT A LITTLE TESTING.
I'M A DEAD DUCK.
YOU KNOW ME. ALWAYS LOOKING OUT FOR YOUR BEST INTERESTS. I KNOW HOW KOOKY YOU CAN GET.

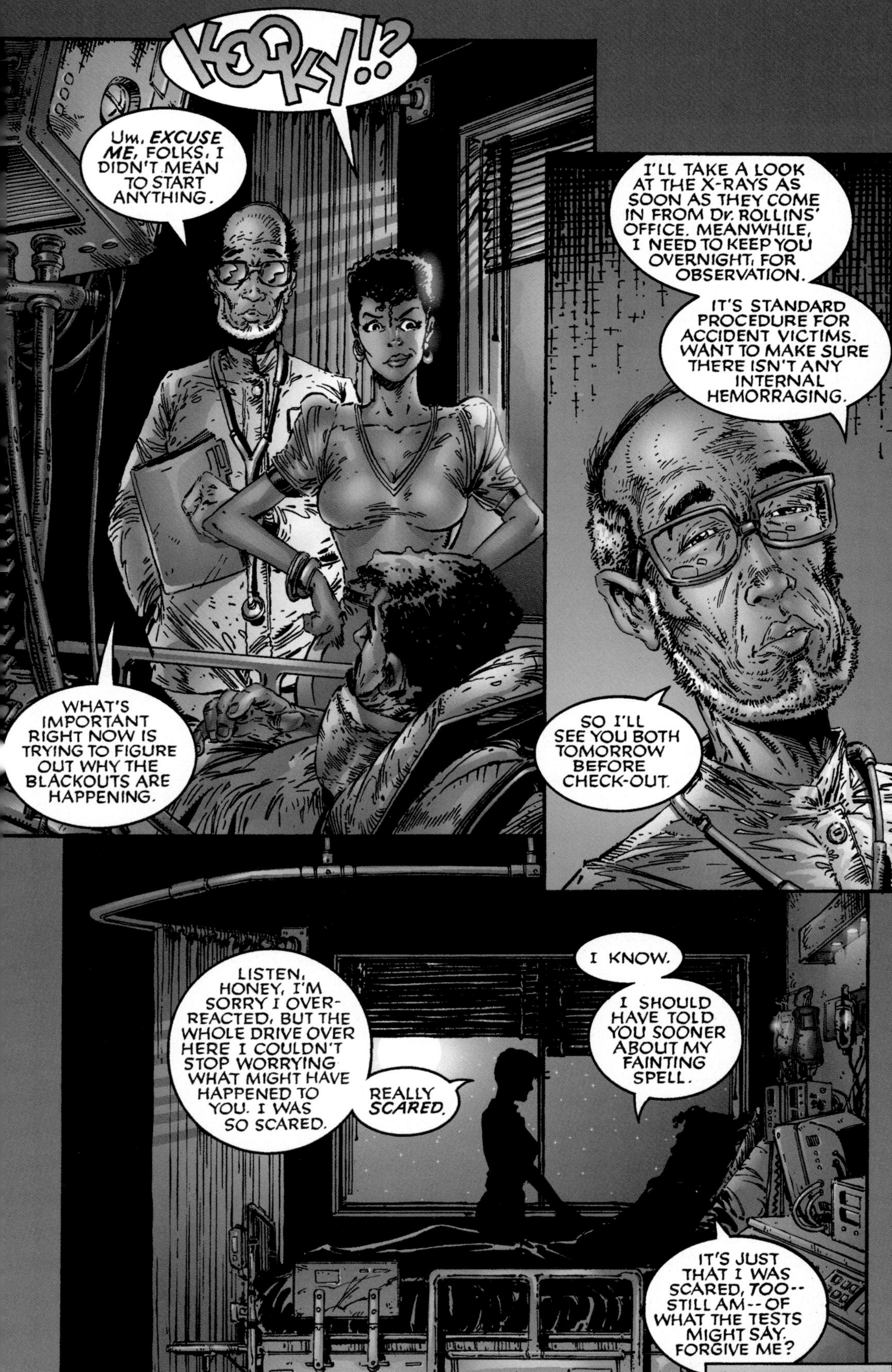
KOOKY!?
UM, EXCUSE ME, FOLKS, I DIDN'T MEAN TO START ANYTHING.
WHAT'S IMPORTANT RIGHT NOW IS TRYING TO FIGURE OUT WHY THE BLACKOUTS ARE HAPPENING.
I'LL TAKE A LOOK AT THE X-RAYS AS SOON AS THEY COME IN FROM Dr. ROLLINS' OFFICE. MEANWHILE, I NEED TO KEEP YOU OVERNIGHT, FOR OBSERVATION.
IT'S STANDARD PROCEDURE FOR ACCIDENT VICTIMS. WANT TO MAKE SURE THERE ISN'T ANY INTERNAL HEMORRAGING.
SO I'LL SEE YOU BOTH TOMORROW BEFORE CHECK-OUT.
LISTEN, HONEY, I'M SORRY I OVER-REACTED, BUT THE WHOLE DRIVE OVER HERE I COULDN'T STOP WORRYING WHAT MIGHT HAVE HAPPENED TO YOU. I WAS SO SCARED.
REALLY SCARED.
I KNOW.
I SHOULD HAVE TOLD YOU SOONER ABOUT MY FAINTING SPELL.
IT'S JUST THAT I WAS SCARED, TOO-- STILL AM-- OF WHAT THE TESTS MIGHT SAY. FORGIVE ME?
SHE ALWAYS HAS.

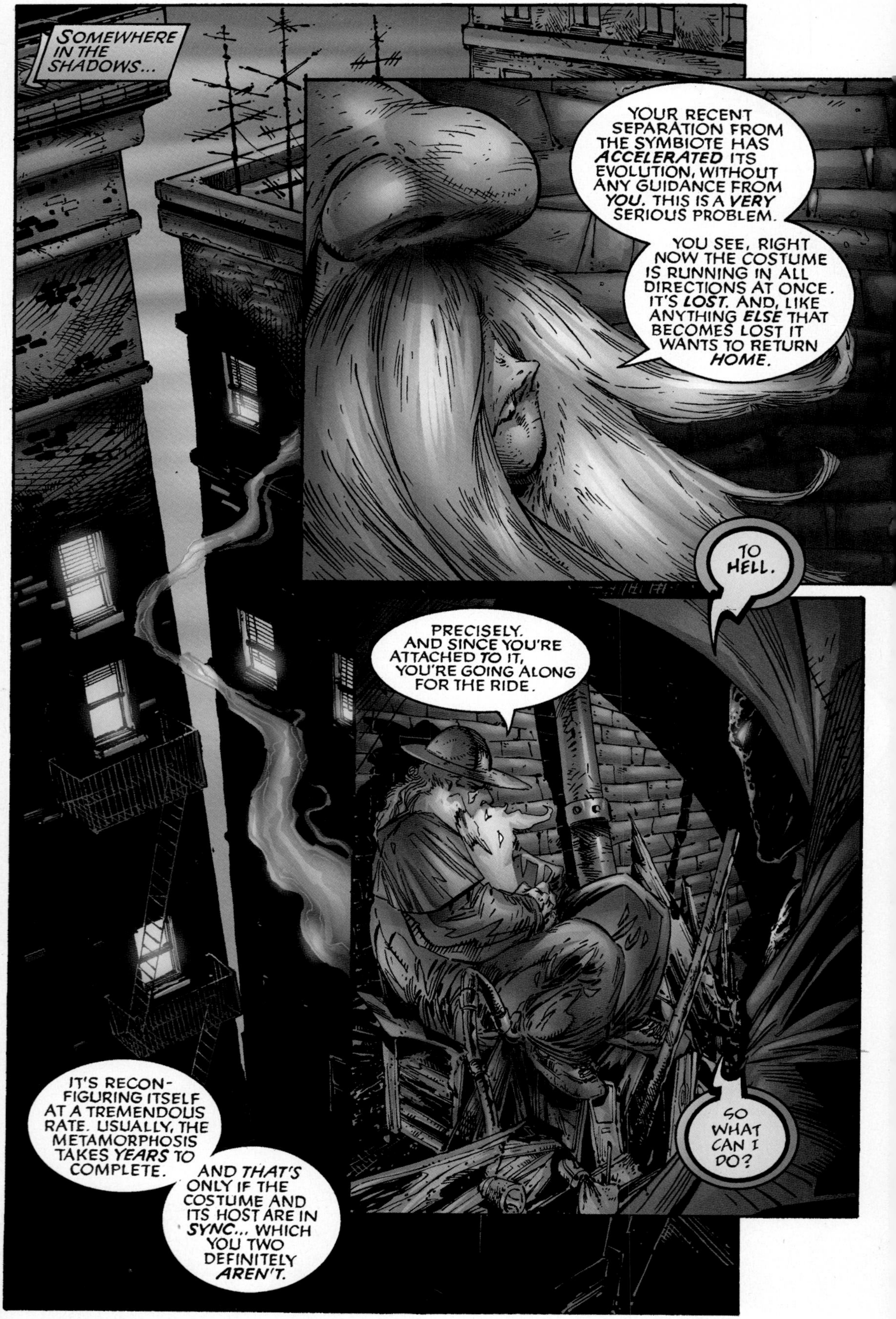
SOMEWHERE IN THE SHADOWS...
YOUR RECENT SEPARATION FROM THE SYMBIOTE HAS ACCELERATED ITS EVOLUTION, WITHOUT ANY GUIDANCE FROM YOU. THIS IS A VERY SERIOUS PROBLEM.
YOU SEE, RIGHT NOW THE COSTUME IS RUNNING IN ALL DIRECTIONS AT ONCE. IT'S LOST. AND, LIKE ANYTHING ELSE THAT BECOMES LOST IT WANTS TO RETURN HOME.
TO HELL.
PRECISELY. AND SINCE YOU'RE ATTACHED TO IT, YOU'RE GOING ALONG FOR THE RIDE.
SO WHAT CAN I DO?
IT'S RECON-FIGURING ITSELF AT A TREMENDOUS RATE. USUALLY, THE METAMORPHOSIS TAKES YEARS TO COMPLETE.
AND THAT'S ONLY IF THE COSTUME AND ITS HOST ARE IN SYNC... WHICH YOU TWO DEFINITELY AREN'T.

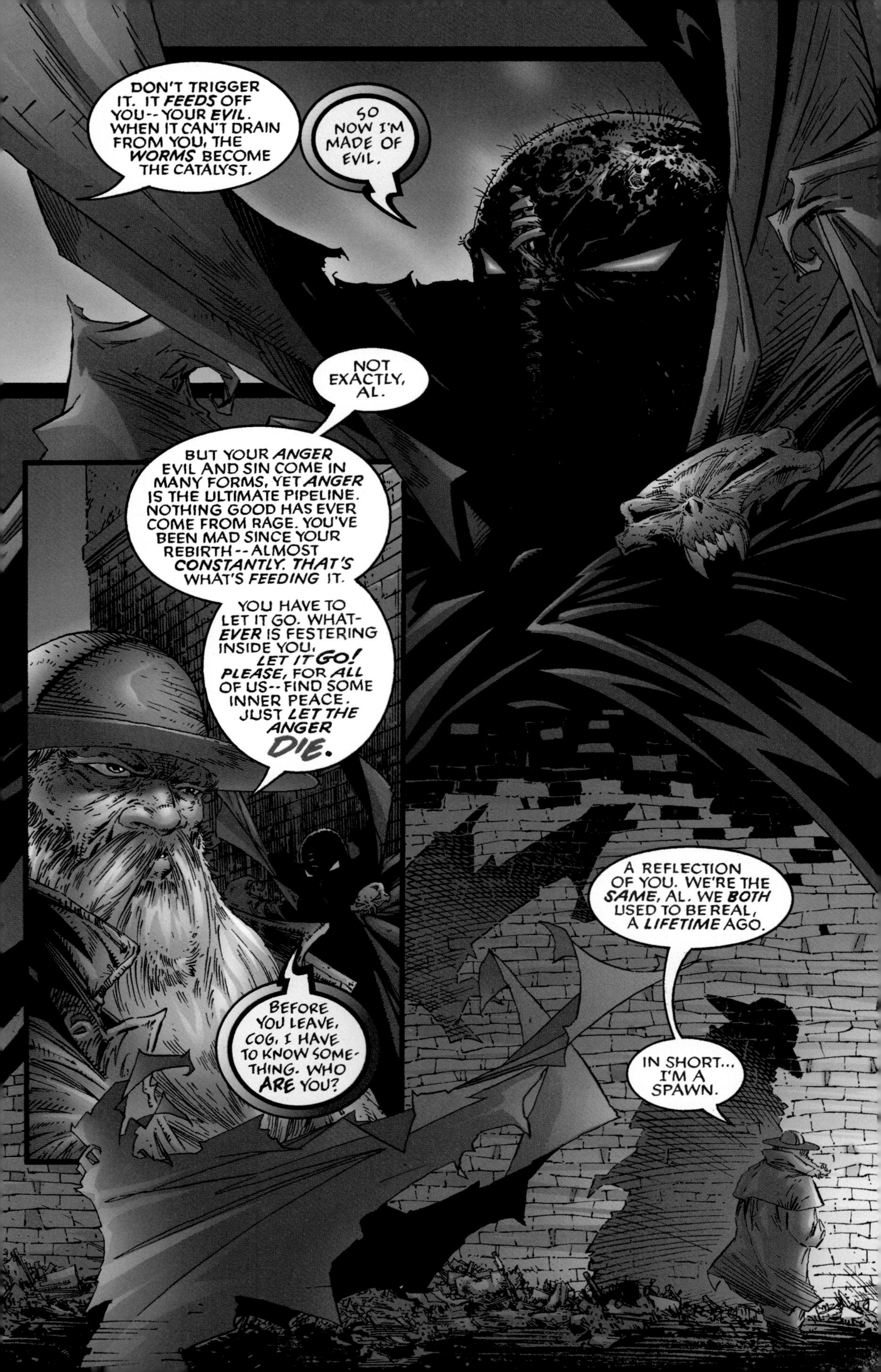
DON'T TRIGGER IT. IT FEEDS OFF YOU-- YOUR EVIL. WHEN IT CAN'T DRAIN FROM YOU, THE WORMS BECOME THE CATALYST.
SO NOW I'M MADE OF EVIL.
NOT EXACTLY, AL.
BUT YOUR ANGER EVIL AND SIN COME IN MANY FORMS, YET ANGER IS THE ULTIMATE PIPELINE. NOTHING GOOD HAS EVER COME FROM RAGE. YOU'VE BEEN MAD SINCE YOUR REBIRTH -- ALMOST CONSTANTLY. THAT'S WHAT'S FEEDING IT.
YOU HAVE TO LET IT GO. WHAT-EVER IS FESTERING INSIDE YOU, LET IT GO! PLEASE, FOR ALL OF US-- FIND SOME INNER PEACE. JUST LET THE ANGER DIE.
BEFORE YOU LEAVE, COG, I HAVE TO KNOW SOME-THING. WHO ARE YOU?
A REFLECTION OF YOU. WE'RE THE SAME, AL. WE BOTH USED TO BE REAL, A LIFETIME AGO.
IN SHORT... I'M A SPAWN.

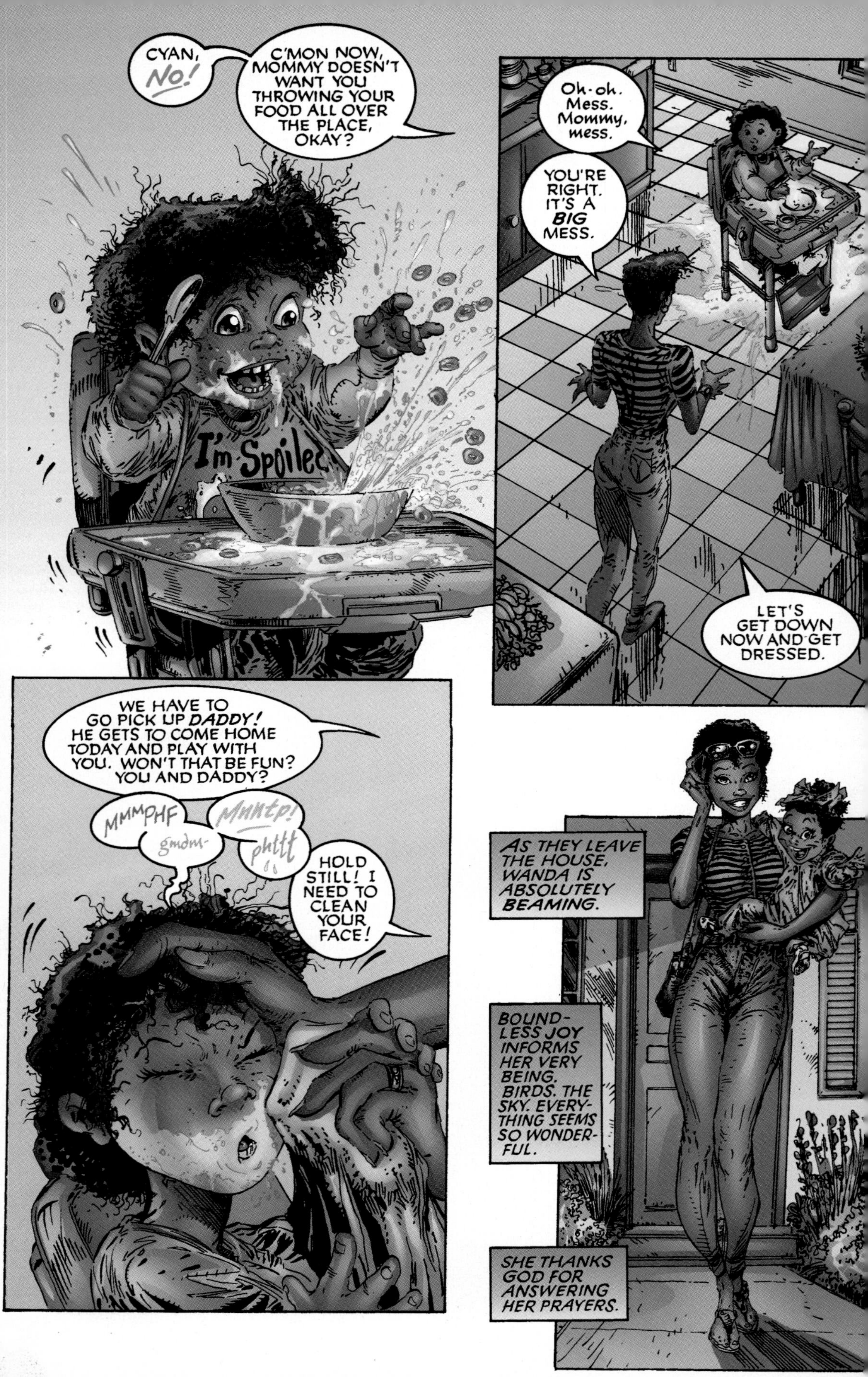
CYAN, NO!
C'MON NOW, MOMMY DOESN'T WANT YOU THROWING YOUR FOOD ALL OVER THE PLACE, OKAY?
I'm Spoiled
Oh-oh. Mess. Mommy, mess.
YOU'RE RIGHT. IT'S A BIG MESS.
LET'S GET DOWN NOW AND GET DRESSED.
WE HAVE TO GO PICK UP DADDY! HE GETS TO COME HOME TODAY AND PLAY WITH YOU. WON'T THAT BE FUN? YOU AND DADDY?
MMMPHF
gmdm-
Mmntp!
phttt
HOLD STILL! I NEED TO CLEAN YOUR FACE!
AS THEY LEAVE THE HOUSE, WANDA IS ABSOLUTELY BEAMING.
BOUNDLESS JOY INFORMS HER VERY BEING. BIRDS. THE SKY. EVERYTHING SEEMS SO WONDERFUL.
SHE THANKS GOD FOR ANSWERING HER PRAYERS.

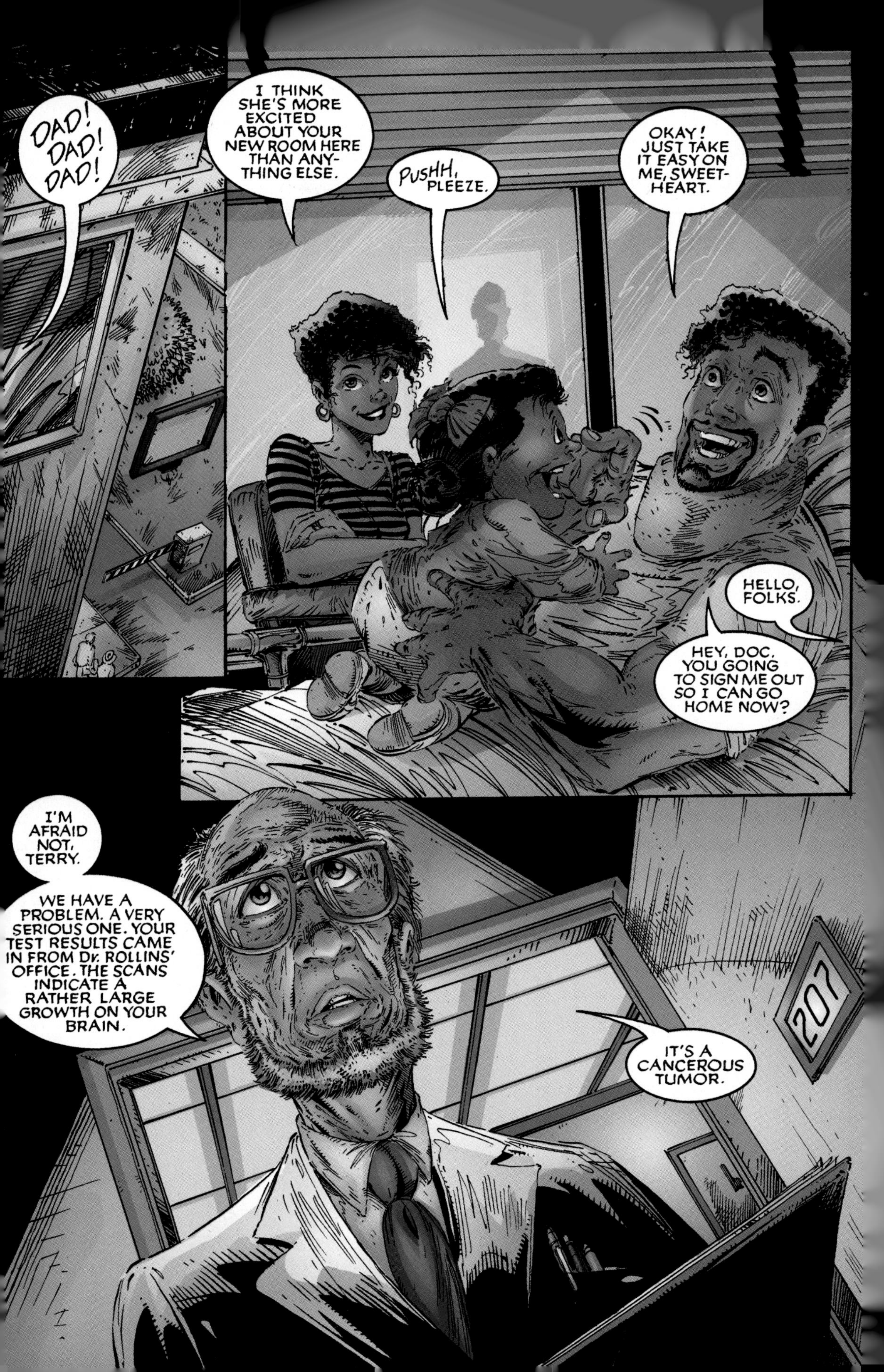
DAD! DAD! DAD!
I THINK SHE'S MORE EXCITED ABOUT YOUR NEW ROOM HERE THAN ANY-THING ELSE.
PUSHH, PLEEZE.
OKAY! JUST TAKE IT EASY ON ME, SWEET-HEART.
HELLO, FOLKS.
HEY, DOC. YOU GOING TO SIGN ME OUT SO I CAN GO HOME NOW?
I'M AFRAID NOT, TERRY.
WE HAVE A PROBLEM. A VERY SERIOUS ONE. YOUR TEST RESULTS CAME IN FROM Dr. ROLLINS' OFFICE. THE SCANS INDICATE A RATHER LARGE GROWTH ON YOUR BRAIN.
IT'S A CANCEROUS TUMOR.
207

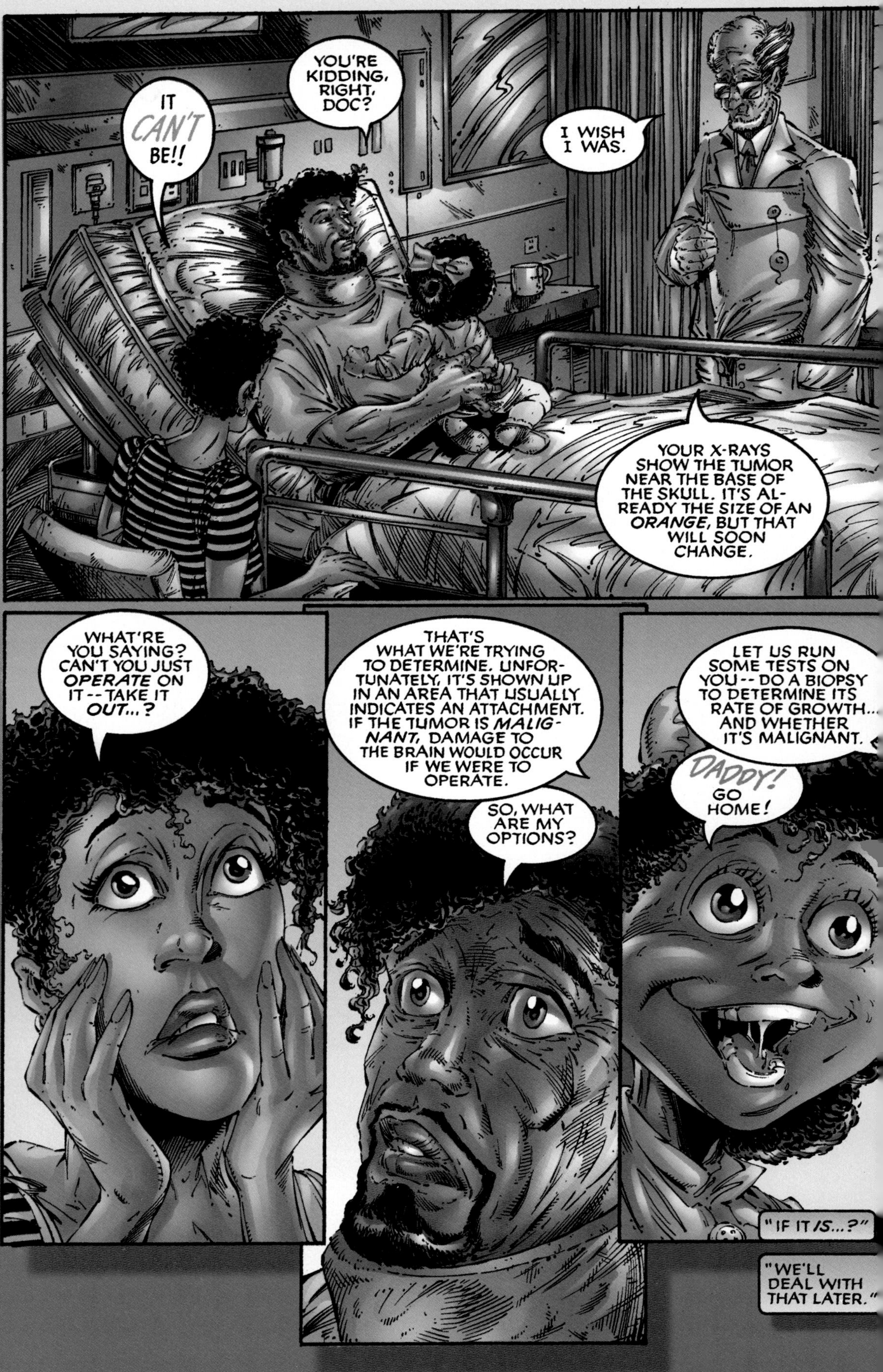
IT CAN'T BE!!
YOU'RE KIDDING, RIGHT, DOC?
I WISH I WAS.
YOUR X-RAYS SHOW THE TUMOR NEAR THE BASE OF THE SKULL. IT'S AL-READY THE SIZE OF AN ORANGE, BUT THAT WILL SOON CHANGE.
WHAT'RE YOU SAYING? CAN'T YOU JUST OPERATE ON IT -- TAKE IT OUT...?
THAT'S WHAT WE'RE TRYING TO DETERMINE. UNFOR-TUNATELY, IT'S SHOWN UP IN AN AREA THAT USUALLY INDICATES AN ATTACHMENT. IF THE TUMOR IS MALIG-NANT, DAMAGE TO THE BRAIN WOULD OCCUR IF WE WERE TO OPERATE.
SO, WHAT ARE MY OPTIONS?
LET US RUN SOME TESTS ON YOU -- DO A BIOPSY TO DETERMINE ITS RATE OF GROWTH... AND WHETHER IT'S MALIGNANT.
DADDY! GO HOME!
"IF IT IS...?"
"WE'LL DEAL WITH THAT LATER."

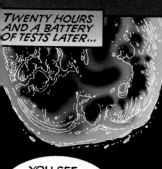

TWENTY HOURS AND A BATTERY OF TESTS LATER...

YOU SEE THIS CLOUDY AREA-- IT REPRESENTS THE CANCER.

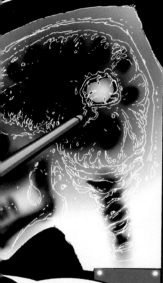

WHEN YOU HAD YOUR COLD, A *VIRUS* ENTERED YOUR SYSTEM. USUALLY, THE BODY COMBATS A VIRUS WITH A NUMBER OF DIFFERENT DEFENSES.

BUT AS YOUR COLD GOT WORSE, IT DEVELOPED INTO AN EARLY STAGE OF *PNEUMONIA.* AS THE VIRUS GREW STRONGER, IT TRIGGERED THE LATENT CELLS OF THE *CANCER* TO GROW.

MEANING YOU'VE ALWAYS HAD THIS IN YOU, JUST IN A DORMANT STATE. YOU, LIKE MILLIONS OF OTHERS, WERE PROBABLY BORN WITH IT.

UNFORTUNATELY, ITS POSITIONING MAKES IT IMPOSSIBLE FOR US TO OPERATE. TO REMOVE IT *ALL,* I'D HAVE TO REMOVE PART OF THE BRAIN, *TOO.* THIS IS COMPOUNDED BY THE FACT THAT THE TUMOR IS *MALIGNANT.*

MALIGNANT.

TERRY SQUEEZES WANDA EVEN HARDER.

SO IT'D JUST GROW BACK, EVEN IF YOU *COULD* REMOVE IT.

YES.

MEANING I'M GOING TO *DIE.* ISN'T THAT RIGHT, DOCTOR? H-HOW MUCH TIME DO I HAVE?

AT ITS CURRENT RATE OF GROWTH, ABOUT TWO MONTHS, BUT THERE IS A SERIES OF PROCEDURES THAT CAN SLOW THE SPREAD OF IT.

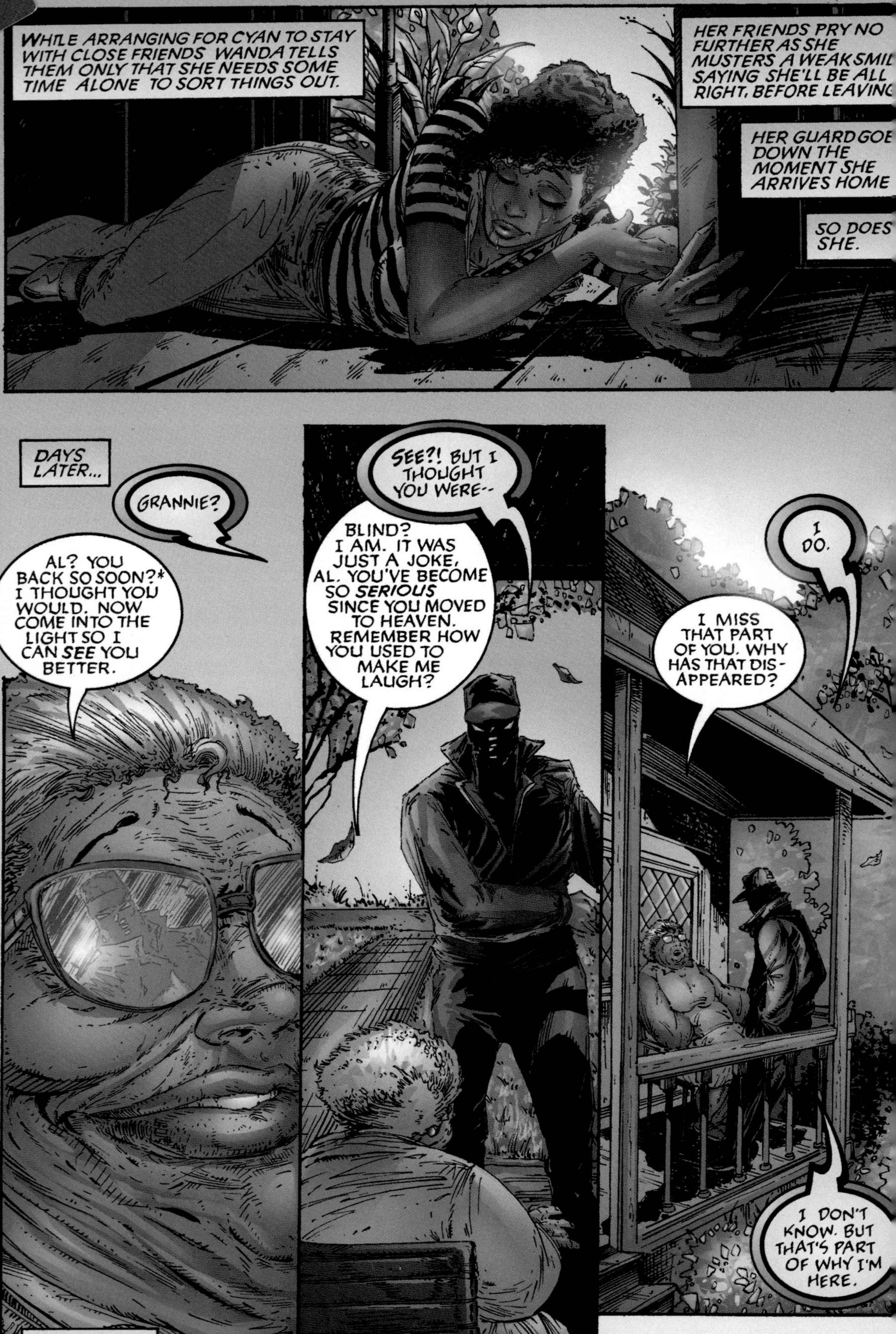

WHILE ARRANGING FOR CYAN TO STAY WITH CLOSE FRIENDS WANDA TELLS THEM ONLY THAT SHE NEEDS SOME TIME ALONE TO SORT THINGS OUT.
HER FRIENDS PRY NO FURTHER AS SHE MUSTERS A WEAK SMIL SAYING SHE'LL BE ALL RIGHT, BEFORE LEAVING
HER GUARD GOE DOWN THE MOMENT SHE ARRIVES HOME
SO DOES SHE.
DAYS LATER...
GRANNIE?
AL? YOU BACK SO SOON?* I THOUGHT YOU WOULD. NOW COME INTO THE LIGHT SO I CAN SEE YOU BETTER.
SEE?! BUT I THOUGHT YOU WERE--
BLIND? I AM. IT WAS JUST A JOKE, AL. YOU'VE BECOME SO SERIOUS SINCE YOU MOVED TO HEAVEN. REMEMBER HOW YOU USED TO MAKE ME LAUGH?
I DO.
I MISS THAT PART OF YOU. WHY HAS THAT DIS-APPEARED?
I DON'T KNOW. BUT THAT'S PART OF WHY I'M HERE.
*LAST ISSUE--Tom

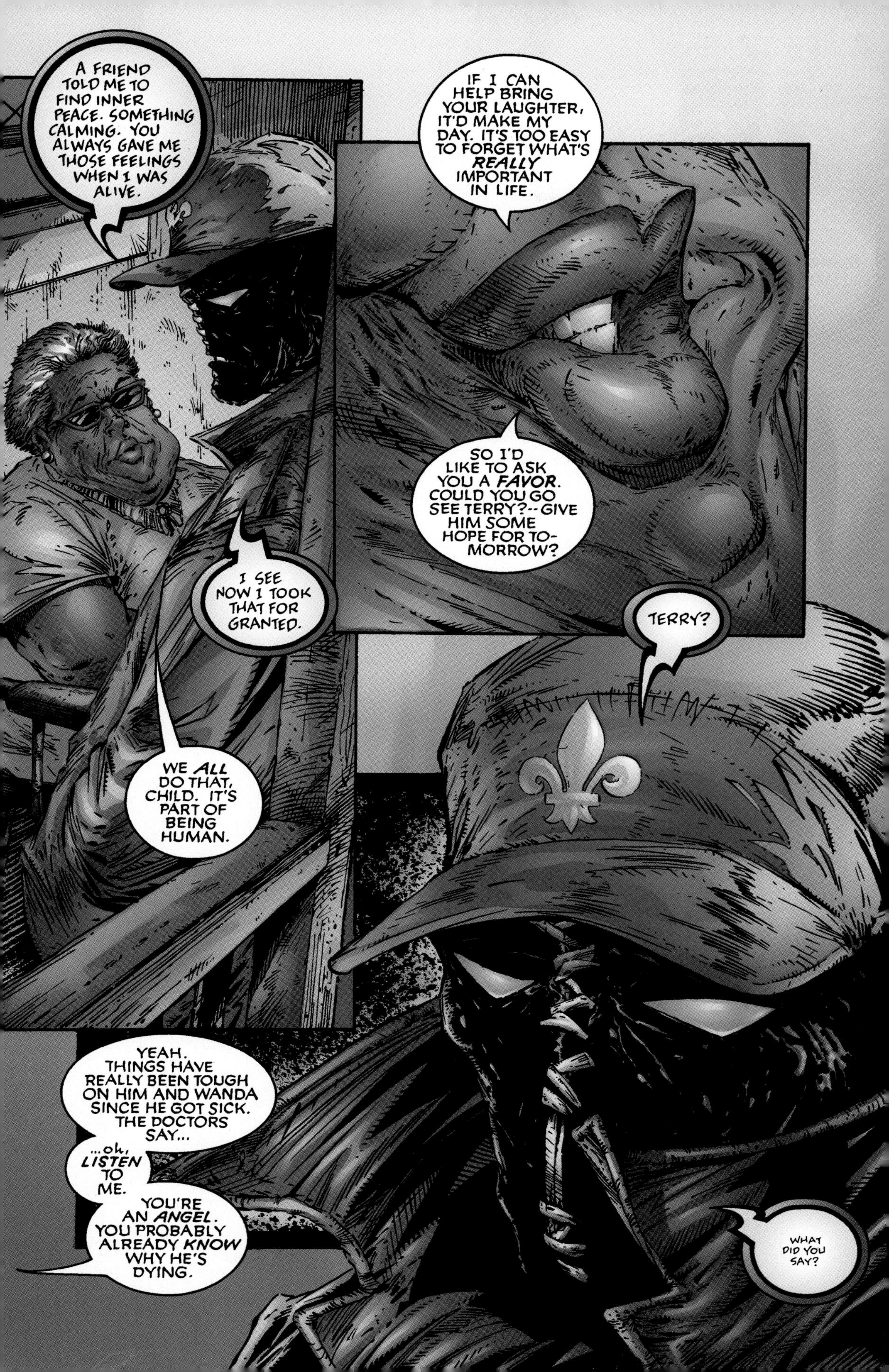
A FRIEND TOLD ME TO FIND INNER PEACE. SOMETHING CALMING. YOU ALWAYS GAVE ME THOSE FEELINGS WHEN I WAS ALIVE.
I SEE NOW I TOOK THAT FOR GRANTED.
WE ALL DO THAT, CHILD. IT'S PART OF BEING HUMAN.
IF I CAN HELP BRING YOUR LAUGHTER, IT'D MAKE MY DAY. IT'S TOO EASY TO FORGET WHAT'S REALLY IMPORTANT IN LIFE.
SO I'D LIKE TO ASK YOU A FAVOR. COULD YOU GO SEE TERRY?-- GIVE HIM SOME HOPE FOR TO-MORROW?
TERRY?
YEAH. THINGS HAVE REALLY BEEN TOUGH ON HIM AND WANDA SINCE HE GOT SICK. THE DOCTORS SAY...
...oh, LISTEN TO ME.
YOU'RE AN ANGEL. YOU PROBABLY ALREADY KNOW WHY HE'S DYING.
WHAT DID YOU SAY?

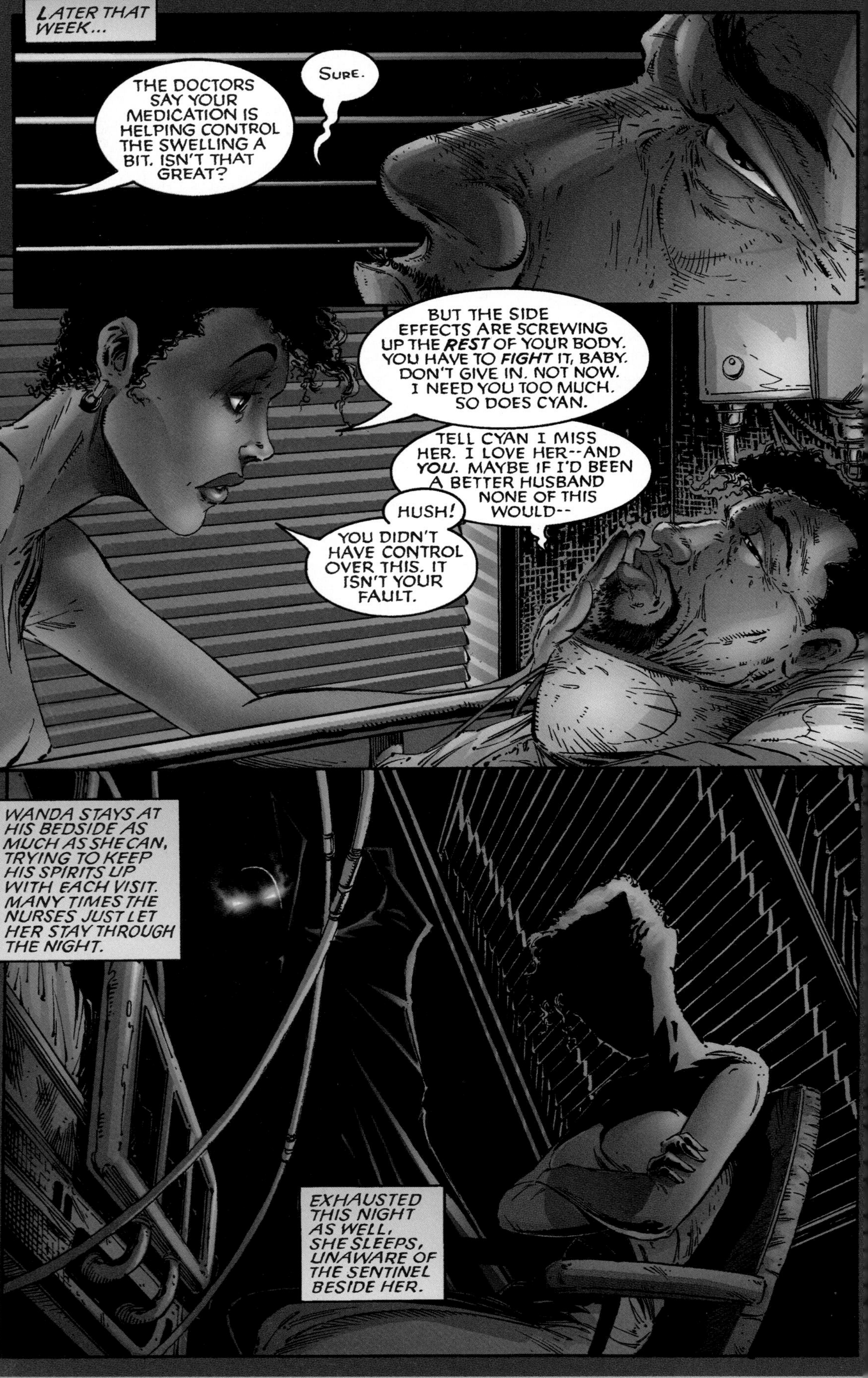
LATER THAT WEEK...
THE DOCTORS SAY YOUR MEDICATION IS HELPING CONTROL THE SWELLING A BIT. ISN'T THAT GREAT?
SURE.
BUT THE SIDE EFFECTS ARE SCREWING UP THE REST OF YOUR BODY. YOU HAVE TO FIGHT IT, BABY. DON'T GIVE IN. NOT NOW. I NEED YOU TOO MUCH. SO DOES CYAN.
TELL CYAN I MISS HER. I LOVE HER--AND YOU. MAYBE IF I'D BEEN A BETTER HUSBAND NONE OF THIS WOULD--
HUSH!
YOU DIDN'T HAVE CONTROL OVER THIS. IT ISN'T YOUR FAULT.
WANDA STAYS AT HIS BEDSIDE AS MUCH AS SHE CAN, TRYING TO KEEP HIS SPIRITS UP WITH EACH VISIT. MANY TIMES THE NURSES JUST LET HER STAY THROUGH THE NIGHT.
EXHAUSTED THIS NIGHT AS WELL, SHE SLEEPS, UNAWARE OF THE SENTINEL BESIDE HER.

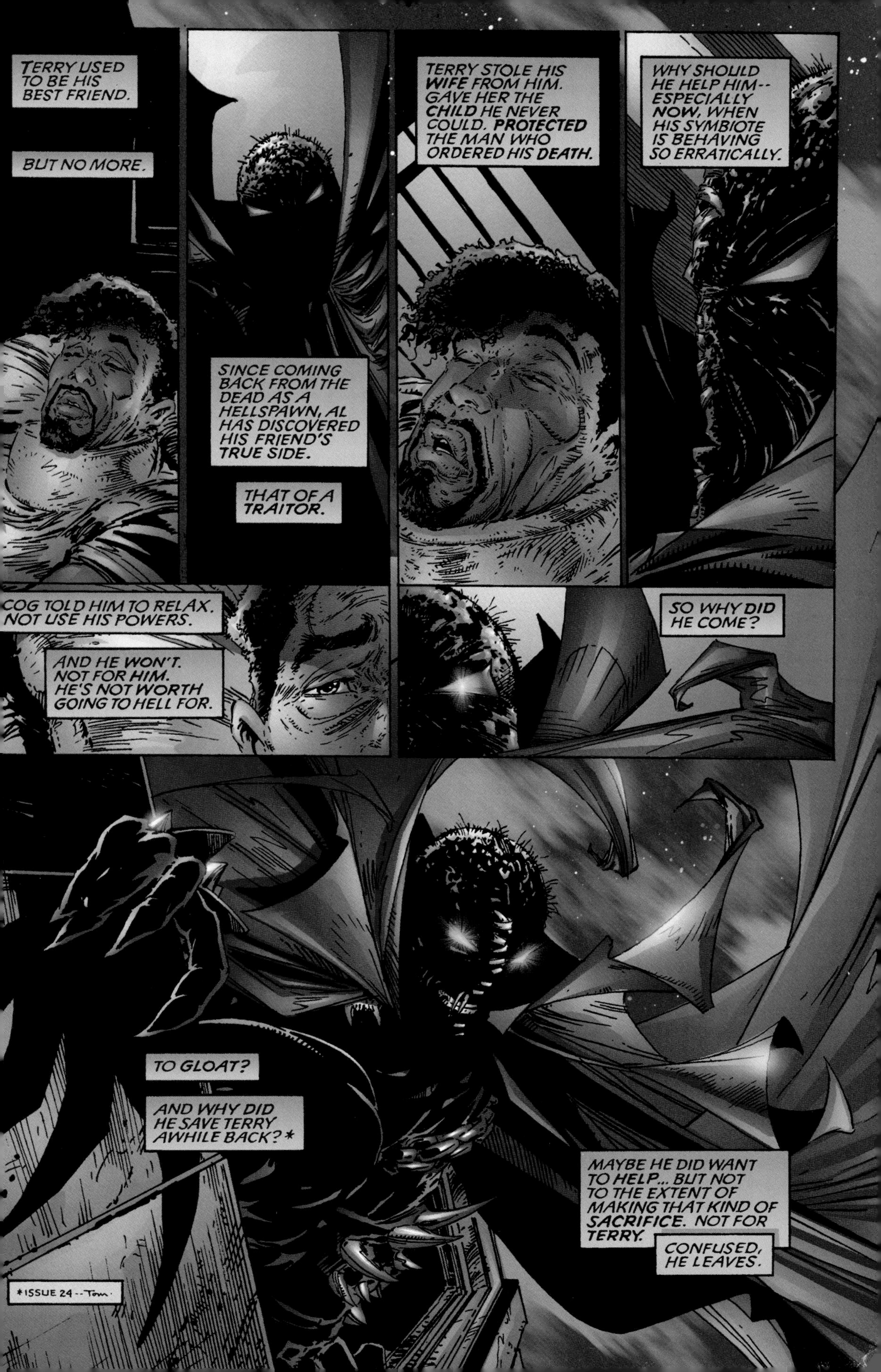
TERRY USED TO BE HIS BEST FRIEND.
BUT NO MORE.
SINCE COMING BACK FROM THE DEAD AS A HELLSPAWN, AL HAS DISCOVERED HIS FRIEND'S TRUE SIDE.
THAT OF A TRAITOR.
TERRY STOLE HIS WIFE FROM HIM. GAVE HER THE CHILD HE NEVER COULD. PROTECTED THE MAN WHO ORDERED HIS DEATH.
WHY SHOULD HE HELP HIM-- ESPECIALLY NOW, WHEN HIS SYMBIOTE IS BEHAVING SO ERRATICALLY.
COG TOLD HIM TO RELAX. NOT USE HIS POWERS.
AND HE WON'T. NOT FOR HIM. HE'S NOT WORTH GOING TO HELL FOR.
SO WHY DID HE COME?
TO GLOAT?
AND WHY DID HE SAVE TERRY AWHILE BACK?*
MAYBE HE DID WANT TO HELP... BUT NOT TO THE EXTENT OF MAKING THAT KIND OF SACRIFICE. NOT FOR TERRY.
CONFUSED, HE LEAVES.
*ISSUE 24 --Tom

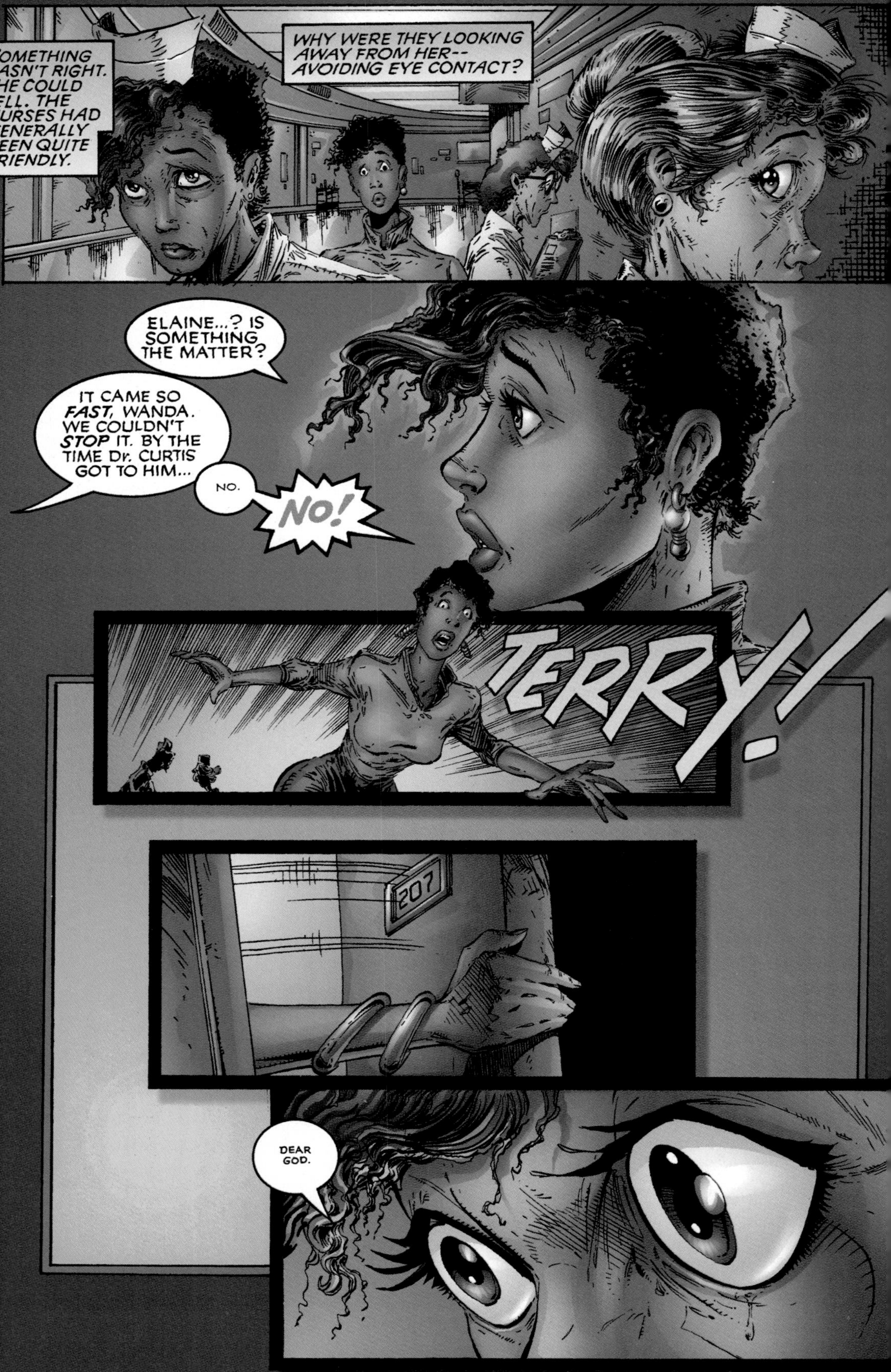
SOMETHING WASN'T RIGHT. SHE COULD TELL. THE NURSES HAD GENERALLY BEEN QUITE FRIENDLY.
WHY WERE THEY LOOKING AWAY FROM HER-- AVOIDING EYE CONTACT?
ELAINE...? IS SOMETHING THE MATTER?
IT CAME SO FAST, WANDA. WE COULDN'T STOP IT. BY THE TIME Dr. CURTIS GOT TO HIM...
NO.
NO!
TERRY!
DEAR GOD.

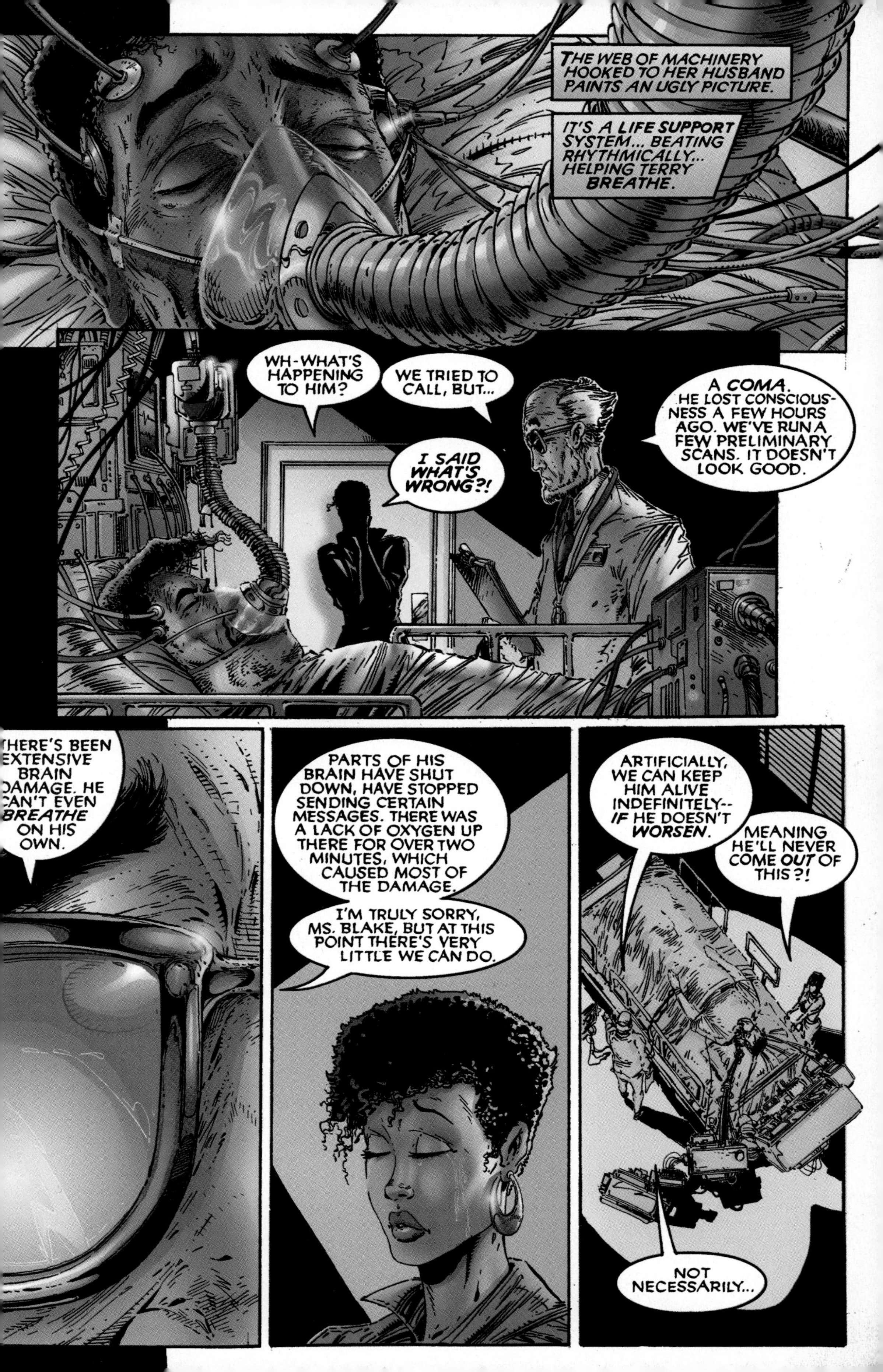
THE WEB OF MACHINERY HOOKED TO HER HUSBAND PAINTS AN UGLY PICTURE.
IT'S A LIFE SUPPORT SYSTEM... BEATING RHYTHMICALLY... HELPING TERRY BREATHE.
WH-WHAT'S HAPPENING TO HIM?
WE TRIED TO CALL, BUT...
I SAID WHAT'S WRONG?!
A COMA. HE LOST CONSCIOUSNESS A FEW HOURS AGO. WE'VE RUN A FEW PRELIMINARY SCANS. IT DOESN'T LOOK GOOD.
THERE'S BEEN EXTENSIVE BRAIN DAMAGE. HE CAN'T EVEN BREATHE ON HIS OWN.
PARTS OF HIS BRAIN HAVE SHUT DOWN, HAVE STOPPED SENDING CERTAIN MESSAGES. THERE WAS A LACK OF OXYGEN UP THERE FOR OVER TWO MINUTES, WHICH CAUSED MOST OF THE DAMAGE.
I'M TRULY SORRY, MS. BLAKE, BUT AT THIS POINT THERE'S VERY LITTLE WE CAN DO.
ARTIFICIALLY, WE CAN KEEP HIM ALIVE INDEFINITELY-- IF HE DOESN'T WORSEN.
MEANING HE'LL NEVER COME OUT OF THIS?!
NOT NECESSARILY...

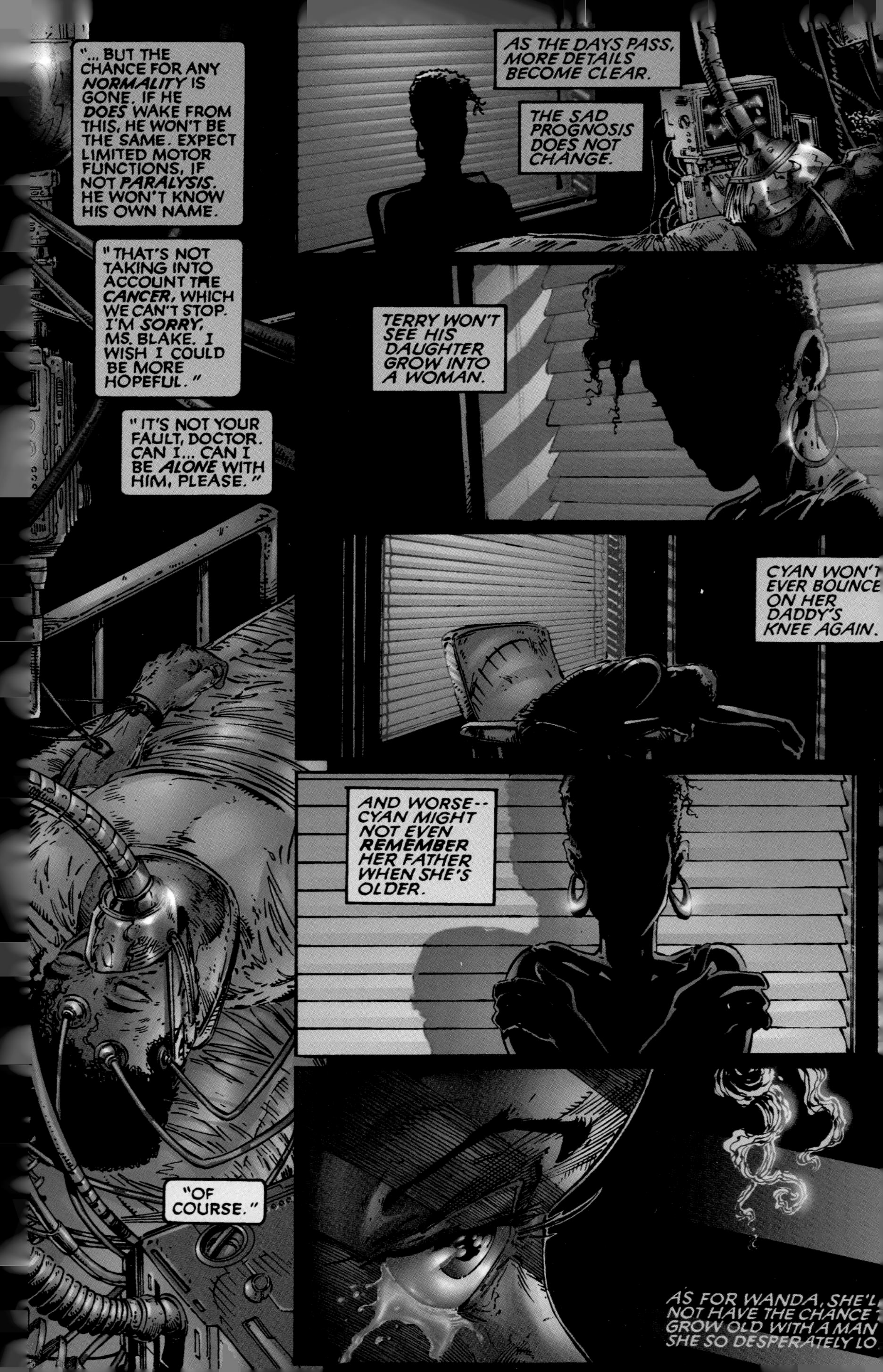
"... BUT THE CHANCE FOR ANY NORMALITY IS GONE. IF HE DOES WAKE FROM THIS, HE WON'T BE THE SAME. EXPECT LIMITED MOTOR FUNCTIONS, IF NOT PARALYSIS. HE WON'T KNOW HIS OWN NAME.
"THAT'S NOT TAKING INTO ACCOUNT THE CANCER, WHICH WE CAN'T STOP. I'M SORRY, MS. BLAKE. I WISH I COULD BE MORE HOPEFUL."
"IT'S NOT YOUR FAULT, DOCTOR. CAN I... CAN I BE ALONE WITH HIM, PLEASE."
"OF COURSE."
AS THE DAYS PASS, MORE DETAILS BECOME CLEAR.
THE SAD PROGNOSIS DOES NOT CHANGE.
TERRY WON'T SEE HIS DAUGHTER GROW INTO A WOMAN.
CYAN WON'T EVER BOUNCE ON HER DADDY'S KNEE AGAIN.
AND WORSE-- CYAN MIGHT NOT EVEN REMEMBER HER FATHER WHEN SHE'S OLDER.
AS FOR WANDA, SHE'L NOT HAVE THE CHANCE GROW OLD WITH A MAN SHE SO DESPERATELY LO

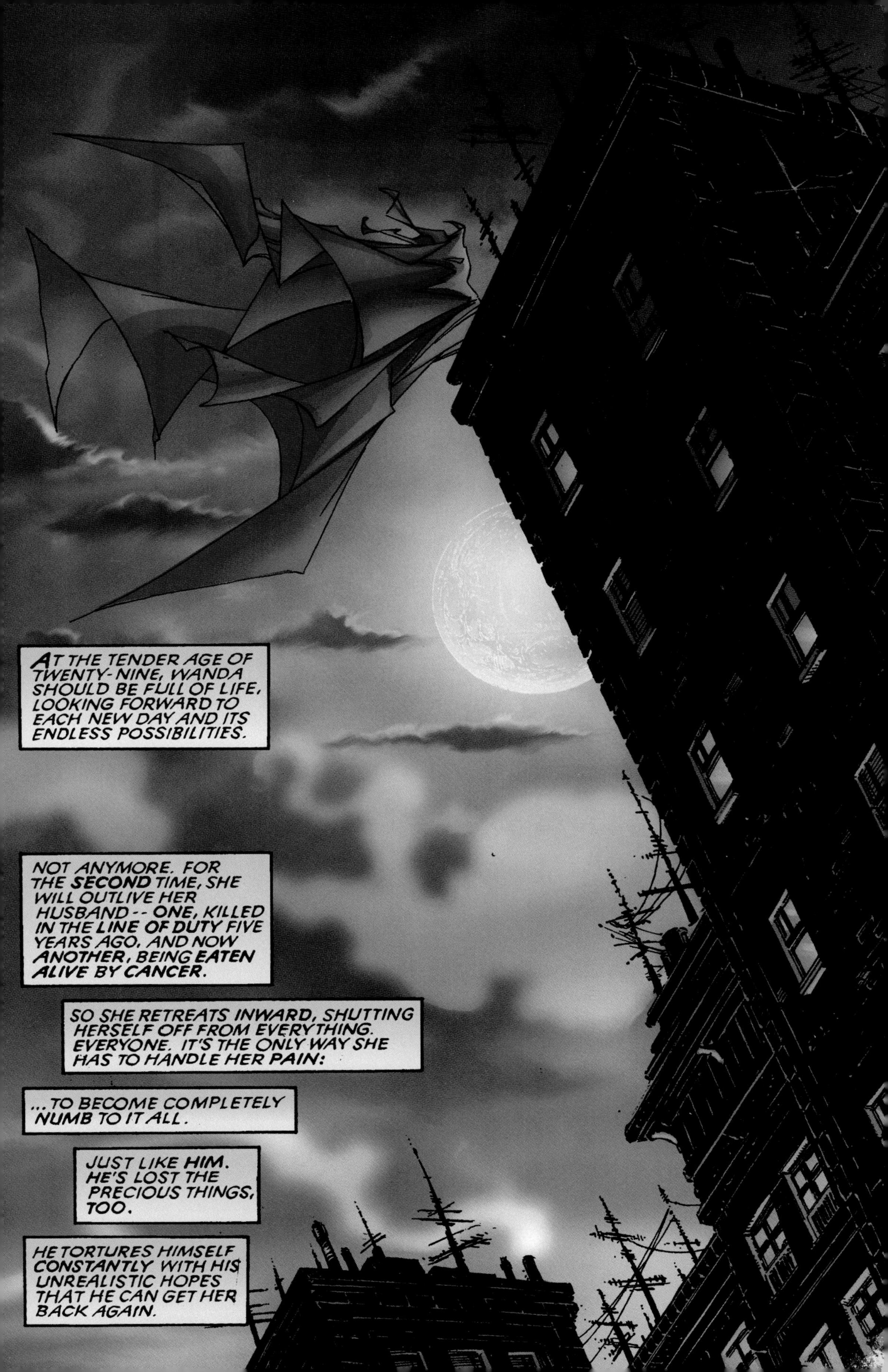
AT THE TENDER AGE OF TWENTY-NINE, WANDA SHOULD BE FULL OF LIFE, LOOKING FORWARD TO EACH NEW DAY AND ITS ENDLESS POSSIBILITIES.
NOT ANYMORE. FOR THE SECOND TIME, SHE WILL OUTLIVE HER HUSBAND -- ONE, KILLED IN THE LINE OF DUTY FIVE YEARS AGO, AND NOW ANOTHER, BEING EATEN ALIVE BY CANCER.
SO SHE RETREATS INWARD, SHUTTING HERSELF OFF FROM EVERYTHING. EVERYONE. IT'S THE ONLY WAY SHE HAS TO HANDLE HER PAIN:
...TO BECOME COMPLETELY NUMB TO IT ALL.
JUST LIKE HIM. HE'S LOST THE PRECIOUS THINGS, TOO.
HE TORTURES HIMSELF CONSTANTLY WITH HIS UNREALISTIC HOPES THAT HE CAN GET HER BACK AGAIN.

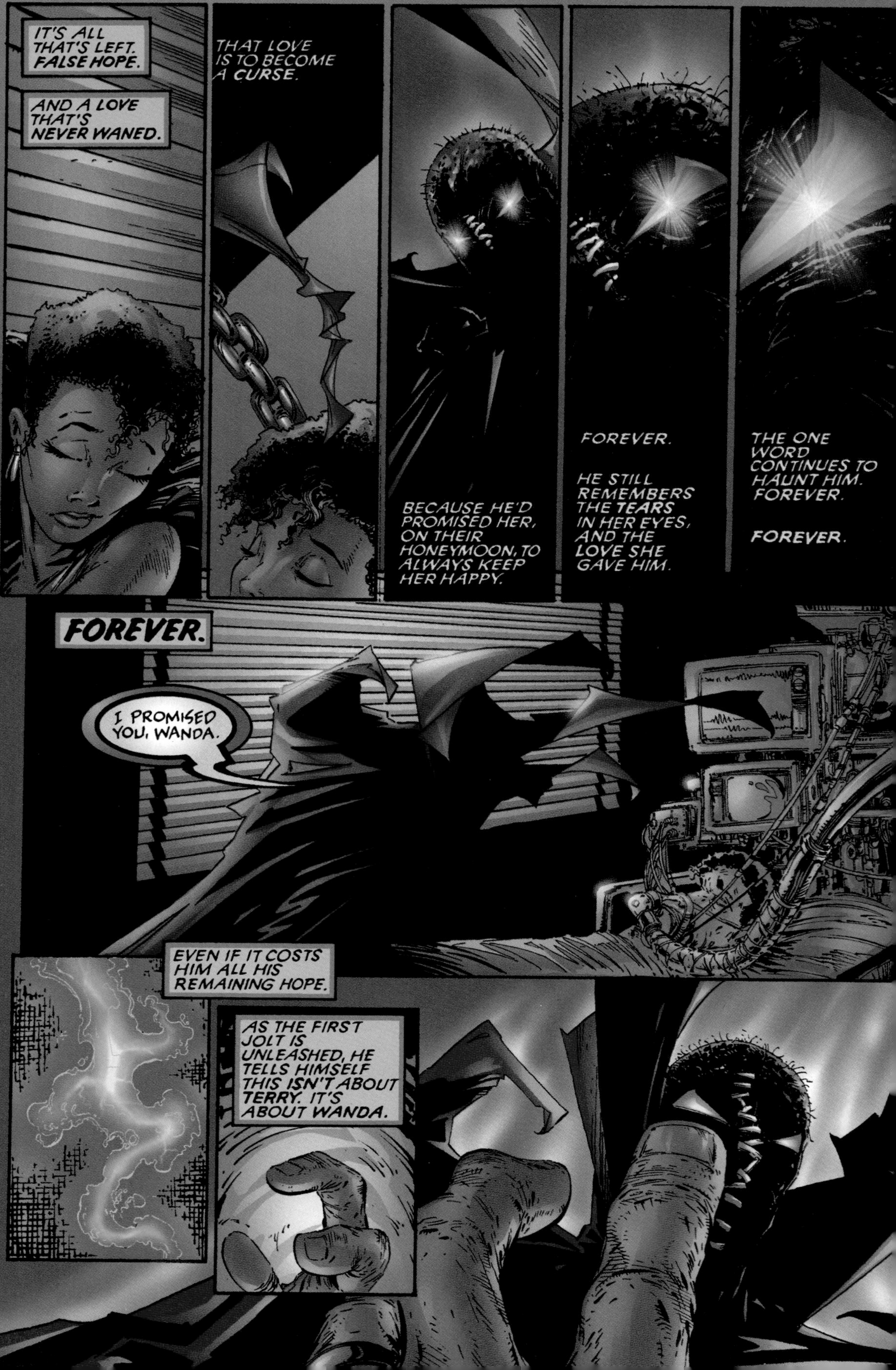
IT'S ALL THAT'S LEFT. FALSE HOPE.
AND A LOVE THAT'S NEVER WANED.
THAT LOVE IS TO BECOME A CURSE.
BECAUSE HE'D PROMISED HER, ON THEIR HONEYMOON, TO ALWAYS KEEP HER HAPPY.
FOREVER.
HE STILL REMEMBERS THE TEARS IN HER EYES, AND THE LOVE SHE GAVE HIM.
THE ONE WORD CONTINUES TO HAUNT HIM. FOREVER.
FOREVER.
FOREVER.
I PROMISED YOU, WANDA.
EVEN IF IT COSTS HIM ALL HIS REMAINING HOPE.
AS THE FIRST JOLT IS UNLEASHED, HE TELLS HIMSELF THIS ISN'T ABOUT TERRY. IT'S ABOUT WANDA.

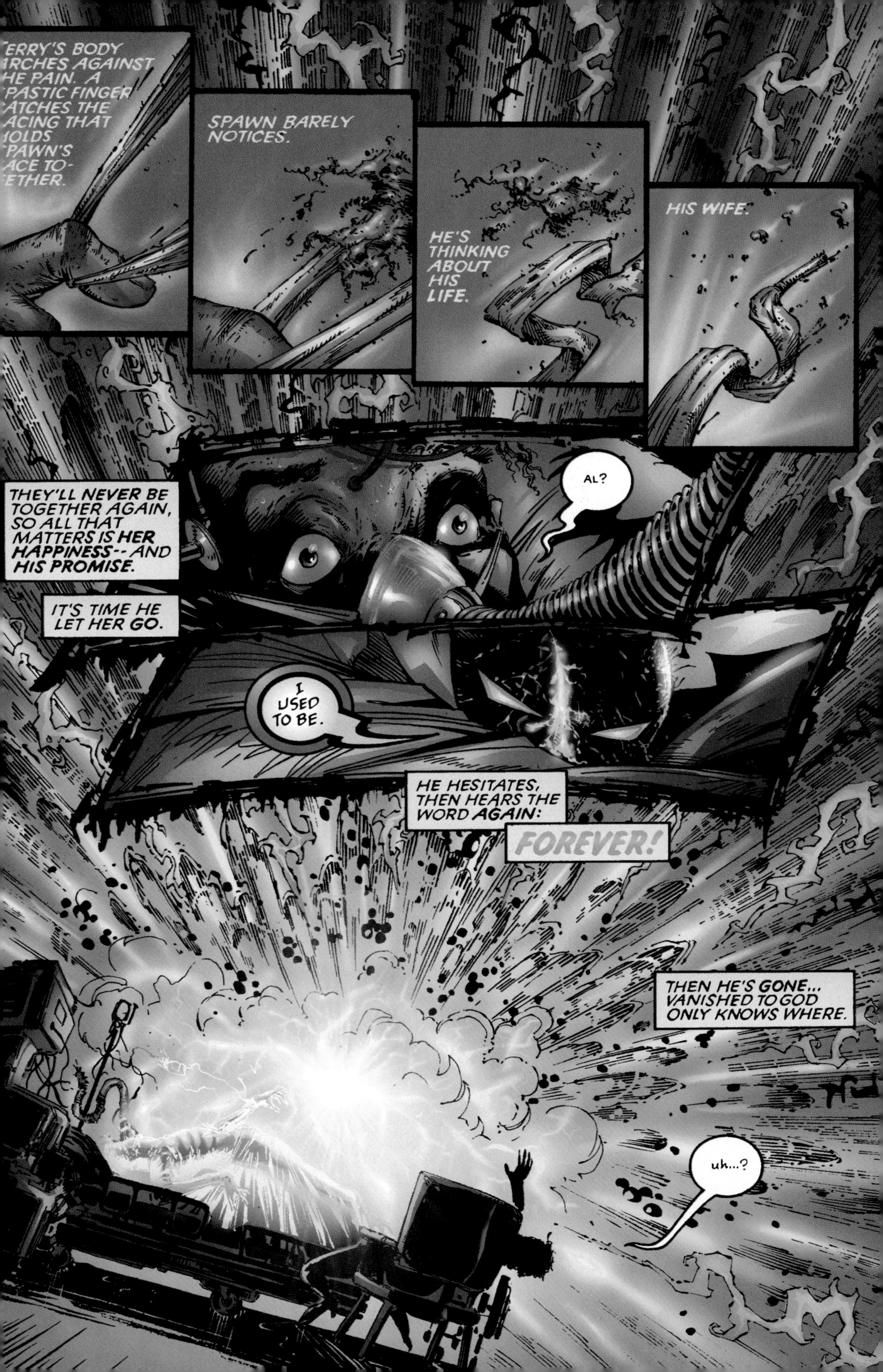

ERRY'S BODY ARCHES AGAINST HE PAIN. A PASTIC FINGER ATCHES THE ACING THAT HOLDS PAWN'S ACE TO-ETHER.
SPAWN BARELY NOTICES.
HE'S THINKING ABOUT HIS LIFE.
HIS WIFE.
AL?
THEY'LL NEVER BE TOGETHER AGAIN, SO ALL THAT MATTERS IS HER HAPPINESS-- AND HIS PROMISE.
IT'S TIME HE LET HER GO.
I USED TO BE.
HE HESITATES, THEN HEARS THE WORD AGAIN:
FOREVER!
THEN HE'S GONE... VANISHED TO GOD ONLY KNOWS WHERE.
uh...?

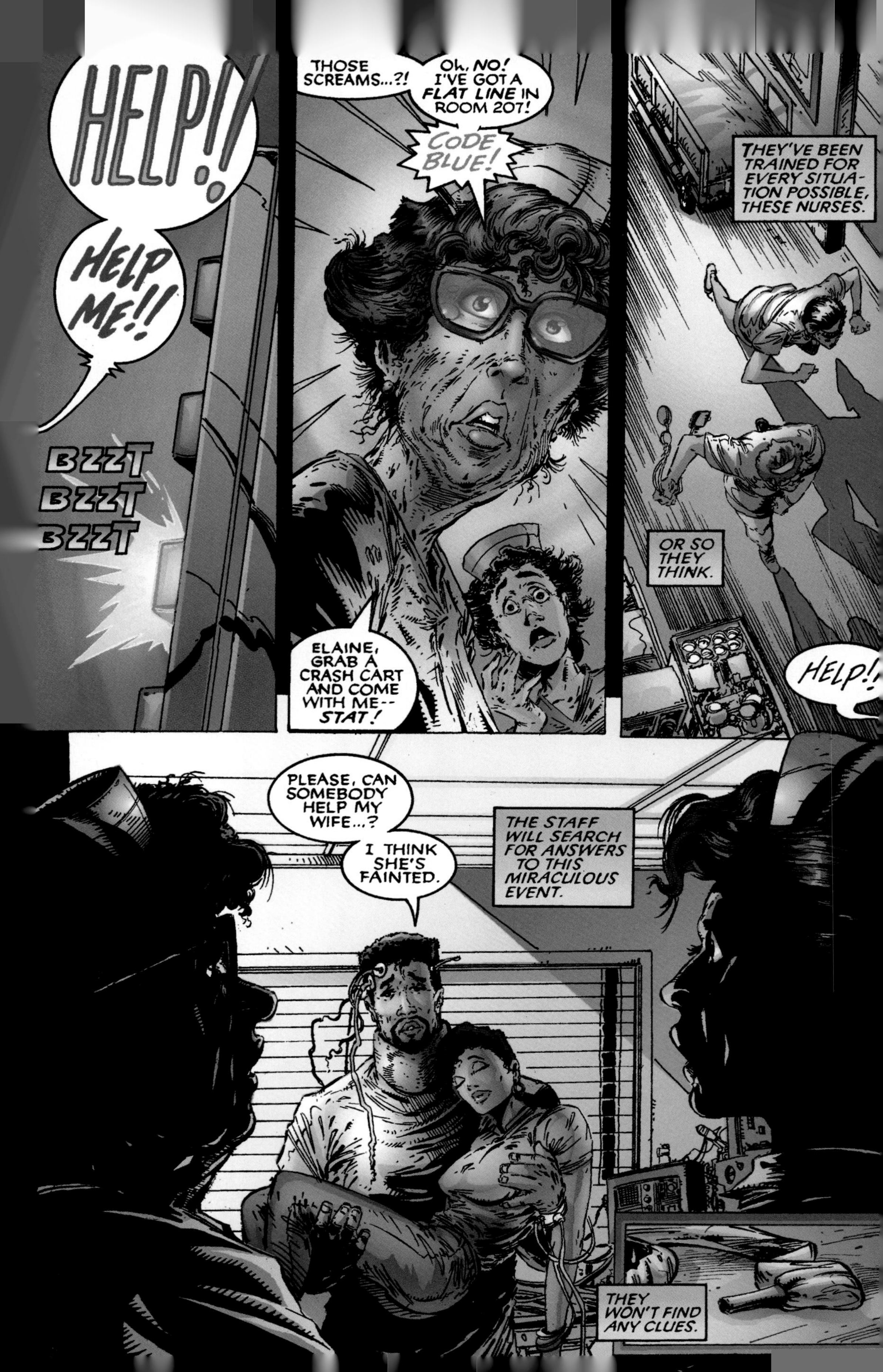
HELP!!
HELP ME!!
BZZT BZZT BZZT
THOSE SCREAMS...?!
Oh, NO! I'VE GOT A FLAT LINE IN ROOM 207!
CODE BLUE!
ELAINE, GRAB A CRASH CART AND COME WITH ME-- STAT!
THEY'VE BEEN TRAINED FOR EVERY SITUATION POSSIBLE, THESE NURSES.
OR SO THEY THINK.
HELP!!
PLEASE, CAN SOMEBODY HELP MY WIFE...?
I THINK SHE'S FAINTED.
THE STAFF WILL SEARCH FOR ANSWERS TO THIS MIRACULOUS EVENT.
THEY WON'T FIND ANY CLUES.

Evil. The worms have always been the most effective sponges for it. Dwelling

underground, hidden from God's light, they absorb the aura of wickedness.

–REVENGE

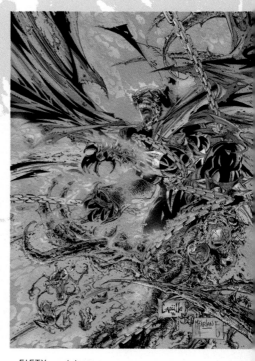

FIFTY part-two

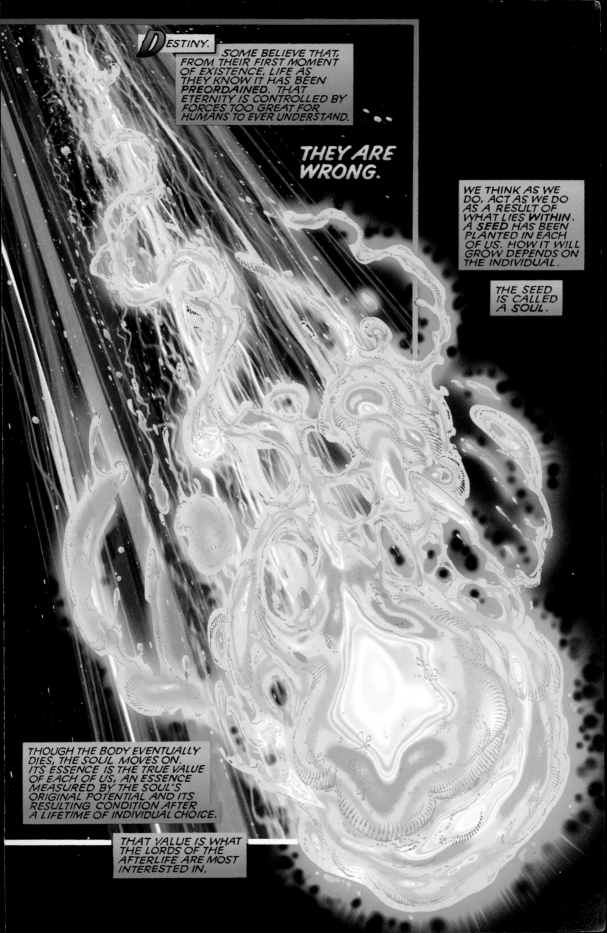

DESTINY. SOME BELIEVE THAT, FROM THEIR FIRST MOMENT OF EXISTENCE, LIFE AS THEY KNOW IT HAS BEEN PREORDAINED. THAT ETERNITY IS CONTROLLED BY FORCES TOO GREAT FOR HUMANS TO EVER UNDERSTAND.

THEY ARE WRONG.

WE THINK AS WE DO, ACT AS WE DO AS A RESULT OF WHAT LIES WITHIN. A SEED HAS BEEN PLANTED IN EACH OF US. HOW IT WILL GROW DEPENDS ON THE INDIVIDUAL.

THE SEED IS CALLED A SOUL.

THOUGH THE BODY EVENTUALLY DIES, THE SOUL MOVES ON. ITS ESSENCE IS THE TRUE VALUE OF EACH OF US, AN ESSENCE MEASURED BY THE SOUL'S ORIGINAL POTENTIAL AND ITS RESULTING CONDITION AFTER A LIFETIME OF INDIVIDUAL CHOICE.

THAT VALUE IS WHAT THE LORDS OF THE AFTERLIFE ARE MOST INTERESTED IN.

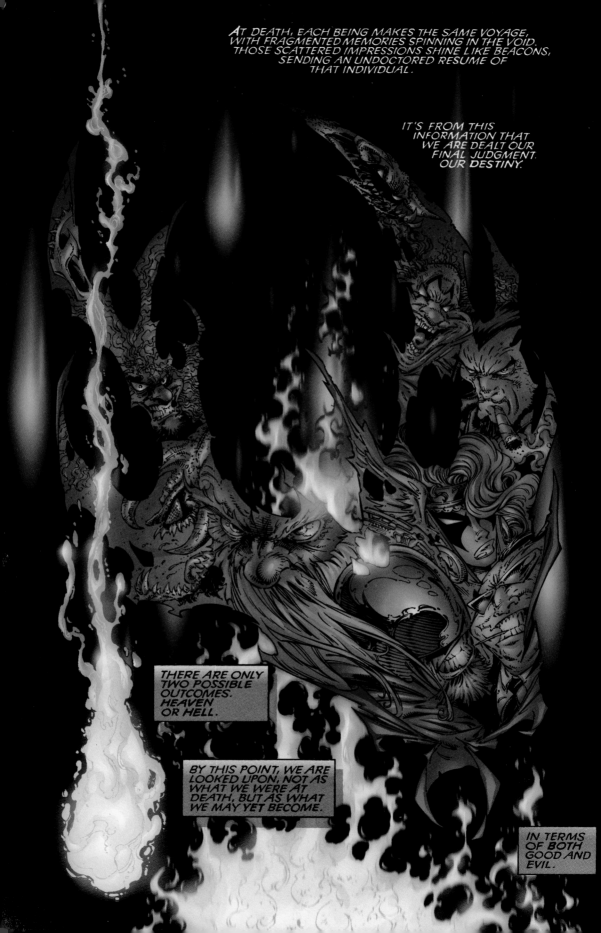

AT DEATH, EACH BEING MAKES THE SAME VOYAGE, WITH FRAGMENTED MEMORIES SPINNING IN THE VOID. THOSE SCATTERED IMPRESSIONS SHINE LIKE BEACONS, SENDING AN UNDOCTORED RESUME OF THAT INDIVIDUAL.

IT'S FROM THIS INFORMATION THAT WE ARE DEALT OUR FINAL JUDGMENT. OUR DESTINY.

THERE ARE ONLY TWO POSSIBLE OUTCOMES. HEAVEN OR HELL.

BY THIS POINT, WE ARE LOOKED UPON, NOT AS WHAT WE WERE AT DEATH, BUT AS WHAT WE MAY YET BECOME.

IN TERMS OF BOTH GOOD AND EVIL.

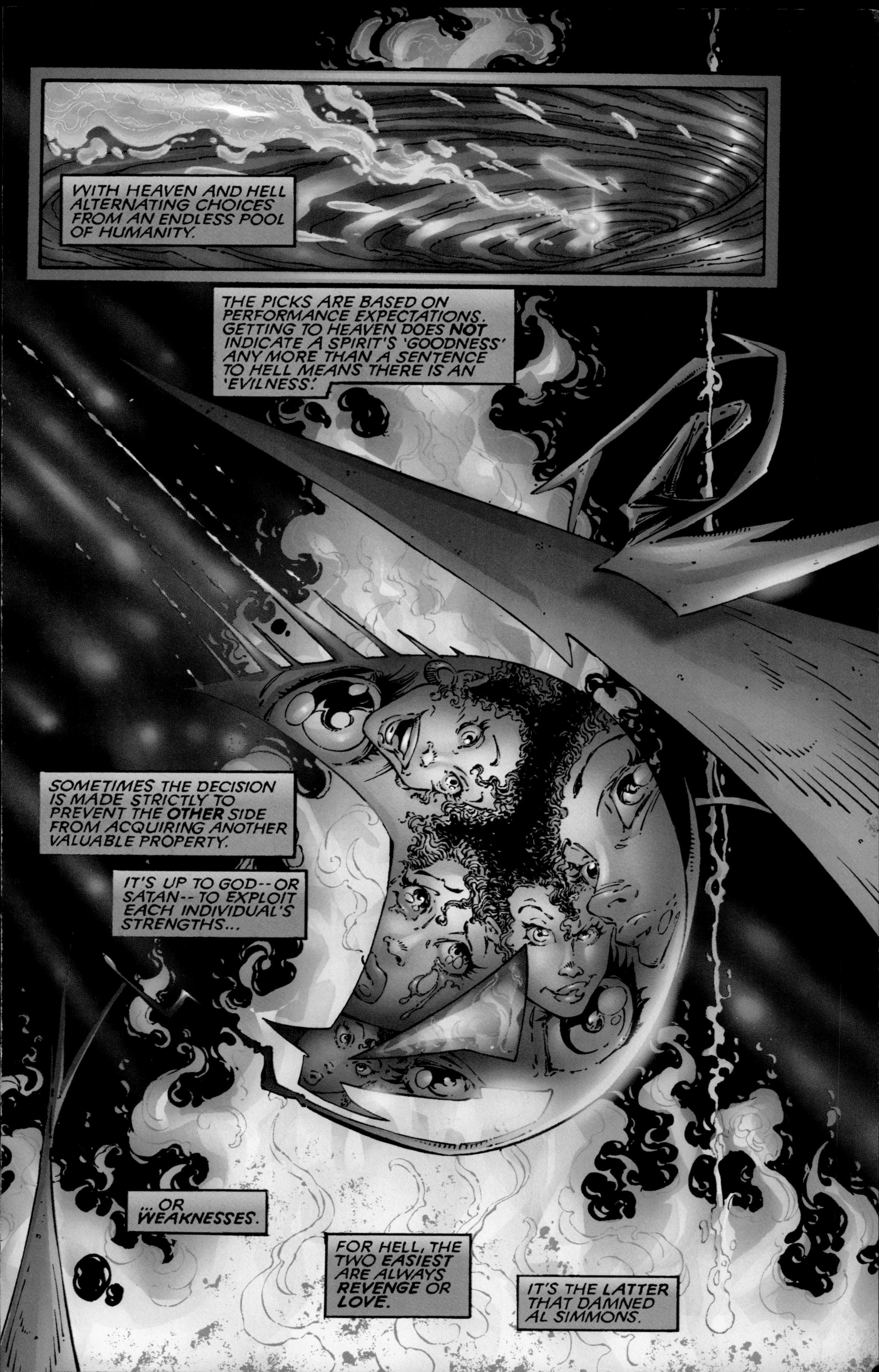
WITH HEAVEN AND HELL ALTERNATING CHOICES FROM AN ENDLESS POOL OF HUMANITY.
THE PICKS ARE BASED ON PERFORMANCE EXPECTATIONS. GETTING TO HEAVEN DOES NOT INDICATE A SPIRIT'S 'GOODNESS' ANY MORE THAN A SENTENCE TO HELL MEANS THERE IS AN 'EVILNESS.'
SOMETIMES THE DECISION IS MADE STRICTLY TO PREVENT THE OTHER SIDE FROM ACQUIRING ANOTHER VALUABLE PROPERTY.
IT'S UP TO GOD--OR SATAN--TO EXPLOIT EACH INDIVIDUAL'S STRENGTHS...
...OR WEAKNESSES.
FOR HELL, THE TWO EASIEST ARE ALWAYS REVENGE OR LOVE.
IT'S THE LATTER THAT DAMNED AL SIMMONS.

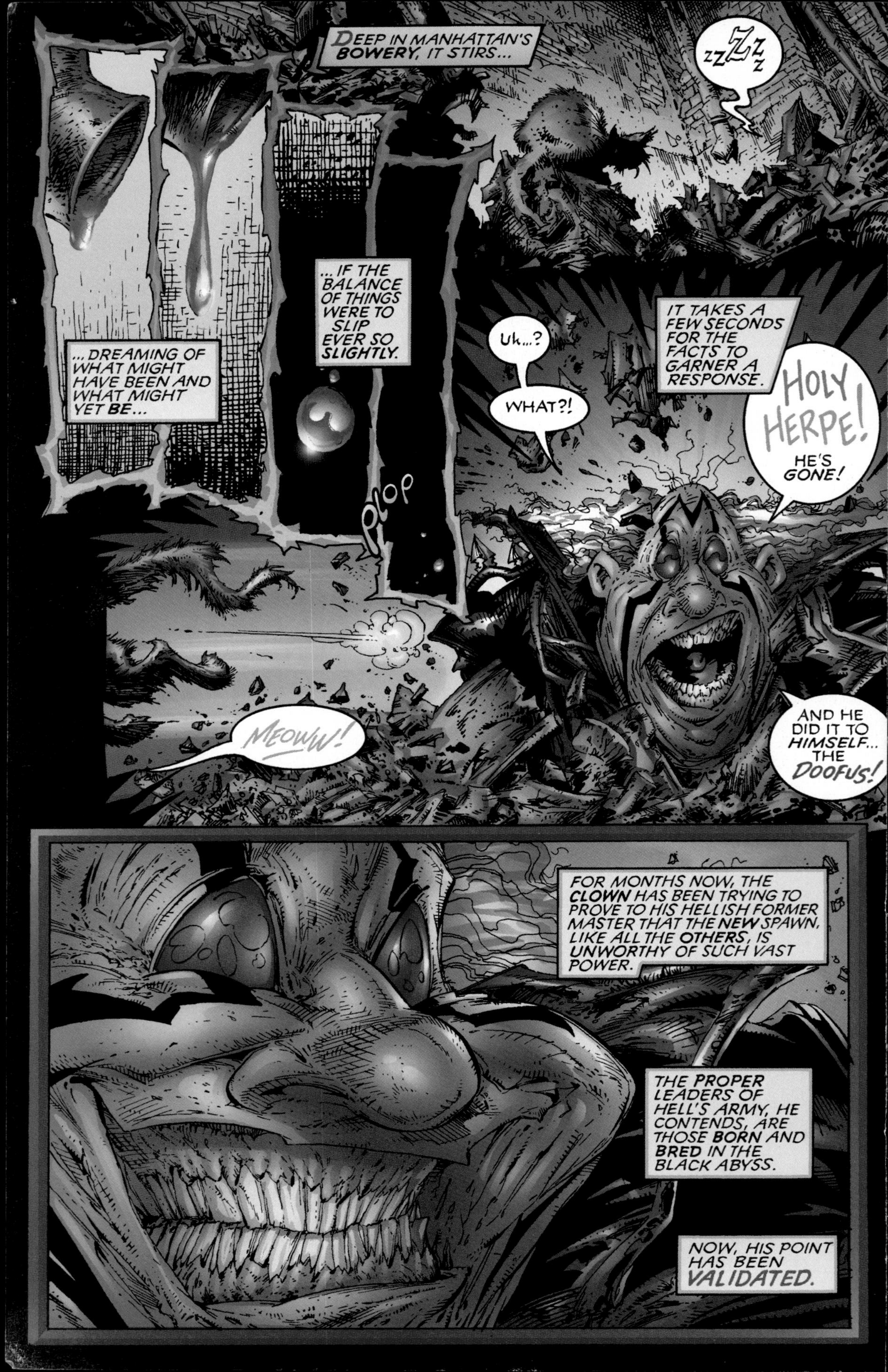
DEEP IN MANHATTAN'S BOWERY, IT STIRS...
zzZZz
...DREAMING OF WHAT MIGHT HAVE BEEN AND WHAT MIGHT YET BE...
...IF THE BALANCE OF THINGS WERE TO SLIP EVER SO SLIGHTLY.
PLOP
Uh...?
WHAT?!
IT TAKES A FEW SECONDS FOR THE FACTS TO GARNER A RESPONSE.
HOLY HERPE! HE'S GONE!
MEOWW!
AND HE DID IT TO HIMSELF... THE DOOFUS!
FOR MONTHS NOW, THE CLOWN HAS BEEN TRYING TO PROVE TO HIS HELLISH FORMER MASTER THAT THE NEW SPAWN, LIKE ALL THE OTHERS, IS UNWORTHY OF SUCH VAST POWER.
THE PROPER LEADERS OF HELL'S ARMY, HE CONTENDS, ARE THOSE BORN AND BRED IN THE BLACK ABYSS.
NOW, HIS POINT HAS BEEN VALIDATED.

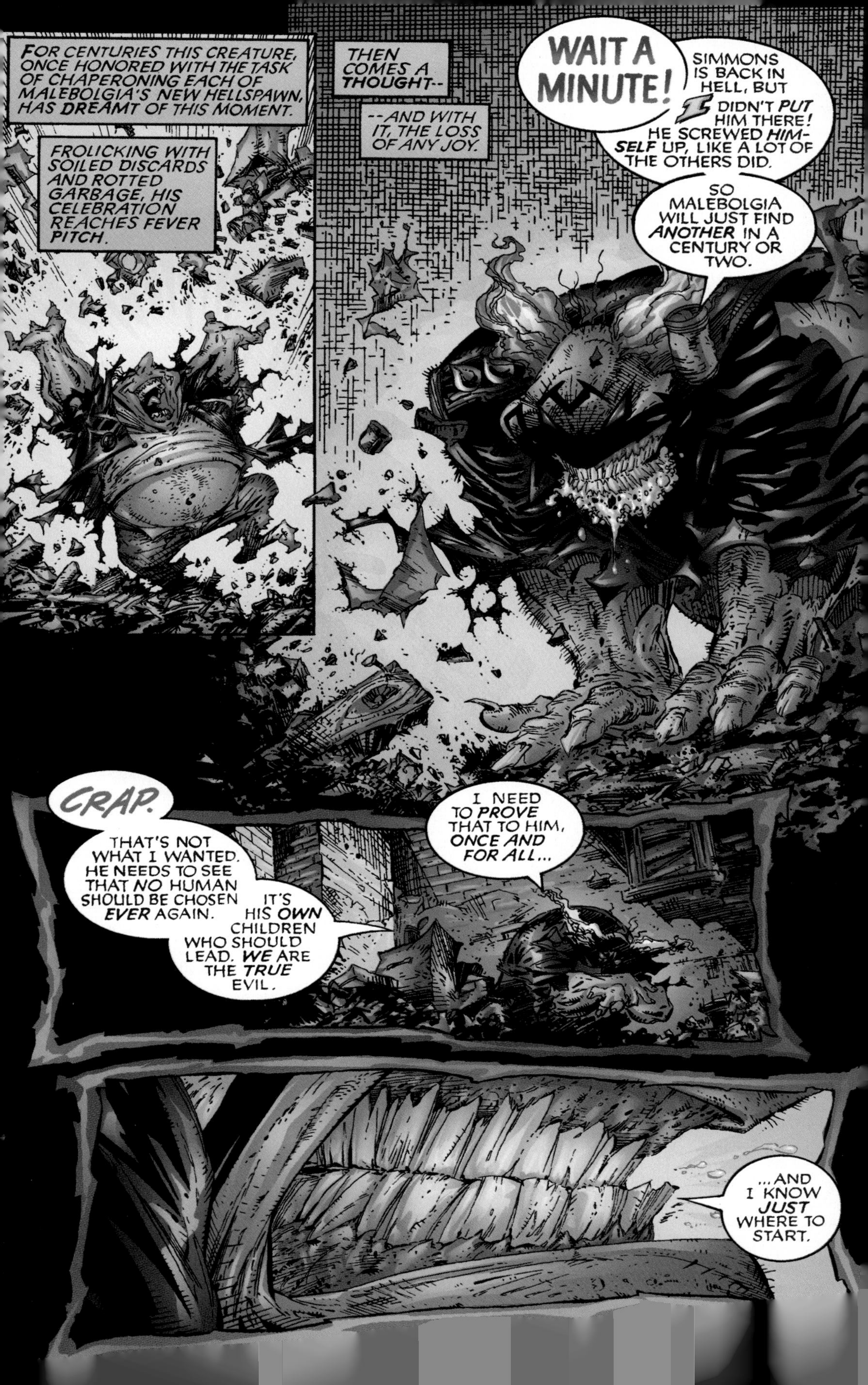
FOR CENTURIES THIS CREATURE, ONCE HONORED WITH THE TASK OF CHAPERONING EACH OF MALEBOLGIA'S NEW HELLSPAWN, HAS DREAMT OF THIS MOMENT.
FROLICKING WITH SOILED DISCARDS AND ROTTED GARBAGE, HIS CELEBRATION REACHES FEVER PITCH.
THEN COMES A THOUGHT--
--AND WITH IT, THE LOSS OF ANY JOY.
WAIT A MINUTE!
SIMMONS IS BACK IN HELL, BUT I DIDN'T PUT HIM THERE! HE SCREWED HIMSELF UP, LIKE A LOT OF THE OTHERS DID.
SO MALEBOLGIA WILL JUST FIND ANOTHER IN A CENTURY OR TWO.
CRAP.
THAT'S NOT WHAT I WANTED. HE NEEDS TO SEE THAT NO HUMAN SHOULD BE CHOSEN EVER AGAIN.
IT'S HIS OWN CHILDREN WHO SHOULD LEAD. WE ARE THE TRUE EVIL.
I NEED TO PROVE THAT TO HIM, ONCE AND FOR ALL...
...AND I KNOW JUST WHERE TO START.

A FEW DAYS LATER...

OUTPATIENT REGISTRATION

AFTERNOON MS. BLAKE.

HELLO, DOCTOR. YOU SAID YOU WANTED TO SEE ME.

YES. I JUST RECEIVED THE RESULTS OF THE LATEST TESTS. AND TO BE QUITE HONEST, THIS WHOLE SITUATION HAS EVERYONE COMPLETELY STUMPED.

THERE'S NO MORE EVIDENCE OF CANCER *ANYWHERE* IN HIS BODY. AS A MATTER OF FACT, THE AREA OF HIS HEAD WHICH WAS AFFECTED IS CLEANER THAN NORMAL. WE'VE RUN EVERY DIAGNOSTIC I CAN THINK OF. EACH RESULT IS *NEGATIVE*.

SO WHAT DOES THAT MEAN?

CALL IT A MIRACLE, BUT TERRY IS 100% CURED. SO, UNLESS EITHER ONE OF YOU HAS ANY OBJECTIONS...

HOLY BIBLE

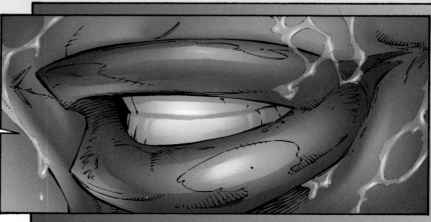

... I'M RELEASING HIM TOMORROW. IT'S TIME HE WENT HOME TO HIS FAMILY.

THANK YOU, DOCTOR. AND IF YOU DON'T MIND, I'D LIKE TO TELL HIM MYSELF.

OF COURSE.

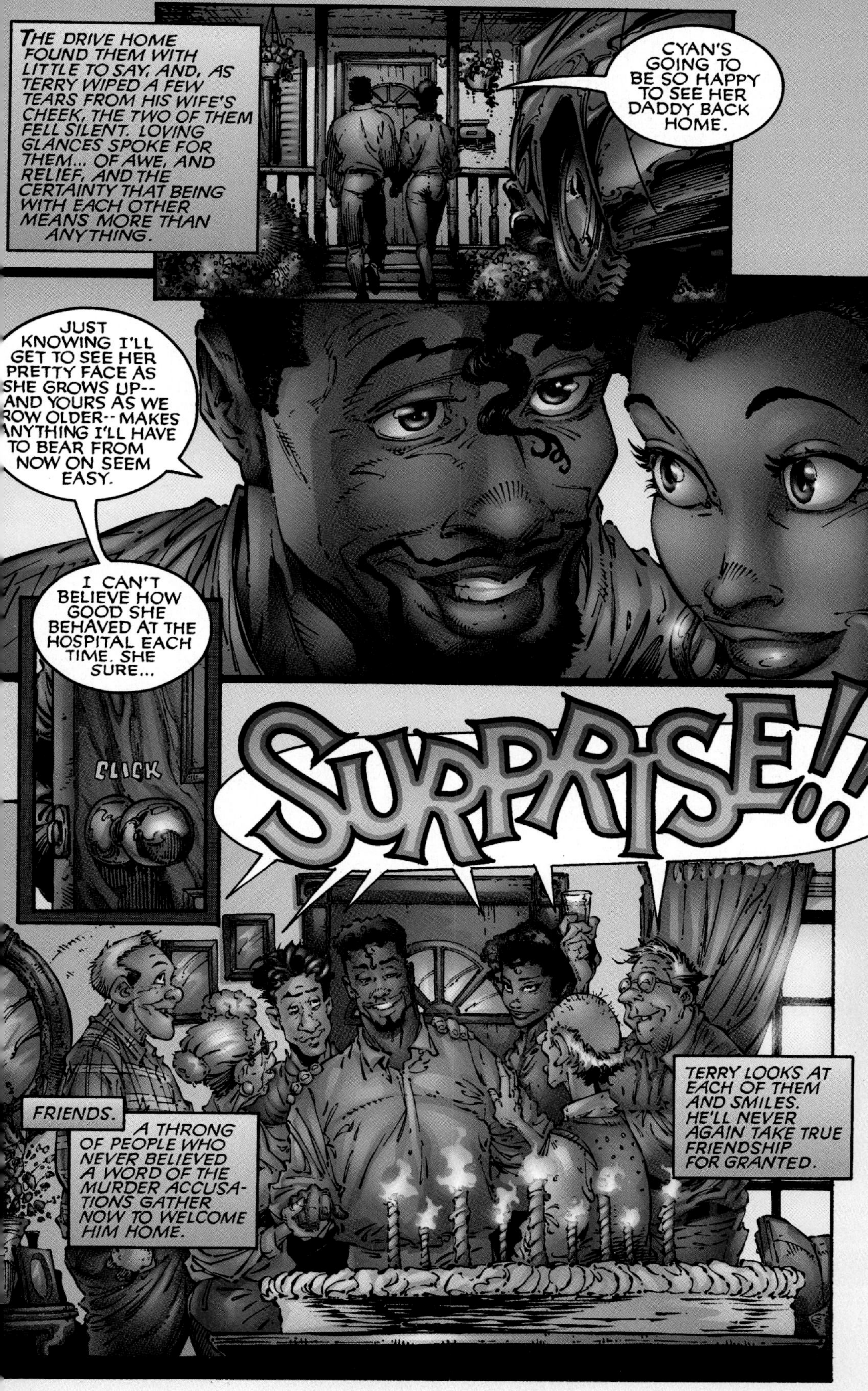
THE DRIVE HOME FOUND THEM WITH LITTLE TO SAY, AND, AS TERRY WIPED A FEW TEARS FROM HIS WIFE'S CHEEK, THE TWO OF THEM FELL SILENT. LOVING GLANCES SPOKE FOR THEM... OF AWE, AND RELIEF, AND THE CERTAINTY THAT BEING WITH EACH OTHER MEANS MORE THAN ANYTHING.
CYAN'S GOING TO BE SO HAPPY TO SEE HER DADDY BACK HOME.
JUST KNOWING I'LL GET TO SEE HER PRETTY FACE AS SHE GROWS UP-- AND YOURS AS WE GROW OLDER-- MAKES ANYTHING I'LL HAVE TO BEAR FROM NOW ON SEEM EASY.
I CAN'T BELIEVE HOW GOOD SHE BEHAVED AT THE HOSPITAL EACH TIME. SHE SURE...
CLICK
SURPRISE!!
FRIENDS.
A THRONG OF PEOPLE WHO NEVER BELIEVED A WORD OF THE MURDER ACCUSATIONS GATHER NOW TO WELCOME HIM HOME.
TERRY LOOKS AT EACH OF THEM AND SMILES. HE'LL NEVER AGAIN TAKE TRUE FRIENDSHIP FOR GRANTED.

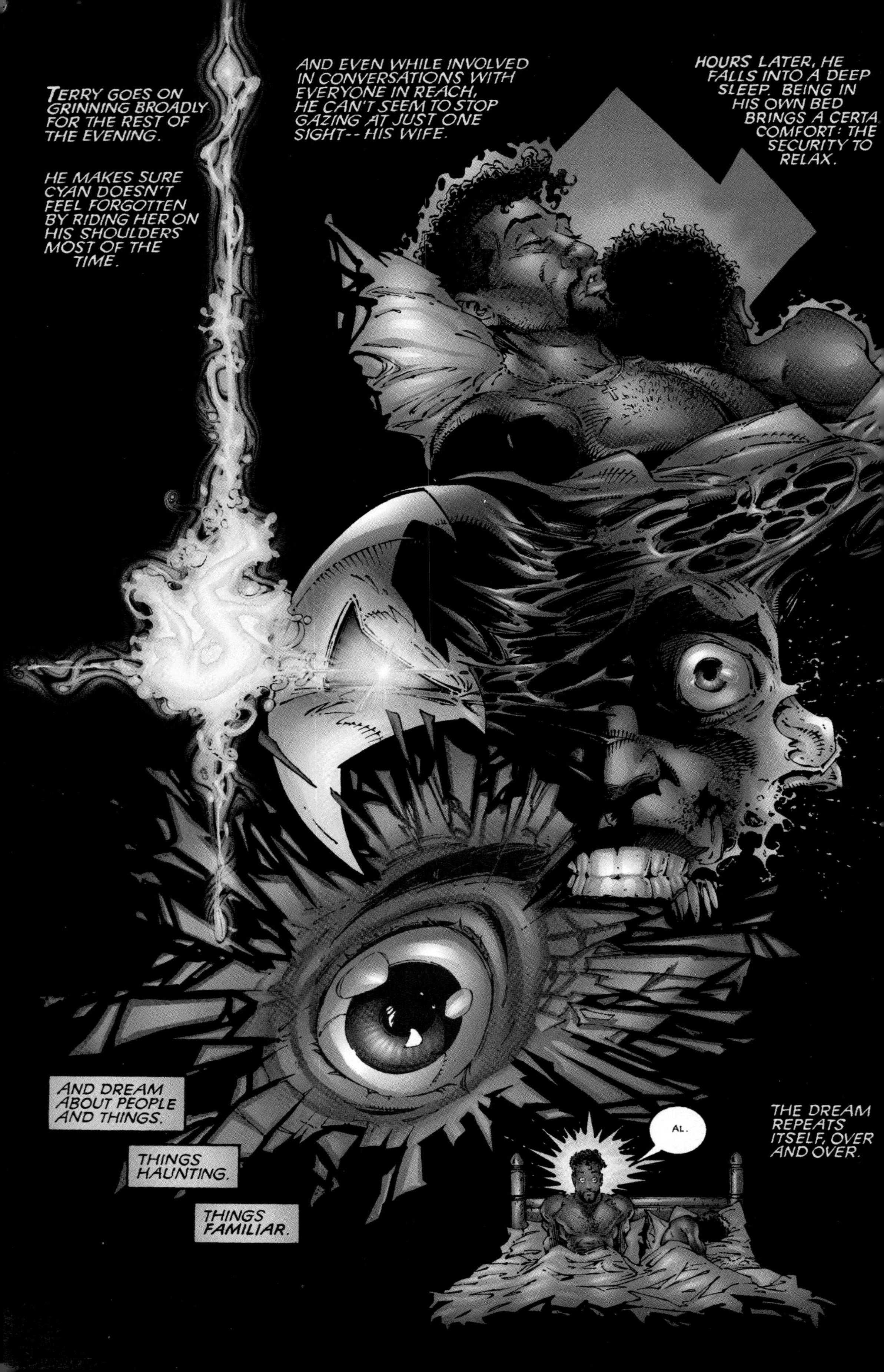
TERRY GOES ON GRINNING BROADLY FOR THE REST OF THE EVENING.
HE MAKES SURE CYAN DOESN'T FEEL FORGOTTEN BY RIDING HER ON HIS SHOULDERS MOST OF THE TIME.
AND EVEN WHILE INVOLVED IN CONVERSATIONS WITH EVERYONE IN REACH, HE CAN'T SEEM TO STOP GAZING AT JUST ONE SIGHT-- HIS WIFE.
HOURS LATER, HE FALLS INTO A DEEP SLEEP. BEING IN HIS OWN BED BRINGS A CERTA COMFORT: THE SECURITY TO RELAX.
AND DREAM ABOUT PEOPLE AND THINGS.
THINGS HAUNTING.
THINGS FAMILIAR.
AL.
THE DREAM REPEATS ITSELF, OVER AND OVER.

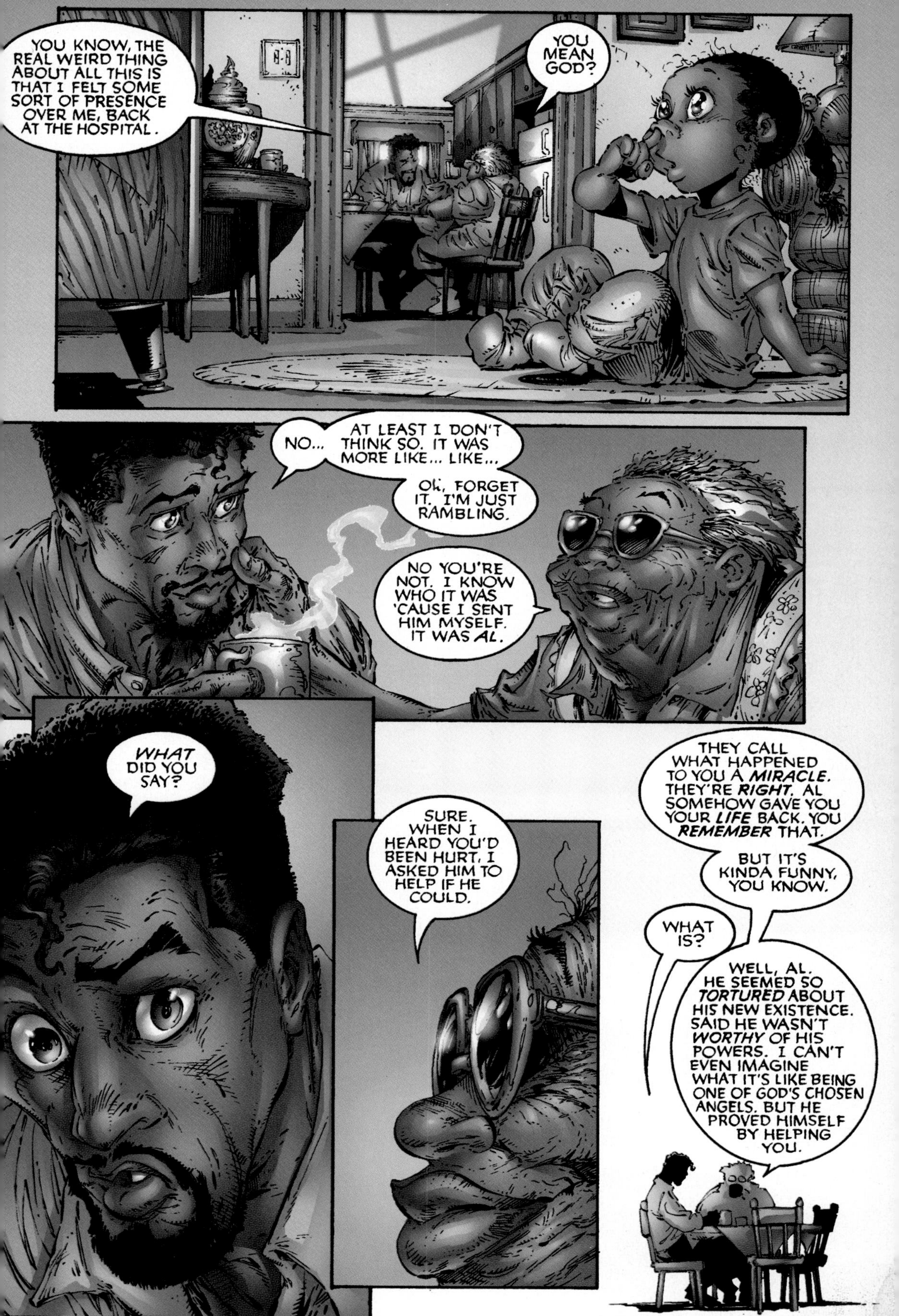
YOU KNOW, THE REAL WEIRD THING ABOUT ALL THIS IS THAT I FELT SOME SORT OF PRESENCE OVER ME, BACK AT THE HOSPITAL.
YOU MEAN GOD?
NO...
AT LEAST I DON'T THINK SO. IT WAS MORE LIKE... LIKE...
OH, FORGET IT. I'M JUST RAMBLING.
NO YOU'RE NOT. I KNOW WHO IT WAS 'CAUSE I SENT HIM MYSELF. IT WAS AL.
WHAT DID YOU SAY?
SURE. WHEN I HEARD YOU'D BEEN HURT, I ASKED HIM TO HELP IF HE COULD.
THEY CALL WHAT HAPPENED TO YOU A MIRACLE. THEY'RE RIGHT. AL SOMEHOW GAVE YOU YOUR LIFE BACK. YOU REMEMBER THAT.
BUT IT'S KINDA FUNNY, YOU KNOW.
WHAT IS?
WELL, AL. HE SEEMED SO TORTURED ABOUT HIS NEW EXISTENCE. SAID HE WASN'T WORTHY OF HIS POWERS. I CAN'T EVEN IMAGINE WHAT IT'S LIKE BEING ONE OF GOD'S CHOSEN ANGELS. BUT HE PROVED HIMSELF BY HELPING YOU.

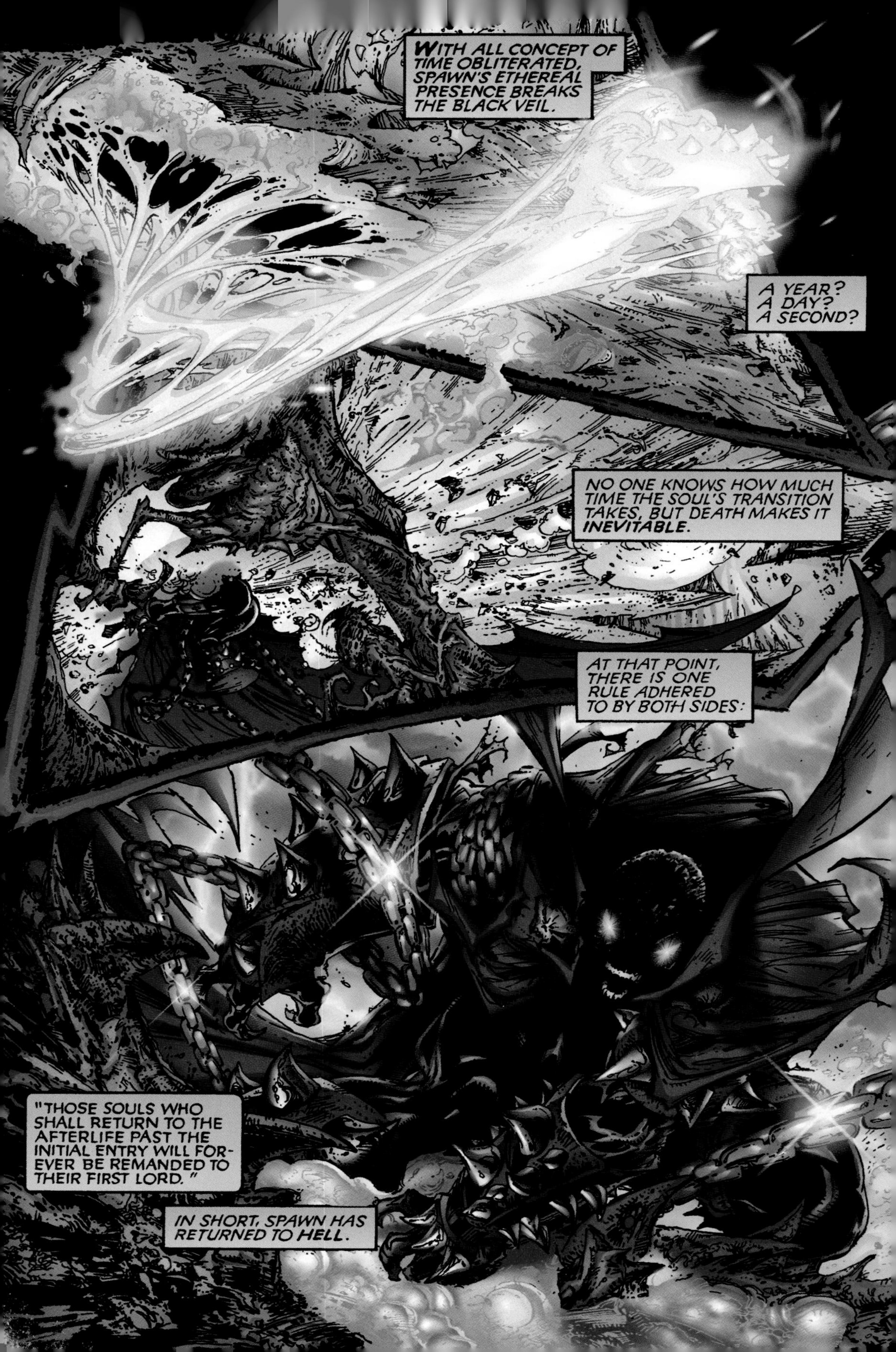
WITH ALL CONCEPT OF TIME OBLITERATED, SPAWN'S ETHEREAL PRESENCE BREAKS THE BLACK VEIL.
A YEAR? A DAY? A SECOND?
NO ONE KNOWS HOW MUCH TIME THE SOUL'S TRANSITION TAKES, BUT DEATH MAKES IT INEVITABLE.
AT THAT POINT, THERE IS ONE RULE ADHERED TO BY BOTH SIDES:
"THOSE SOULS WHO SHALL RETURN TO THE AFTERLIFE PAST THE INITIAL ENTRY WILL FOREVER BE REMANDED TO THEIR FIRST LORD."
IN SHORT, SPAWN HAS RETURNED TO HELL.

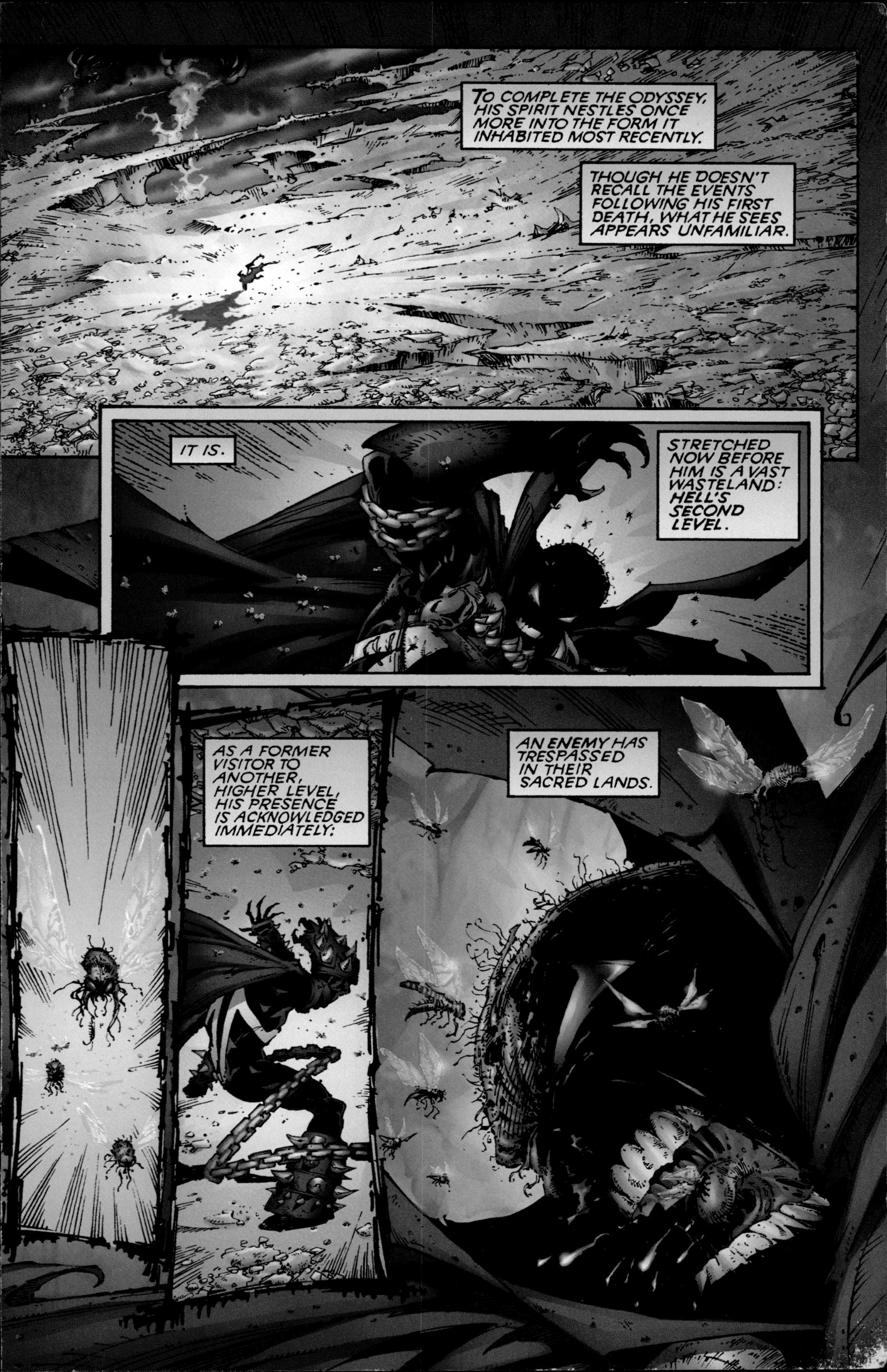
TO COMPLETE THE ODYSSEY, HIS SPIRIT NESTLES ONCE MORE INTO THE FORM IT INHABITED MOST RECENTLY.
THOUGH HE DOESN'T RECALL THE EVENTS FOLLOWING HIS FIRST DEATH, WHAT HE SEES APPEARS UNFAMILIAR.
IT IS.
STRETCHED NOW BEFORE HIM IS A VAST WASTELAND: HELL'S SECOND LEVEL.
AS A FORMER VISITOR TO ANOTHER, HIGHER LEVEL, HIS PRESENCE IS ACKNOWLEDGED IMMEDIATELY:
AN ENEMY HAS TRESPASSED IN THEIR SACRED LANDS.

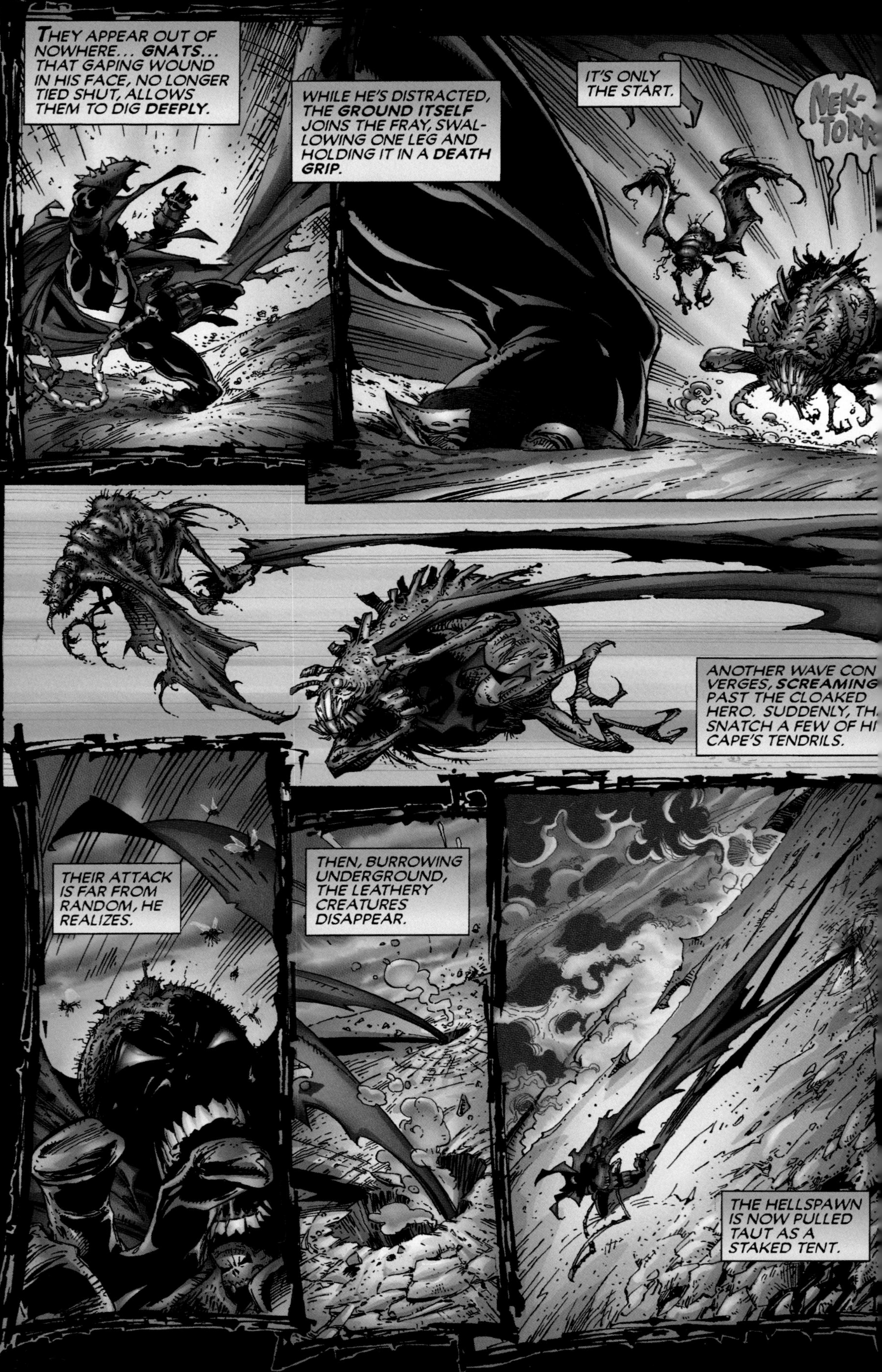

THEY APPEAR OUT OF NOWHERE... GNATS... THAT GAPING WOUND IN HIS FACE, NO LONGER TIED SHUT, ALLOWS THEM TO DIG DEEPLY.
WHILE HE'S DISTRACTED, THE GROUND ITSELF JOINS THE FRAY, SWAL-LOWING ONE LEG AND HOLDING IT IN A DEATH GRIP.
IT'S ONLY THE START.
NEK-TORR
ANOTHER WAVE CON VERGES, SCREAMING PAST THE CLOAKED HERO. SUDDENLY, TH SNATCH A FEW OF HI CAPE'S TENDRILS.
THEIR ATTACK IS FAR FROM RANDOM, HE REALIZES.
THEN, BURROWING UNDERGROUND, THE LEATHERY CREATURES DISAPPEAR.
THE HELLSPAWN IS NOW PULLED TAUT AS A STAKED TENT.

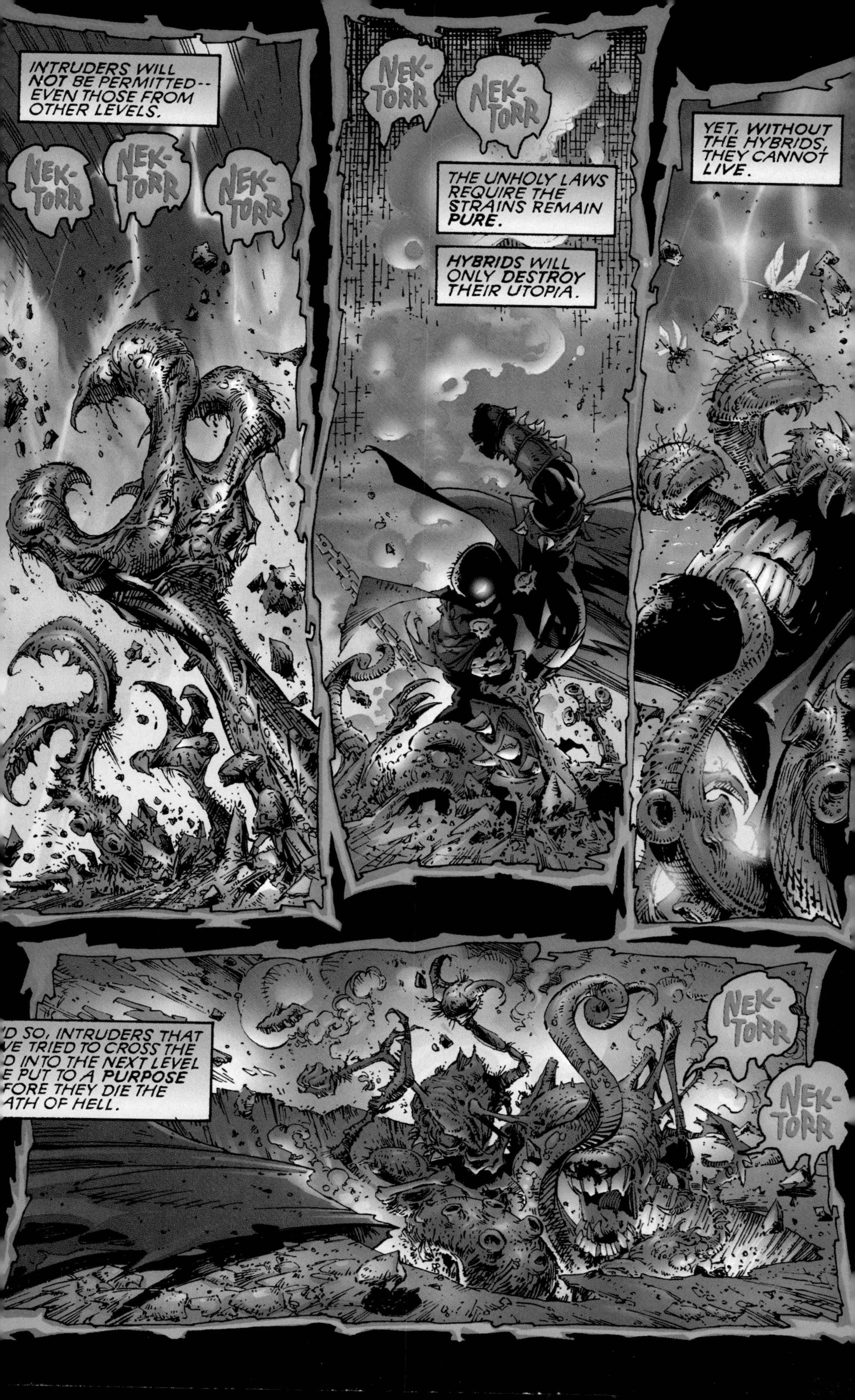
INTRUDERS WILL NOT BE PERMITTED-- EVEN THOSE FROM OTHER LEVELS.
NEK-TORR
NEK-TORR
NEK-TORR
NEK-TORR
NEK-TORR
THE UNHOLY LAWS REQUIRE THE STRAINS REMAIN PURE.
HYBRIDS WILL ONLY DESTROY THEIR UTOPIA.
YET, WITHOUT THE HYBRIDS, THEY CANNOT LIVE.
'D SO, INTRUDERS THAT
VE TRIED TO CROSS THE
D INTO THE NEXT LEVEL
E PUT TO A PURPOSE
FORE THEY DIE THE
ATH OF HELL.
NEK-TORR
NEK-TORR

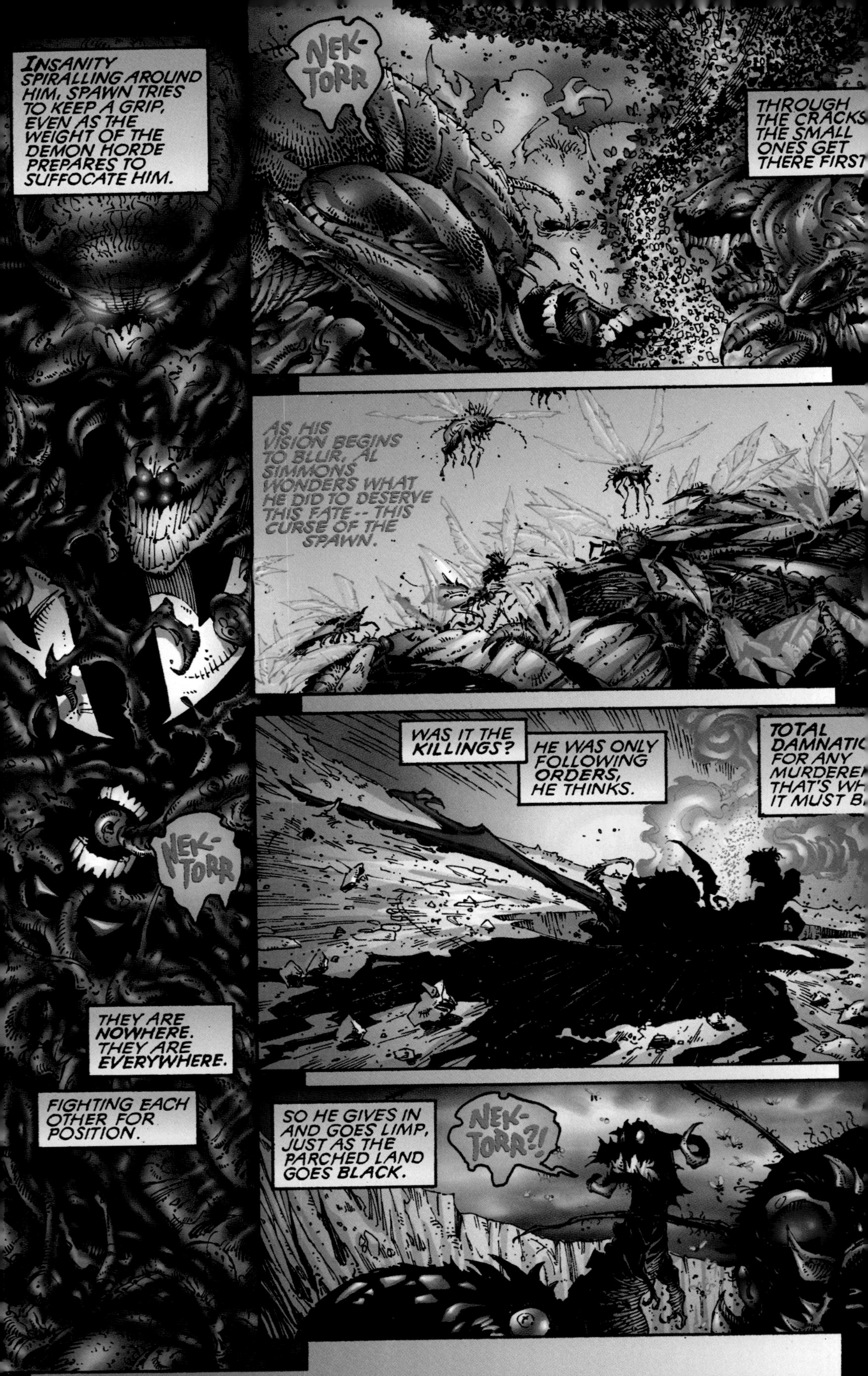
INSANITY SPIRALLING AROUND HIM, SPAWN TRIES TO KEEP A GRIP, EVEN AS THE WEIGHT OF THE DEMON HORDE PREPARES TO SUFFOCATE HIM.
NEK-TORR
THROUGH THE CRACKS THE SMALL ONES GET THERE FIRST
AS HIS VISION BEGINS TO BLUR, AL SIMMONS WONDERS WHAT HE DID TO DESERVE THIS FATE -- THIS CURSE OF THE SPAWN.
NEK-TORR
WAS IT THE KILLINGS?
HE WAS ONLY FOLLOWING ORDERS, HE THINKS.
TOTAL DAMNATIC FOR ANY MURDERE THAT'S WH IT MUST B
THEY ARE NOWHERE. THEY ARE EVERYWHERE.
FIGHTING EACH OTHER FOR POSITION.
SO HE GIVES IN AND GOES LIMP, JUST AS THE PARCHED LAND GOES BLACK.
NEK-TORR?!

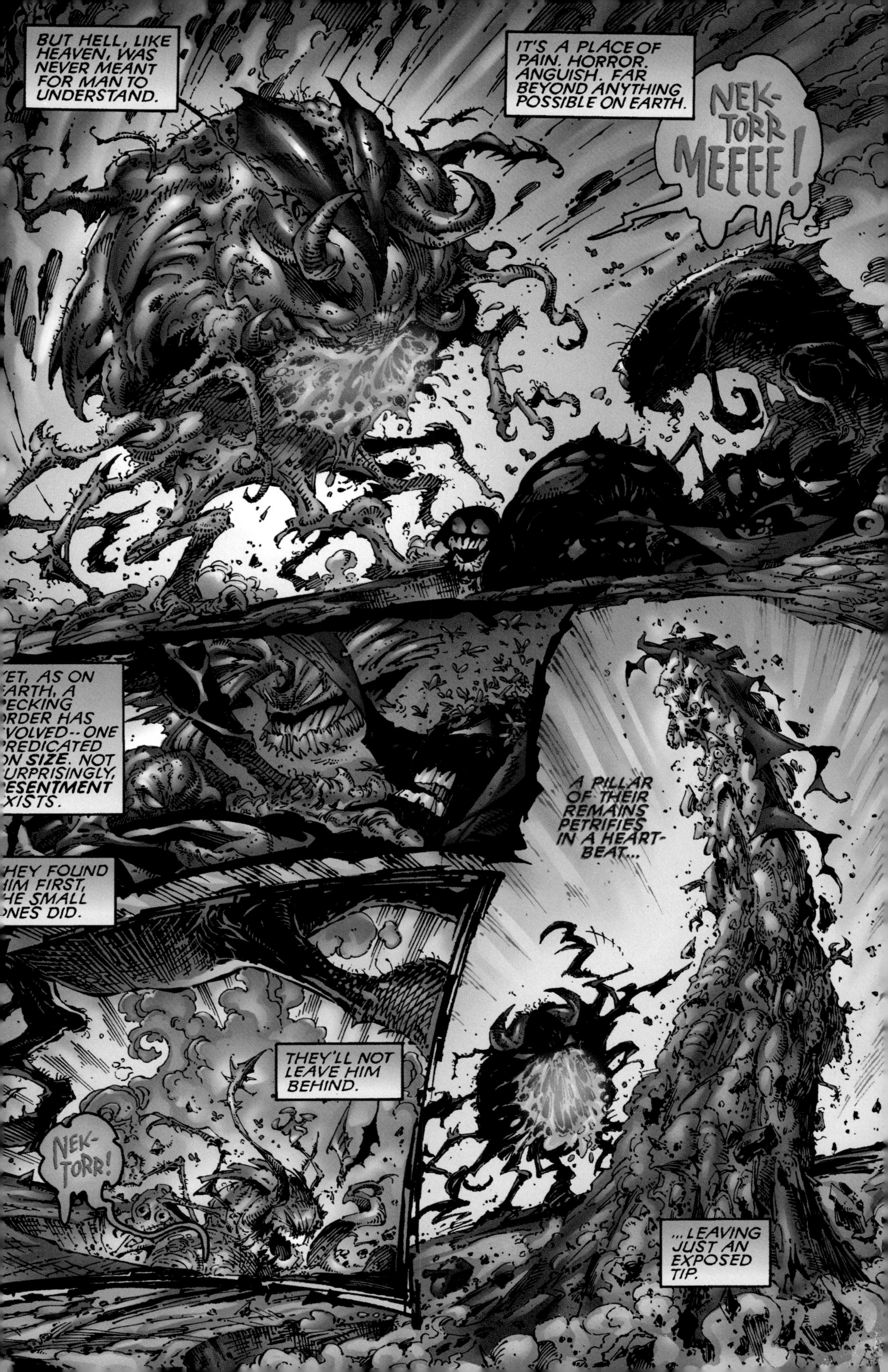
BUT HELL, LIKE HEAVEN, WAS NEVER MEANT FOR MAN TO UNDERSTAND.
IT'S A PLACE OF PAIN. HORROR. ANGUISH. FAR BEYOND ANYTHING POSSIBLE ON EARTH.
NEK-TORR MEEEE!
ET, AS ON ARTH, A ECKING RDER HAS VOLVED--ONE REDICATED N SIZE. NOT URPRISINGLY, ESENTMENT XISTS.
A PILLAR OF THEIR REMAINS PETRIFIES IN A HEART-BEAT...
HEY FOUND IM FIRST, HE SMALL NES DID.
THEY'LL NOT LEAVE HIM BEHIND.
NEK-TORR!
...LEAVING JUST AN EXPOSED TIP.

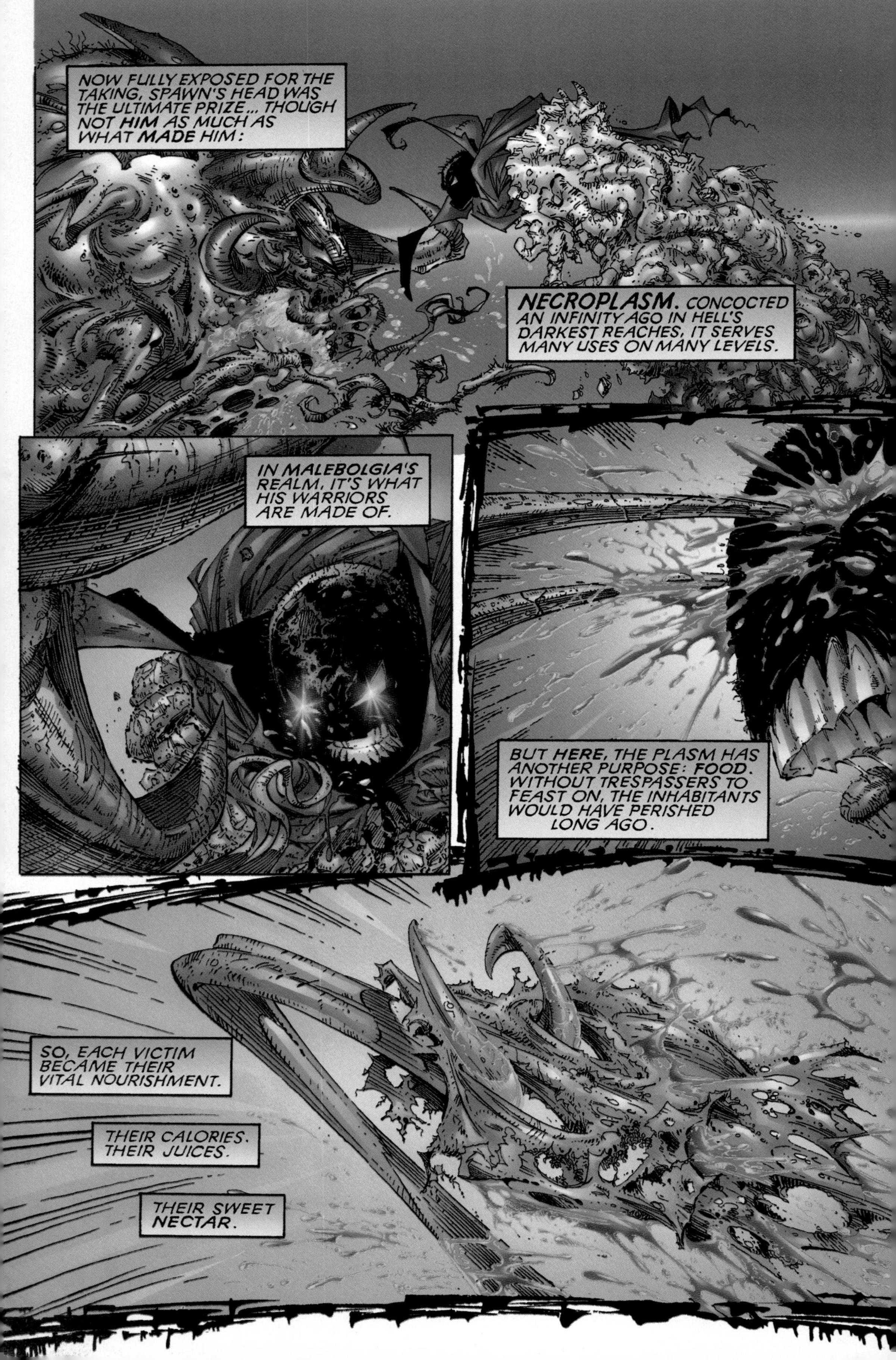
NOW FULLY EXPOSED FOR THE TAKING, SPAWN'S HEAD WAS THE ULTIMATE PRIZE... THOUGH NOT HIM AS MUCH AS WHAT MADE HIM:
NECROPLASM. CONCOCTED AN INFINITY AGO IN HELL'S DARKEST REACHES, IT SERVES MANY USES ON MANY LEVELS.
IN MALEBOLGIA'S REALM, IT'S WHAT HIS WARRIORS ARE MADE OF.
BUT HERE, THE PLASM HAS ANOTHER PURPOSE: FOOD. WITHOUT TRESPASSERS TO FEAST ON, THE INHABITANTS WOULD HAVE PERISHED LONG AGO.
SO, EACH VICTIM BECAME THEIR VITAL NOURISHMENT.
THEIR CALORIES. THEIR JUICES.
THEIR SWEET NECTAR.

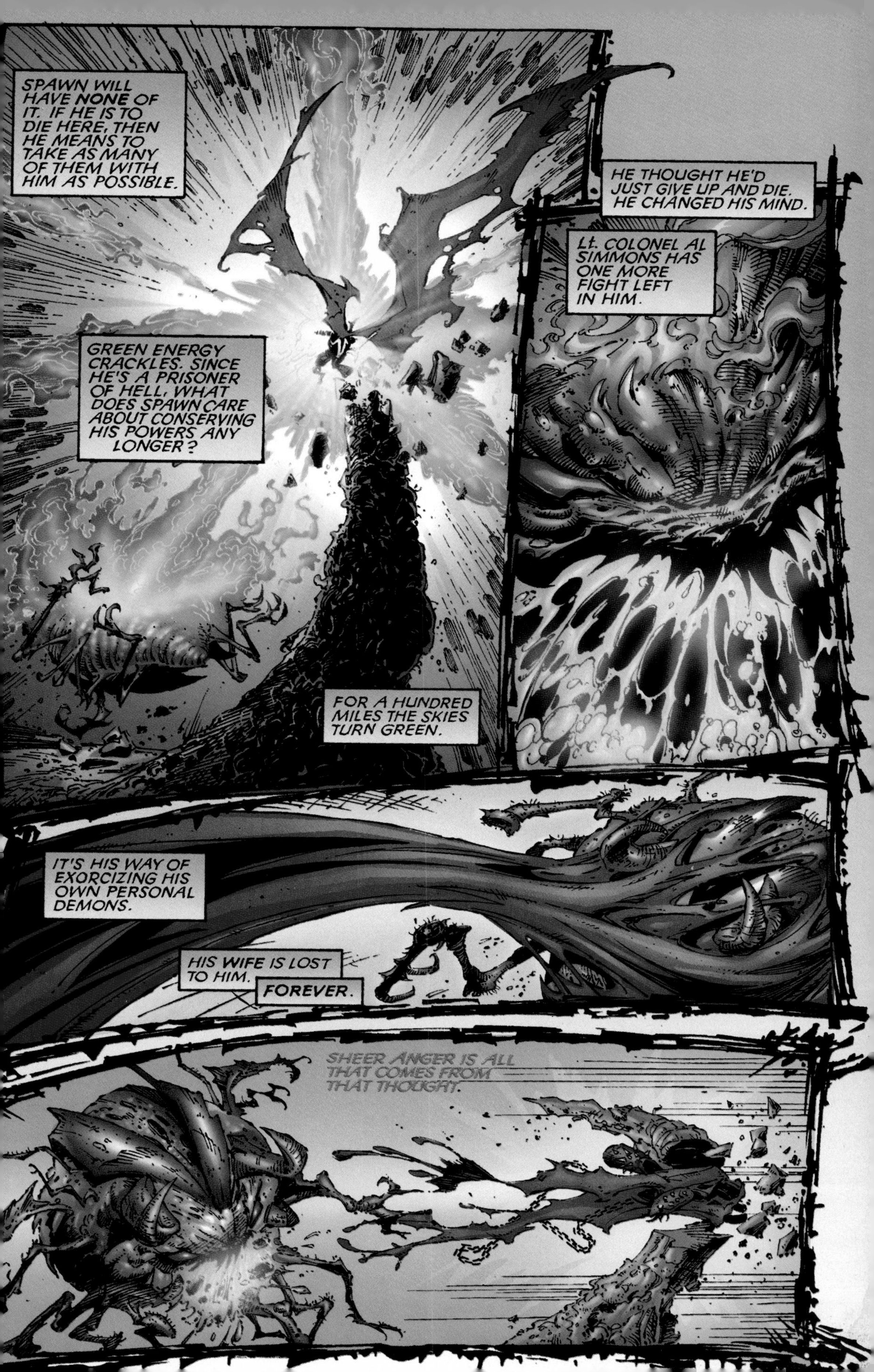
SPAWN WILL HAVE **NONE** OF IT. IF HE IS TO DIE HERE, THEN HE MEANS TO TAKE AS MANY OF THEM WITH HIM AS POSSIBLE.
GREEN ENERGY CRACKLES. SINCE HE'S A PRISONER OF HELL, WHAT DOES SPAWN CARE ABOUT CONSERVING HIS POWERS ANY LONGER?
FOR A HUNDRED MILES THE SKIES TURN GREEN.
HE THOUGHT HE'D JUST GIVE UP AND DIE. HE CHANGED HIS MIND.
Lt. COLONEL AL SIMMONS HAS ONE MORE FIGHT LEFT IN HIM.
IT'S HIS WAY OF EXORCIZING HIS OWN PERSONAL DEMONS.
HIS **WIFE** IS LOST TO HIM.
FOREVER.
SHEER ANGER IS ALL THAT COMES FROM THAT THOUGHT.

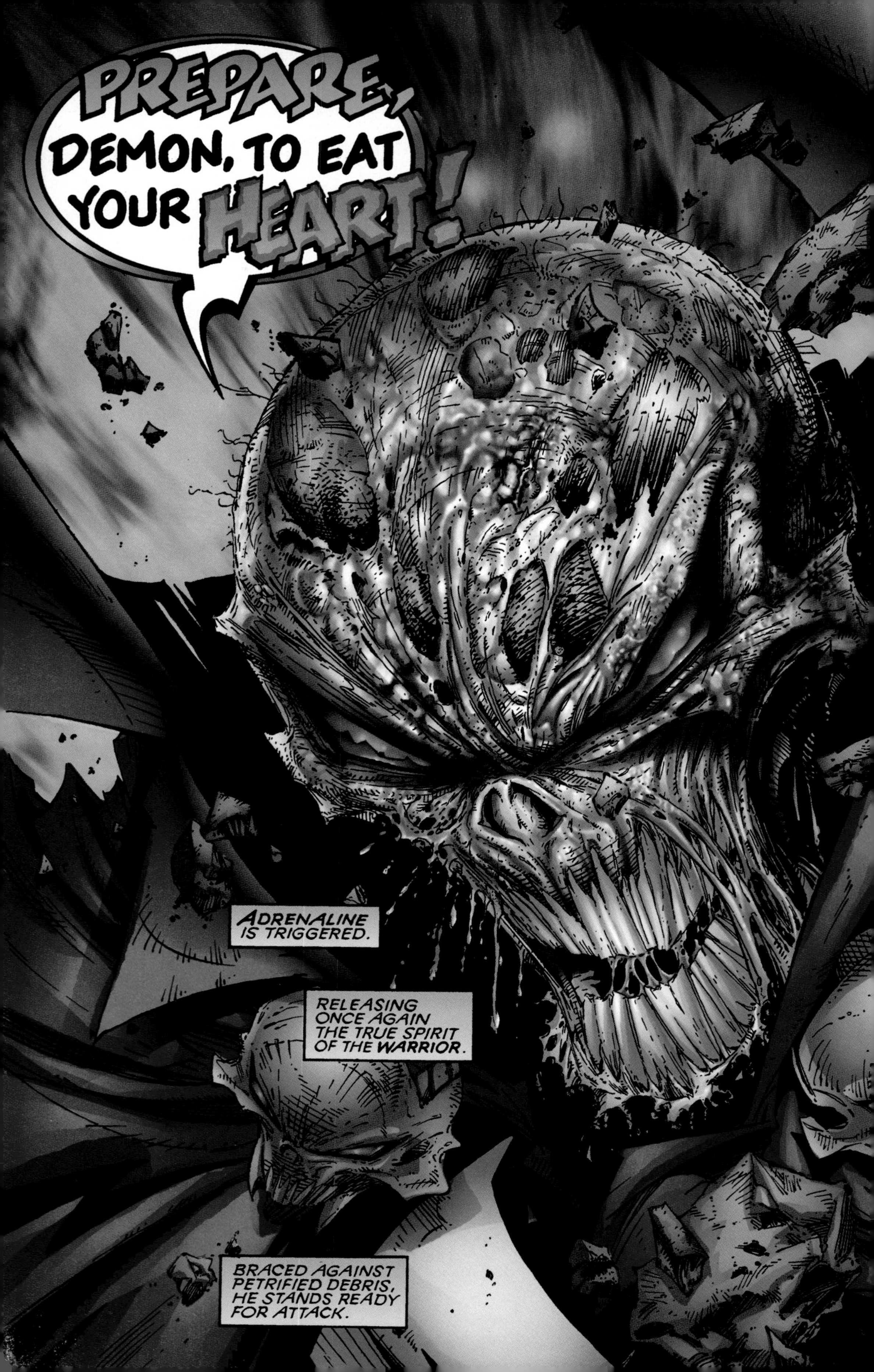
PREPARE, DEMON, TO EAT YOUR HEART!
ADRENALINE IS TRIGGERED.
RELEASING ONCE AGAIN THE TRUE SPIRIT OF THE WARRIOR.
BRACED AGAINST PETRIFIED DEBRIS, HE STANDS READY FOR ATTACK.

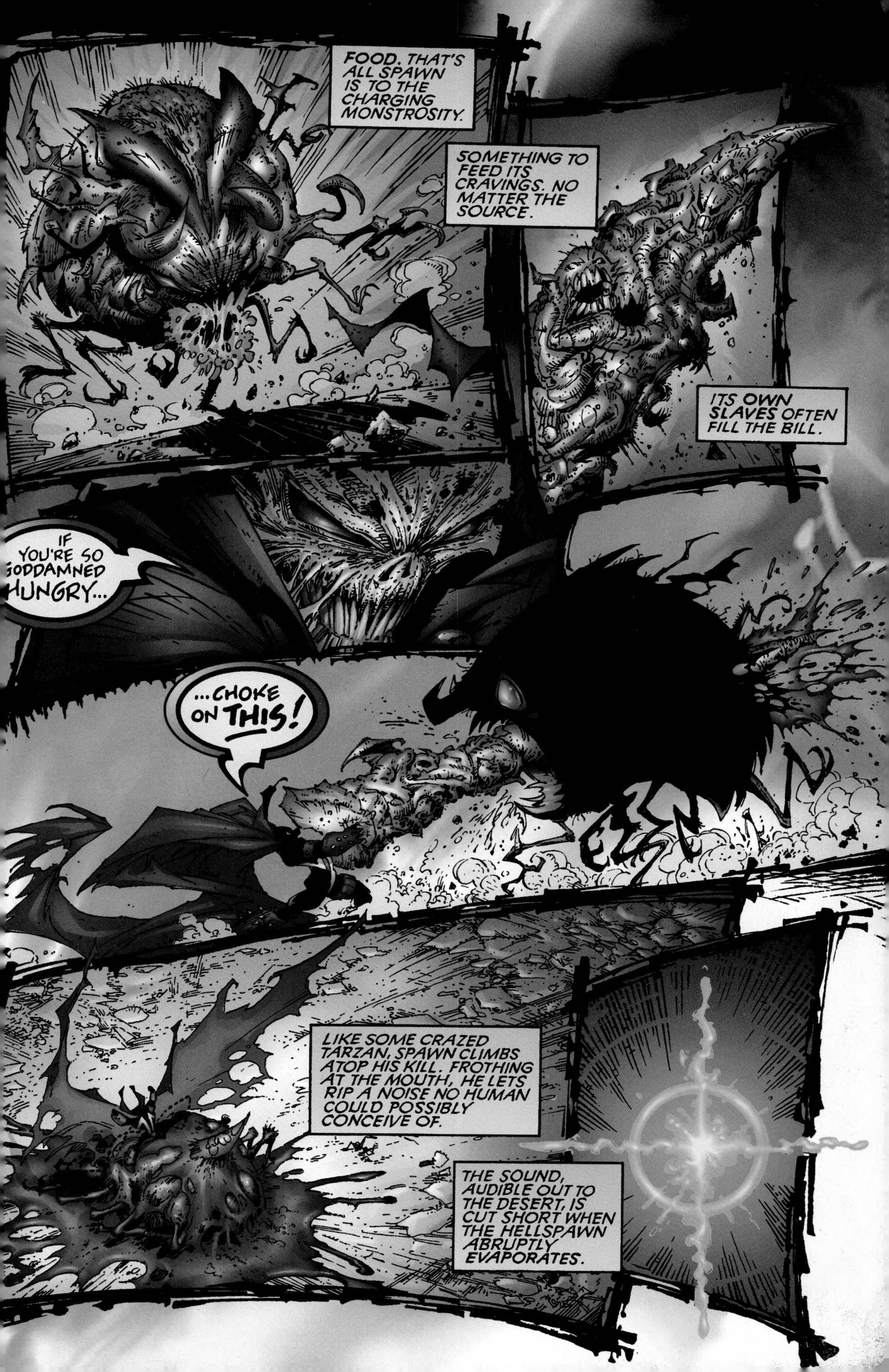
FOOD. THAT'S ALL SPAWN IS TO THE CHARGING MONSTROSITY.
SOMETHING TO FEED ITS CRAVINGS. NO MATTER THE SOURCE.
ITS OWN SLAVES OFTEN FILL THE BILL.
IF YOU'RE SO GODDAMNED HUNGRY...
...CHOKE ON THIS!
LIKE SOME CRAZED TARZAN, SPAWN CLIMBS ATOP HIS KILL. FROTHING AT THE MOUTH, HE LETS RIP A NOISE NO HUMAN COULD POSSIBLY CONCEIVE OF.
THE SOUND, AUDIBLE OUT TO THE DESERT, IS CUT SHORT WHEN THE HELLSPAWN ABRUPTLY EVAPORATES.

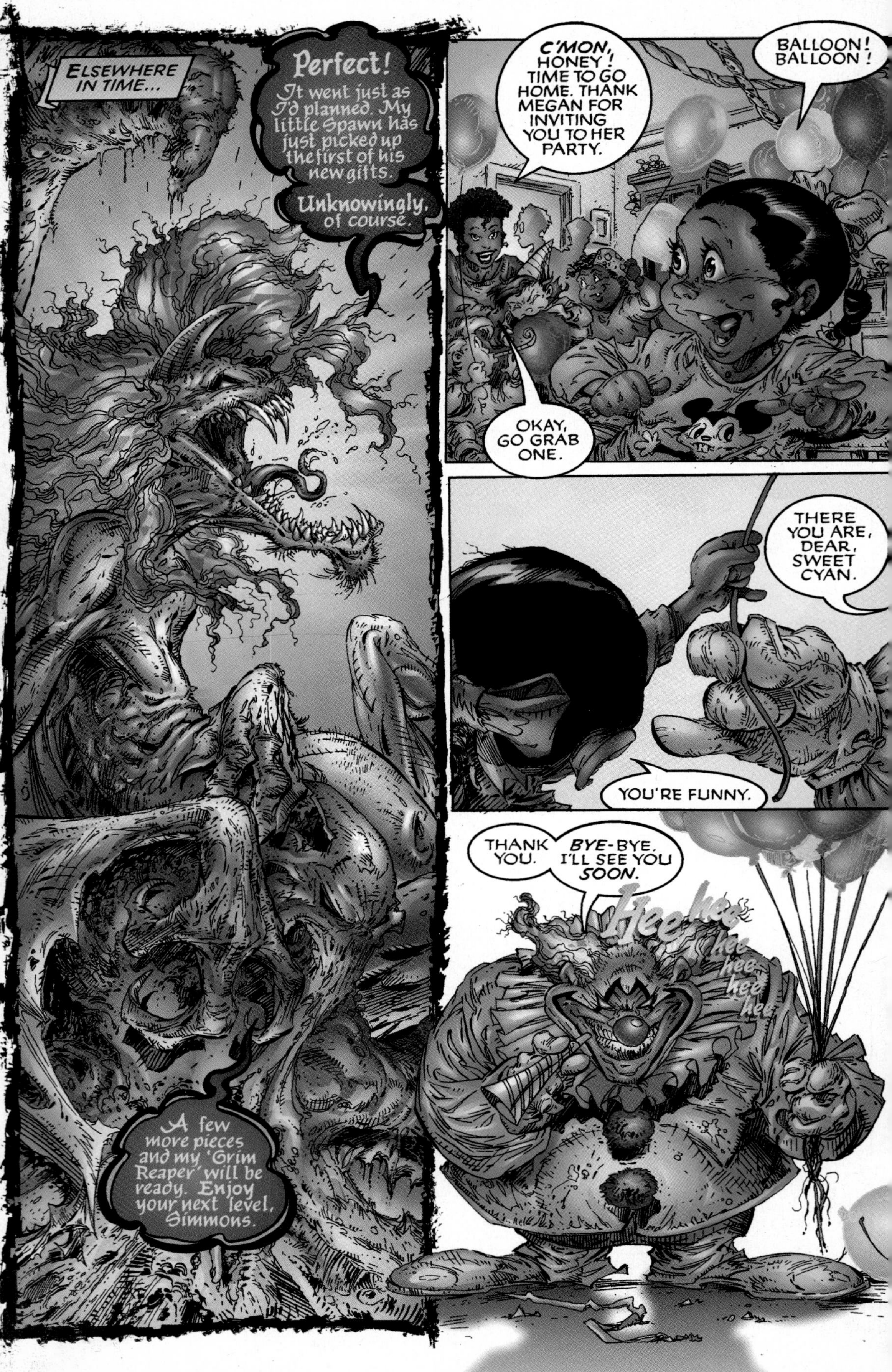
ELSEWHERE IN TIME...
Perfect! It went just as I'd planned. My little Spawn has just picked up the first of his new gifts.
Unknowingly, of course.
A few more pieces and my 'Grim Reaper' will be ready. Enjoy your next level, Simmons.
C'MON, HONEY! TIME TO GO HOME. THANK MEGAN FOR INVITING YOU TO HER PARTY.
BALLOON! BALLOON!
OKAY, GO GRAB ONE.
THERE YOU ARE, DEAR, SWEET CYAN.
YOU'RE FUNNY.
THANK YOU.
BYE-BYE. I'LL SEE YOU SOON.
Hee hee hee hee hee hee

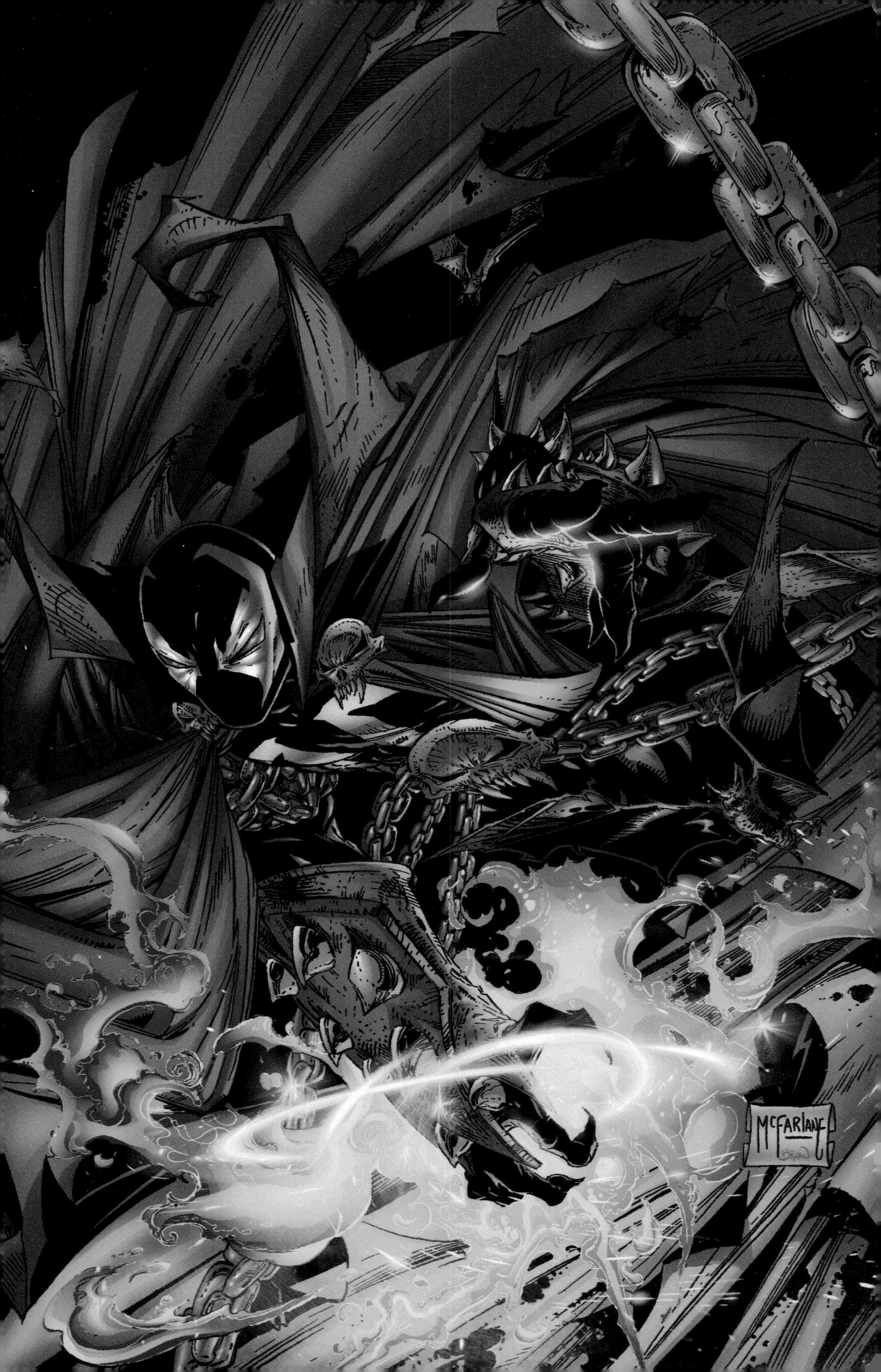
McFARLANE

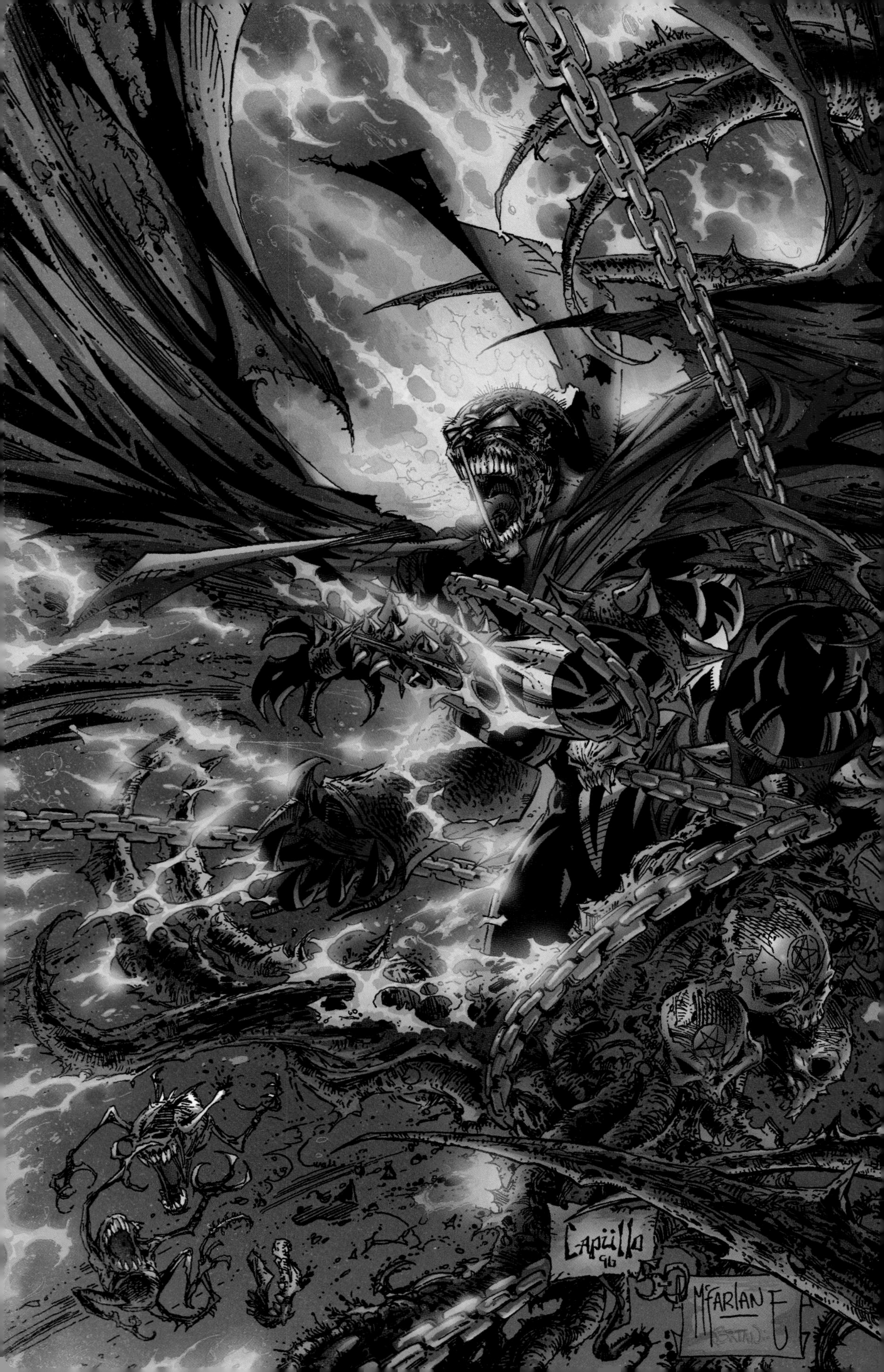
Capullo 96